CHRISTOPHER COLUMBUS
Master of the Atlantic

CHRISTOPHER COLUMBUS

Master of the Atlantic

DAVID A. THOMAS

ANDRE DEUTSCH

First published in 1991 by
André Deutsch Limited
105–106 Great Russell Street
London WC1B 3LJ

British Library Cataloguing in Publication Data

Thomas, David A. (David Arthur), *1925 –*
  Christopher Columbus: Master of the Atlantic.
  I. Title
  970.015092
ISBN 0 233 98724 X

Printed in Hong Kong by Dah Hua Printing

Contents

Acknowledgements

I WISH to acknowledge the help and wise counsel of a number of people who kindly put their services and knowledge at my disposal in a manner quite above what one could reasonably expect. Every researcher is aware of the debt he or she owes to those many librarians and archivists who make a book possible. In particular I am indebted to the staff of the Reading Room at the National Maritime Museum for their unfailing help and courtesy over a very long period of research.

I am appreciative, too, of the help given by the staff of the reference libraries of the County of Essex at Chelmsford and Harlow, to the staff of the Cambridge University Library, and especially to the staff of the Central Reference Library of the London Borough of Redbridge who are a model of patience and forbearance.

I owe a debt of gratitude to all those whose books, articles and picture collections are cited in the work. It is invidious to pick out a few names among so many referred to yet it would be patently ungracious not to express an obligation to the late Samuel Eliot Morison, eminent author of *Admiral of the Ocean Sea: A Life of Christopher Columbus*, Little, Brown & Co; to the late Gianni Granzotto for his *Christopher Columbus: The Dream and the Obsession*, Doubleday; to Dr Robert H. Fuson for his *The Log of Christopher Columbus*, Ashford Press Publishing; and to Paolo Taviani, author of *Christopher Columbus: The Grand Design*, Orbis Publishing.

I am also grateful to the following for allowing me to quote extracts from their works: Rutgers University of New Brunswick, *The Life of Admiral Christopher Columbus*, by his son Ferdinand Columbus: Jarrolds Publishing, *Christopher Columbus: The Journal of His First Voyage to America*.

Special thanks are due to the numerous agencies which have drawn upon their collections to provide the fine photographs in the book. All of them, especially the curator at La Rábida Monastery at Huelva, went out of their way to be helpful.

I wish also to express my thanks to Juan Ruiz-Palma for his unfailing help in translations from Spanish and Portuguese.

David A. Thomas
Sheering, Essex

Picture Credits

PICTURE CREDITS

Patrimonio Nacional, Madrid

La Rábida Monastery, Huelva

Museo Civico, Como

Archive Simancas, Valladolid

Biblioteca Columbina, Seville

El Escorial, Madrid

Princess Cruises Ltd, London

Museo Naval, Pegli-Genoa

The Library of Congress, Washington

British Library, London

National Graphics Center, Virginia

National Maritime Museum, London

Biblioteca Nacional Gerencia, Madrid

Spanish National Tourist Office, London

Metropolitan Museum of Art, New York

Museu Nacional de Arte Antiga, Lisbon

Comision de Quinto Centenaria, Santo Domingo

Barclay Stratton (Jamaica Tourist Office), London

Oficina de Informacion y Turismo, Granada

Oficina de Turismo, Valladolid

Trinidad and Tobago Tourist Office

Icelandic Embassy

British Virgin Islands Tourist Board

The cover engraving is a detail from *The Pearl Fisheries of Margerita Island* by Jean de Bry. The cover portrait of Columbus is reproduced by kind permission of the monastery of La Rábida at Huelva.

Chronology

1451 Christopher Columbus was born in Genoa, Italy, the son of Domenico Columbus and his wife Susannah Fontanarosa. The precise date may be disputed, but Genoa is now generally accepted as his birthplace, despite the claims of other competing towns throughout Europe.

1464 Probably at the age of thirteen Christopher began his maritime career making short trading trips. His formal education has not been documented but it is believed he learnt the rudiments of reading, writing, spelling and drawing or painting from the local friars — as was the custom.

1470 First documentary evidence naming Christopher and his father, dated 22 September and headlined Genoa.

1474–5 Columbus served aboard a ship trading as far east as Chios, an island off Turkey in the Aegean and at the time a Genoese possession.

1475 or 1476 Columbus became involved in a corsair enterprise off Tunisia in an attempt to capture an Aragonese ship.

1476 Columbus voyaged to England — Bristol and London — but en route the Genoese ship in which he served, which formed part of a convoy, was intercepted by a French corsair squadron. Columbus's ship was sunk but he survived by swimming ashore near Cape St Vincent, 13 August.

1477 Columbus arrived in England in December 1476. Spent the winter and the spring of 1477 there. Embarked at Bristol in a ship bound for Iceland.

That summer/autumn he returned to Lisbon, Portugal, and settled there.

1478 Columbus made a trading voyage to Madeira, commissioned by the influential Paola di Negro. The deal was soured and in the following year Columbus testified in Genoa in a lawsuit, 25 August 1479.

1479 September/October is the preferred date for the marriage of Columbus to Felipa Moniz Perestrello, daughter of the governor of Porto Santo.

1480–82 First son Diego was born. Columbus made trading voyages to the Canaries and Azores.

1482–3 He sailed to Guinea, the Gold Coast and Cape Verde Islands. Returned to Lisbon. He had by now formulated his plan to sail to the west to discover the islands of Japan and the Indies.

1483–4 King John II of Portugal rejected Columbus's plans.

1485 Henry VII ascended the English throne. Columbus's wife, Felipa, was dead by now. Practically destitute, Columbus moved with Diego to Palos and La Rábida.

1486 January: Columbus presented his plans to the Catholic Sovereigns. While a commission scrutinised his plans throughout 1487 he lived for months in Córdoba and came to know Beatrice Enríquez de Harana.

1487 August: the plans were rejected.

1488 Ferdinand was born to the unmarried Beatrice and Columbus.

1489–91 Columbus sought sponsorship from the wealthy Andalusian dukes and King John of Portugal.

1492 Surrender of the Moors at Granada completed the reconquest of the Iberian peninsula. After more rejections, King Ferdinand and Queen Isabella finally approved Columbus's Capitulations.
May: fitting out of the expedition started at Palos.
3 August: *Santa Maria*, *Pinta* and *Niña* sailed on the first stage of the first voyage of discovery.
8 September: the ocean crossing began.
12 October: at 2 am land was sighted. Columbus landed at dawn on the island of Guanahani in the Bahamas group.
October/December: discovered Cuba and Hispaniola.
24–25 December: *Santa Maria* was shipwrecked.

1493 16 January: return voyage started.
4 March: Columbus arrived at the estuary of the Tagus, then on to Lisbon.
End of April: the Discoverer was received in Barcelona by the Catholic Sovereigns.
25 September: second voyage of discovery began from Cádiz. The voyage lasted till 11 June 1496 – nearly 3 years. It included the discovery of countless islands, and in June 1495 the sending home of five shiploads of Indians – the start of the slave trade.

1496 11 June: Columbus arrived at Cádiz.
October: finance allocated for the third voyage.

1498 February: death of Columbus's father.
30 May: third voyage of discovery began.
31 July: Columbus arrived at the island of Trinidad, and the following day ne sighted the mainland of South America.

1499 Rebellion in Hispaniola. The discoverer Alonso de Ojeda sailed (with Amerigo Vespucci aboard) and discovered Venezuela.

1500 Columbus was arrested and returned to Cádiz. He was soon freed and returned to favour.

1502 May: Columbus started on his fourth voyage from Cádiz. He followed the coastline of today's Panama, Costa Rica, Nicaragua and Honduras.

1503 He reached Jamaica.

1504 7 November: the fourth voyage ended when Columbus landed at Sanlúcar de Barrameda.
26 November: Queen Isabella died.

1506 Christopher Columbus died at Valladolid.

1542 Columbus's remains were exhumed and taken to Hispaniola.

1898 His remains were taken to Seville Cathedral.

1 Background to a Genius

RARELY are historians and scholars unanimous about anything Columbian, and therein lies much of the attraction of Christopher Columbus. Today, most are agreed about the date and place of his birth, even though a shadowy doubt may cloud the issue in some quarters. It is important that we examine, however briefly, some of the far-fetched and unfounded claims regarding the great Admiral's birth, and the early life and casual up-bringing of one of the world's most imaginative explorers and navigators.

Until a hundred years ago a strong body of opinion accepted Washington Irving's* submission that Columbus's year of birth was 1435, which was based on the statement by Friar Andrés Bernáldez, a contemporary and friend of Columbus: 'He died in Valladolid,' he recorded, 'in the year 1506, in the month of May, in a good old age, being seventy years old, a little more or less.'

Bernáldez allowed himself the escape clause − 'a little more or less' − but as a friend he should have been better qualified than most to assess the explorer's age. Bernáldez's views find favour with few scholars today. J.B. Thacher in his three-volume biography originally published in 1903 suggests a birth date of 1446, and this date is perpetuated in the 1967 edition.

However, much more persuasive about the year of birth is Paolo Taviani† in his thoroughly researched life and career of the Admiral up to the departure of the first expedition in 1492. He places the date between 25 August and 31 October 1451. As evidence, he refers to two unquestionably authentic

*See Irving's entry in the bibliography.

†*Christopher Columbus: The Grand Design* by Paolo Taviani, Orbis Publishers, 1985.

THE CALENDAR IN 1492

AT THE time of Columbus's voyages of discovery the Christian world used the Julian calendar, and had been doing so for nearly fifteen hundred years. By 1492 the astronomical year was out of phase with the calendar because each year was eleven minutes and fourteen seconds too long. A year had been set at 365.25 days rather than 365.242199 days. These errors had accumulated to nine days, so all Columbian dates need this number of days added to bring them into line with modern calendars.

Pope Gregory XIII proclaimed a new calendar which was adopted by the Catholic world in 1582. England, with her conservative resistance to change, clung to the past for more than a century and a half until 1752 (by which time the error had grown to eleven days), confusing historians as well as the general reader.

Curiously, Columbus Day is still celebrated on the Old Style (OS) rather than the New Style (NS) date of 21 October.

THE NAME'S THE SAME

A FEATURE of all the world's literature relating to Columbus is the variety of spellings of his name. The Anglicised version is CHRISTOPHER COLUMBUS, but *El Almirante*, the Admiral of the Ocean Sea, arguably the world's greatest explorer and navigator, has had his name spelled with various combinations of the following:

CRISTOBAL COLON, COULON or COULLON; COLOMB; CHRISTOPHE COLOMB; COLUMBA; CHRISTOFORUS COLUMBUS; CHRISTOVAL COLON; CRISTOFORO COLOMO; CHRISTOVAM; CHRISTOFEL COLONUS; COLOMBO.

It could well be asked how did Columbus make his signature: presumably that would give the definitive style? Not so. Columbus did nothing if not to leave people mystified: a separate box feature will try to untangle his signature. When in Spain he adopted what was supposed to have been the original Roman name of the family, COLONUS, which he abbreviated to COLON in order to adapt it to the Castilian tongue. Hence, he is known throughout Spanish history as CRISTÓBAL COLÓN, and the pronunciation is emphasised as indicated. Throughout the whole of the English-speaking world he is recognised by the Anglicised version — CHRISTOPHER COLUMBUS.

documents. One, dated 31 October 1470, bears Columbus's declaration that he is nineteen years old. The other is dated 25 August 1479 and declares he was 'about twenty-seven'.

There is uncertainty, too, as to the exact house where the great event took place. The persistent Taviani has made intensive efforts to identify the building, but has not been able to point to it with complete assurance. What is known with historical accuracy is that Columbus spent his childhood and early formative years in a street called Vico Diritto near the gate of Sant'Andrea in Genoa, the important trading port of that region of Italy known as Liguria.

To find out how the Columbus family came to live in this part of Genoa we need to go back to Christopher's grandfather. Documentary evidence reveals that in 1429 Giovani Columbus was a resident of Quinto, a village on the outskirts of Genoa though long since absorbed into the urban sprawl of the city. Giovani had been born in a small village named Mocónesi in the upper Fontanabuona valley. In 1429 he apprenticed his eleven-year-old son Domenico to a Mocónesi weaver for six years.

Domenico — Christopher's father — duly took up the craft of weaving and traded in his woollen goods. He prospered sufficiently in his business to enable him to buy a modest amount of land and some property; we know, for example, that some years later he owned an inn, for he was described as a tavern-keeper as well as a weaver. But it would be wrong to describe his prosperity as anything grander than modest.

What brought him into some sort of prominence in local Genoese affairs was his interest in politics, in which he took an active part although his interests lay more on the fringes than at the heart of party politics. Nevertheless, this earned him the appointment of warder of the Porta dell'Olivella — a tower and a gate in the wall of the ancient city. His duties have never been defined.

Presumably by the time that Christopher was born, Domenico had married Susannah Fontanarosa: no records of the marriage exist, and the first piece of documentary evidence of Christopher's mother comes some twenty years later

It is claimed that this is the house in Genoa where Columbus spent his boyhood and youth.

in 1471. During this interval the family had moved from Genoa further west round the Gulf of Genoa to Savona. It was evidently an unsatisfactory arrangement because the family soon moved back to Genoa. Domenico could probably read and write despite not having had much formal education, and he had had much recourse to lawyers throughout his business life: his name appears in no less than seventy-seven surviving notarial documents, suggesting an active and energetic life style.

In Genoa, Domenico became embroiled in a legal dispute, was arrested, imprisoned and tried: it cost him dear — a fine of thirty-five lire which necessitated his selling some land in Ginestreto.

He lived to a fine old age, probably not long enough to see in the new century but certainly long enough to celebrate the great discoveries of his son in 1492—3, and perhaps those of the second voyage ending in 1496. His had been an active and moderately successful life in trading and in politics, and judged by the standards of the day he had fared well in buying land and property.

Christopher's mother, Susannah, simply does not come to life, despite intensive research into the available archives. Her only documentary references are sparse and legalistic, giving no picture of the woman at all. We know she raised five children — Christopher and Bartholomew (who both took an early fancy for the sea), Giovani and Giacomo (who were content to stay with the

NVLLA · DOMVS · TITVLO · DIGNIOR
HEIC
PATERNIS · IN · AEDIBVS
CHRISTOPHORVS · COLVMBVS
PVERITIAM
PRIMAMQVE · IVVENTAM · TRANSEGIT

This plaque decorates the humble house in Genoa where Columbus spent his childhood and youth.

family looms) and a daughter, Bianchinetta. Infant mortality in those times was high and it is likely that Susannah bore other children who died in infancy.

Nothing more is known of Christopher's antecedents. It is a pity that Ferdinand, son and biographer of his famous father, failed lamentably to provide us with a true picture of the family's past. He was best fitted to do so, but instead he cloaked the truth to a greater degree even than his father. Christopher Columbus was, to use a modern phrase, economical with the truth. Repeatedly the researcher encounters examples of his deception: his daily falsification of his flagship's log readings is a case in point. Columbus was so devious in this respect that one biographer went so far as to question whether or not he was a pathological liar.

In the biography of his father* Ferdinand almost goes too far in attributing to his father family connections and social distinctions which were not altogether true. This was done by implication rather than by direct statement, and clouded rather than illuminated the story of the Admiral's antecedents. Perhaps this is forgiveable. At the time of his writing the biography (of a greatly honoured father by a devoted son) Ferdinand was a man of considerable wealth, which stemmed in large measure from his father's successes and business acumen, including the revenue from the work of four hundred slaves in Hispaniola. He enjoyed several royal sinecures, he was an aristocrat of long standing, a man of learning, a bibliophile who had amassed one of the greatest libraries of the world. It is understandable that such a man would not wish to have his father's predecessors paraded as low-born, uneducated weavers living

*The Life of Admiral Christopher Columbus, Ferdinand Columbus, trans Benjamin Keen, The Folio Society, 1960.

close to poverty. Instead, Ferdinand, like his father, took refuge in fantasy. Christopher had once boasted a much more noble lineage to which he said he was entitled. He claimed that he was 'not the first admiral of my line'. He was patently wrong — and he was aware of it.

Ferdinand fuelled the fire. Shrewdly he attributed to others the suggestion of his father's noble line stemming from a Roman consul, and included for good measure a French admiral of the reign of Louis XI. With a touch more truth, Ferdinand described Christopher's parents (his own grandparents) as 'persons of worth who had been reduced to poverty by the factions and wars of Lombardy'.

Much has been written about Christopher's Jewish ancestry; that he was, in fact, a Spanish Jew converted to Christianity, one who was known as a *converso*. The notable Spanish historian Salvador de Madariaga wrote a formidable and plausible biography of Columbus* which was marred by its anti-Semitic slant. Columbus was not, as alleged, an emigré Catalan Jew forced by racial discrimination to flee Genoa and adopt the Catholic faith. What is much more convincing are all the accounts of Columbus's fervent devotion to the Virgin and to St Francis. The so-called evidence of his aquiline nose, the Jewishness of his mother's name and a tendency to the miserly care of his earnings (an almost universal trait) do not amount to a row of beans.

Ferdinand referred to his father's Christian virtues:†

> He was so strict in matters of religion that for fasting and saying prayers he might have been taken for a member of a religious order. He was so great an enemy of swearing and blasphemy that I give my word I never heard him utter any oath other than 'By St Ferdinand!' and when he grew very angry with someone his rebuke was to say 'God take you!' . . . If he had to write anything, he always began by writing these words: *IESUS CUM MARIA sit nobis in via.*

The facts are that Christopher Columbus came from very humble, Catholic origins and it is due to his father's and his own endeavours that he rose above those beginnings to the riches and honours and distinctions which he earned throughout his great life. These became the envy of Europe, and claimants have clamoured for recognition as the birthplace of Columbus. The exact location has never been established beyond a reasonable doubt, but to all but the blinkered, Columbus was Genoese through and through, and the supporting documentation is irrefutable.

---

*Christopher Columbus, Being The Life of The Very Magnificent Lord Don Cristobal Colón, Hodder & Stoughton, 1939.
†Ferdinand Columbus, p.35.

2 Early Days at Sea: Pirates, Corsairs and Shipwreck

CHRISTOPHER Columbus tells us that he went to sea at the age of fourteen, but even this simple statement is disputed. Indeed, it is surprising that he was not younger: after all, the sea, ships, sailors and the general maritime ambience of a great port like Genoa would have made going to sea second nature for the boy. Much of this is confirmed in this excerpt from a letter Columbus wrote to the Catholic Sovereigns many years later in 1501:*

> From a very early age I began to follow the sea and have continued to do so to this day . . . I have passed more than forty years in the business† and have travelled to every place where there is navigation up to the present time. I have had dealings and conversation with learned men, priests and laymen, Latins and Greeks, Jews and Moors, and many others of other Sects. I find Our Lord . . . granted me the gift of knowledge. He made me skilled in seamanship, equipped me abundantly with the sciences of astronomy, geometry and arithmetic and taught my mind and hand to draw this sphere and upon it the cities, rivers, mountains, islands and ports, each in its proper place. Thus Our Lord revealed to me that it was feasible to sail from here to the Indies, and placed in me a burning desire to carry out this plan.

Yet another mystery at this stage of Christopher's adolescence needs examination. Many sources state that he studied at Pavia University. What should be regarded as one of the most authoritative sources — Ferdinand Columbus — states quite categorically‡ that his father 'studied enough at the University of Pavia, to understand the geographers, of whose teaching he was very fond; for this reason he also gave himself to the study of astronomy and geometry . . .'

Perhaps such extravagant claims from Ferdinand are predictable. However, there is no documentary evidence — such as matriculation records — to support them. The placing of Christopher among the alumni of Pavia seems a pure invention by Ferdinand, and the error or deception has been perpetuated ever since.

Much more believable is the suggestion that Christopher received a modest and quite ordinary education, probably at the local elementary school which

---

* Ferdinand Columbus, p.35–6.

†This suggests he became associated with the sea at the age of about ten.

‡ Ferdinand Columbus, p.35.

BIRTHPLACE

AT ONE stage or another towns all over Europe have claimed to be the birthplace of Christopher Columbus. Claimants have come from Italy, Spain, Portugal, France, England, the Netherlands, Greece, Switzerland and Turkey.

A plaque in Calvi, Corsica, makes the erroneous claim: '*Ici est né, en 1441, Christophe Colomb, immortalisé par la découverte du Nouveau Monde, alors que Calvi était sous la domination génoise. Mort à Valladolid le 20 mai 1500.*' Columbus did not die in 1500: the date was 1506. The birth date is wrong by ten years. Calvi was not under Genoese domination. And, finally, Columbus was not born in Calvi.

A Greek writer claimed that the great explorer was a fifteenth-century Greek corsair in the service of France with the assumed name of Coulon.

An English claimant published a book in 1682 which stated that Columbus had been 'born in England but was resident in Genoa.' A Lisbon claimant declared that Columbus was no other than the Portuguese nobleman Gonzales Zarco.

Specific towns and villages which have laid claim to the great Genoese Discoverer are:
Nervi, close to Genoa
Bugiasco
Genoa, the true claimant
Piacenza, north-west of Genoa towards Cremona
Quinto, near Vicenza, west of Venice
Albissola, close by Savona
Oneglia, near Imperia, towards Monaco
Cosseria
Chiavari, east along the coast from Genoa towards La Spezia
Milan, north of Genoa
Calvi, on the north-west coast of Corsica
Tortosa, south-east along the coast from Barcelona
Plascencia, south of Salamanca, near the Portuguese border
Pontevedra, north-east Spain, near Santiago
Cogoleto
Savona, west of Genoa
Cuccaro
Finale, near Rapallo
Novara, just west of Milan
Modena, near Bologna

the clothiers' guild had opened for the sons of its members. Nor is there any evidence that Christopher was anything other than a perfectly ordinary young pupil.

However, education of a high order did come his way, instigated by an insatiable curiosity; a self-induced education which his intelligent brain sought to improve and extend. It was far from purely academic. Christopher himself admits to learning the science of navigation through direct contact with the sea, by listening carefully and eagerly to old salts' tales — the pilots and sailors of the Mediterranean.

As well as the sciences of geography, geometry, mathematics, cosmography, astronomy and navigation, Christopher Columbus taught himself to draw, a more than useful adjunct to navigation, enabling him to capture the scenes of harbours and other coastal features, for much charting in the fifteenth century relied heavily upon descriptive and artistic representations of places visited.

It was also in his formative years that the young Columbus studied Latin, mastering it well enough to enable him to understand books on cosmography. Christopher's friend, Andrés Bernáldez, the academic cleric, considered Columbus to be a man of great intellect, but little education. This seems a little simplistic. After all, Columbus taught himself Latin not only well enough to study books and documents but to be able to debate obscure and abstruse matters with scholars at both the Portuguese and the Spanish courts.

Another aspect of his learning touches upon the claims for his origins to have been centred on Spain rather than Italy. It is a fact that — other than Latin — the only surviving evidence of his writings is in Spanish, not Italian. The conclusion has been drawn, therefore, that Spanish was his native tongue. There is no very satisfactory answer to this argument, except that because of

Columbus's evident intelligence, and his apparent ability to learn Latin with such facility, it seems not inconceivable that he should be able to learn Spanish comfortably once he had convinced himself of the necessity of doing so in order to pursue his dreams.

It appears that what Columbus lacked was a formal *disciplined* education: his was too random, like a rudderless ship, discarding at will, hopping from one interest or obsession to another, lacking discernment. As one biographer put it: 'He selected his reading matter not intellectually but obsessively, reading only what related to his own favourite theories, rejecting or distorting whatever failed to support his prejudices.'* And this resulted in an imbalance which became an obsession and which contributed partly at least to his subsequent failures and even his downfall.

Madrid's naval museum describes this chart of Spanish and Portuguese waters as contemporaneous with Columbus — probably very early 16th century.

In his letter to the Catholic Sovereigns dated 1501, Columbus refers obliquely to having travelled 'to every place where there is navigation up to the present time'. During the years 1465 to 1479 (when aged between fourteen and twenty-

* Felipe Fernandez-Armesto, *Columbus and the Conquest of the Impossible*, Weidenfeld and Nicolson, 1974, p. 25.

eight), Columbus became embroiled in the bustling maritime busyness of the Mediterranean. 'Wherever ship has sailed,' he once claimed grandly, 'there have I voyaged.'

We do know that during many of these years in question Columbus was assisting his father's woollen business, working ashore as well as at sea travelling by ship, presumably selling the wares and buying stocks. It is unlikely that he was younger than twenty before he undertook a voyage of any real consequence.

One of the first of any consequence took place about 1474–5, when he was in his early to mid-twenties. The island of Chios or Khios, which is sometimes called 'the garden of the Aegean', slumbers comfortably in the sunshine of the eastern Mediterranean about forty miles from Smyrna, close to the Turkish mainland, almost on the same latitude as Athens. The island is mountainous, verdant and smelling of spices, pines, powerful orange blossom and the aromatic gum mastic bush which Columbus examined carefully because it was such a valuable crop and which he compared many years later to a similar plant found in Cuba.

Two expeditions went from Italy to Chios, one in 1474 and the second in the following year. We know that Columbus visited the island, which was at the time one of the eastern strongholds against the Turkish advance to the west. The first expedition sailed on 25 May 1474; the second left in September 1475 carrying reinforcements to help protect the island from Turkish aggression.

One of the ships on this second expedition belonged to Paolo di Negro, and another belonged to Nicola Spinola. Both families were known to Christopher, all were close friends and the heirs to both men are mentioned in Columbus's will.

Whether Columbus went to Chios with the first expedition and lived there for the next sixteen months or more before returning with the second expedition is not known. One source says firmly that Columbus spent about a year there, seeking his fortune, although this source admits it seems a long time ashore and failed to give Columbus the seafaring experience he was seeking. Nor is it known what he was doing there anyway. Whether he travelled as a seaman, a merchant, a ship's captain or as a pilot – or in whatever capacity – we shall probably never know. As with all things Columbian, mystery accompanies Columbus's association with Chios. Although his name fails to appear on any roll call for either of the expeditions, Columbus made several well-documented references in his writings to his visit. A further puzzling reference is his own statement that he saw the mastic harvest in March. This can only have been a mistake of a date (which he was prone to do) or an error of transcription, for the mastic was never – in hundreds of years – harvested before the spring.

The importance of Chios to the Columbus story is that this beautiful, aromatic island captivated the explorer's mind and imagination, as did the income from the production and sale of the gum mastic. Chios displayed an opulence, colour and variety which sombre, sullen Genoa lacked. Columbus could only gaze and wonder at the island. Further east, beyond Chios, lay the Orient, hiding the measureless wealth and jewels of the sub-continent of India, and further still the unknown vastness of the kingdom of China, ruled by the mighty, inscrutable, mysterious emperor, the Great Khan.

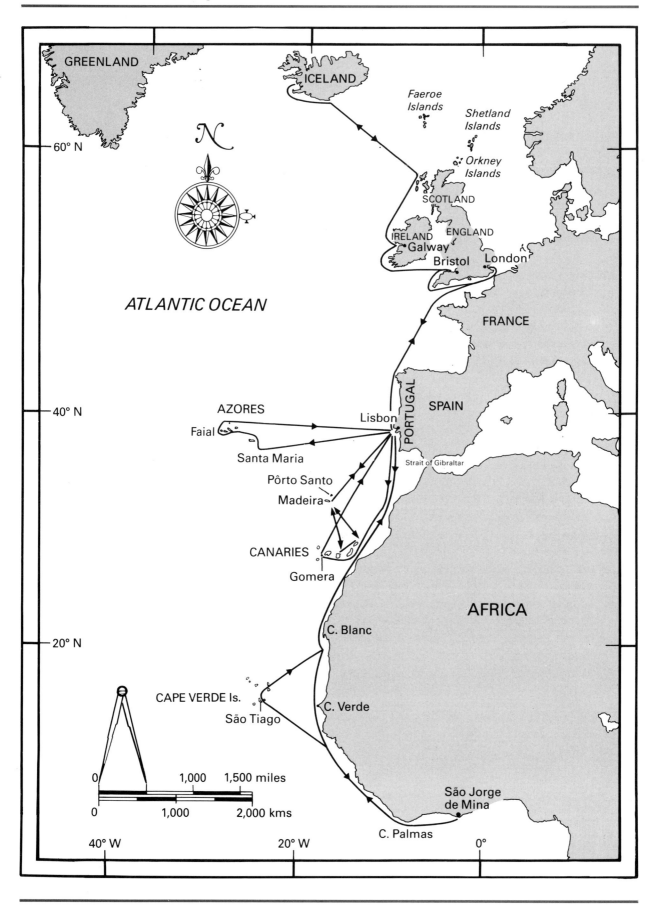

GREENLAND

ICELAND

Faeroe Islands

Shetland Islands

Orkney Islands

SCOTLAND

IRELAND   ENGLAND

Galway

Bristol

London

ATLANTIC OCEAN

FRANCE

AZORES

Faial

Santa Maria

Lisbon

PORTUGAL   SPAIN

Strait of Gibraltar

Pôrto Santo

Madeira

CANARIES

Gomera

AFRICA

C. Blanc

CAPE VERDE Is.

São Tiago

C. Verde

São Jorge de Mina

C. Palmas

0	1,000	1,500 miles	
0	1,000	2,000 kms	

40° W   20° W   0°

60° N

40° N

20° N

Two curious incidents in the Columbus story obtrude at about this time. The first relates to an adventure off Tunis and the second to a shipwreck off Cape St Vincent. The Tunis escapade could only have taken place after the Chios expedition, from which Columbus would have returned to Genoa at the end of 1475. Thus, a likely date for the Tunis story is the following year — 1476. To be precise, it could not have taken place in 1477 when we know Columbus was off Iceland, nor could it have been the summer of 1478 when he was known to be at Madeira. It could have followed thereafter, but the general belief is that it took place earlier rather than later. So, we are looking critically at the years 1475–7.

This coincides with what is believed to have been a period of much sailing experience for Columbus in the Mediterranean, even though supporting documentation is lacking. It is thought that Columbus would have visited scores of the numerous ports, islands, bays and gulfs along the thousands of miles of the Mediterranean coastline. Yet, curiously, the only names for which there is documentary evidence of Columbus's having visited are Naples, Marseilles, the island Hyères, Cape Creus in Catalonia, the bay of Narbonne, Sardinia and the Barbary Coast. There is no reference at all to the hundred-and-one other ports he must have visited during these years of apprenticeship and learning. Such absence of evidence is worrying if only because it raises twinges of doubt. It does not seem possible that Columbus did *not* visit scores of other Mediterranean ports during his early days at sea: for him to have become the great astronomer, navigator and explorer that he was he simply must have had a long and fruitful experience of sailing ... but the evidence is not there.

By now, too, he was accompanying his father's shipments of woven goods and purchases of wool, negotiating with buyers and suppliers, bartering and dealing for merchandise, visiting coastal towns and villages throughout the Gulf of Genoa such as Savona, Voltri, Varazze, Noli, Albenga, and on the gulf's eastern side, Camogli, Sestri and Lerici.

Evidence does exist, however, for both the Tunis adventure and the Cape St Vincent shipwreck — and yet both incidents, despite the evidence, leave nagging doubts. Let us consider the Tunis episode first.

The Tunisian corsair incident came to light in a letter allegedly written by Columbus from Hispaniola in January 1495 to the Catholic Sovereigns. Ferdinand, writing his father's biography, claims to have unearthed this letter, a copy of which was seen by Bishop Las Casas when researching *his* biography of Columbus. No one appears to have seen the original letter, which is supposed to have read:*

> It happened to me that King René [René of Anjou was known as the Good and lived 1409–80] ... sent me to Tunis to capture the galleass *Fernandina*; and when I was off the island of San Pietro, near Sardinia, a vessel informed me there were two ships and a carrack with the said

* Ferdinand Columbus, p.36.

In the years before his voyages of discovery Columbus gained ocean-going experience in places as far apart as the near-equatorial heat of the Gulf of Guinea in the south, and the icy, inhospitable waters off Iceland in the north.

galleass, which frightened my people, and they resolved to go no
further but to return to Marseilles to pick up another ship and more
men. I, seeing that I could do nothing against their wills without some
ruse, agreed to their demand, and changing the point of the compass,
made sail at nightfall; and at sunrise the next day we found ourselves
off Cape Carthage, while all aboard were certain we were bound for
Marseilles.

To begin to understand this incident it is necessary to appreciate that during
this period of the fifteenth century there was a cold war that occasionally flared
up into hot activity. Popular sentiment in Genoa regarded Catalonians and the
Aragonese as traditional enemies, and there had been a tenacious hostility
towards the kingdom of Aragon and its raiding parties which descended on
towns and villages along the Ligurian coast, pillaging, killing, disrupting trade,
and competing with the Genoese for the lucrative trade routes of the
Mediterranean.

Leader or king of the Angévins was René d'Anjou and, during a period of
alliance between the Angévins and the Aragonese, Domenico Columbus, an
activist in support of the Anjou element, would have commended himself — so
the story goes — to René. But it seems wholly unlikely that he had the ear of
the king, let alone that he was able to influence him in the placement of his
young son as a ship's captain. Columbus was given express instructions to
embark on a corsair raid to Tunis to capture the Aragonese galleass *Fernandina*
(sometimes *Ferrandina*). Why such a combative commission should be given to
a peaceful young man unused to cannon and weaponry remains unclear. The
story continues: Columbus duly sailed south from Genoa until he reached the
isle of San Pietro in south-west Sardinian waters. Here he received intelligence
of the *Fernandina* being supported by a small squadron of other vessels,
whereupon his crew refused to continue the voyage and asked to return to
Marseilles, not, strangely, to Genoa.

Columbus did not intend complying, and he resorted to subterfuge. He
tampered with the compass, pretending to head the ship to Marseilles but
continuing on a course to the Gulf of Tunis. 'I had them unfurl the sails
shortly before nightfall,' Columbus is alleged to have written, 'and by sunrise
we were passing the Carthaginian headland, all firmly convinced that we were
arriving at Marseilles.'

On arrival, the *Fernandina* and accompanying ships had gone. The mission
was abandoned.

The story lacks the ring of truth yet has just enough verisimilitude to make
one accept it, albeit with considerable reluctance. Historians are almost equally
divided into camps as to whether or not the mission was ever undertaken,
whether or not Columbus commanded it and whether only some or all of its
elements can be believed. Some, allowing that René really did dispatch a ship,
have voiced the opinion that Columbus probably took part in such an
adventure, not as a captain but possibly as a seaman.

The Spanish historian Madariaga refers to Columbus's having resorted to a
ruse to deceive the ship's company: 'That is Columbus all over!' A more telling
argument casts doubt on the whole story. It is this: the original letter — if
Columbus ever wrote it — would have done Columbus no good whatsoever in
the eyes of the Catholic Sovereigns to whom it was supposedly addressed. René

d'Anjou was a sworn enemy of Aragon (Ferdinand's kingdom), thus Columbus was declaring that he had allied himself at one stage in his life with the king's enemy. It would have been a senseless admission of considerable risk to Columbus, and he would have been sufficiently street-wise politically not to make such a grave misjudgement.

A final possibility exists: that Ferdinand Columbus concocted the letter, purporting it to have been written by his father, in which he related a story garbled, in all good faith, as he tried to recollect facts and anecdotes related to him by his father over the years.

The Cape St Vincent shipwreck which Columbus experienced soon after the Tunisian corsair episode is better documented and is universally accepted as having taken place, although some aspects of the story stretch the imagination. Ferdinand Columbus's version of the incident is sadly flawed and, lending some credence to the thought that he may also have misinterpreted the Tunisian episode, he quite wrongly dated the shipwreck as 1485 — an error then perpetuated by later historians.

It was during the summer of 1476 that a small convoy of five Genoese ships sailed westwards from the tiny harbour of Noli, west of Genoa. It was bound for England and Flanders and was commanded by Cristoforo de Franchi Sacco, who carried with him a safe conduct from King Louis XI of France, safeguarding the squadron from corsairs. During the fifteenth century there was a clear distinction between a corsair and a pirate. A pirate operated essentially for private gain: all ships of all nations were fair game. Corsairs operated under a monarch's commission or under the control of an internationally accepted authority, and they were often financed by banking institutions. Groups of small states sometimes acted concertedly by employing corsairs. Corsair captains offered their services like mercenaries, for their own profit as well as for the profit of their employers.

One such investment-cum-corsair captain was the Frenchman Guillaume de Casenove, also known as Coulon and Coulomp. He had assembled a fleet of fifteen vessels to serve in the name of the king of France. His orders were to attack ships of Aragon and Castile, but not ships of the Genoese Republic.

The Genoese convoy of five ships was armed with small cannons and it is thought that Columbus was aboard the flagship, *Bechalla*. The two squadrons clashed off the Portuguese coast between Lagos and Cape St Vincent. The engagement lasted ten hours and included much grappling, fire-raising and destruction. Three of the Genoese ships were sunk, the other two managing to make good their escape to Cádiz. Four or five of the corsair ships were sunk. Fire, the scourge of wooden ships and respecter of neither friend nor foe, created havoc, and for many men jumping overboard into the sea was the only way of preserving themselves from raging fires and certain death.

One such escaper was Columbus who '. . . being an excellent swimmer, and seeing land only a little more than two leagues away, seized an oar which fate offered him . . . and so it pleased God, who was preserving him for greater things, to give him the strength to reach shore'.*

Columbus regarded his survival as a miracle. He landed at Lagos, then a tiny

*Ferdinand Columbus, p. 39.

fishing village, in such an exhausted state that it took him days to recuperate. Once he had recovered his strength, he set off for Lisbon.

This experience off Cape St Vincent proved a watershed in Columbus's life. Genoa, port of his birth and early formative years, was now behind him. No longer was it to play a leading part in his life. Ahead lay Lisbon, adventures and experiences beyond his wildest dreams, and the beginning of his great enterprise, his ordeal with the Atlantic Ocean and his discovery of the New World.

3 Venture into Northern Waters

W HEN THE Portuguese seamen and fishermen from Lisbon and the Algarve gazed towards the west where the sun disappeared every evening they saw the empty void of the Atlantic with its long, relentless rollers crashing against the rocky shore of the Iberian peninsula having travelled unknown thousands of miles. They knew that the group of islands known as the Azores lay hundreds of miles out into that ocean, but further still there was a boundless expanse of water. Columbus, meditating in his solitude, became obsessively occupied with thoughts about the unexplained emptiness of the ocean.

There was hardly a single person of education who did not believe the earth was round. With his lively spirit of enquiry and adventure, Columbus formed images of the globe and its expanses of sea and land and continents. He wondered, dreamed and fantasised about travelling to the east by following the westering sun.

His Lisbon years (from the age of twenty-five to thirty-three) were heady times, spent in intensive study and self-education, feeding his appetite for knowledge of the sea, ships, cosmography, navigation (in which he seemed to develop a sixth sense), chart-making, the works of the world's travellers and explorers.

Taviani considers that the poet and dreamer in Columbus would have sensed an ethereal atmosphere in this Lisbon period of his life, something in the soul of Portugal and the Portuguese, and he marks the calendar of 13 August 1476 as a watershed in Columbus's life. Thereafter his destiny was decided: the western horizon beckoned and enchanted him, challenged him just as it had the Portuguese, and especially one — Henry the Navigator. He was a man of enormous importance and, apart from his own countrymen, shamelessly neglected by the civilised world.

He was the third child of King John I of Portugal and Philippa, granddaughter of Edward III of England. He was born in 1394 and lived till 1460, distinguishing himself in the war with Morocco at the capture of Ceuta in 1415. He became captivated by the sight of the African coastline, stretching south, washed by the same Atlantic breakers that struck the shore of Portugal. He devoted his time to maritime discovery and commerce.

His influence on maritime technical matters, upon cartography and the design of ships — he was instrumental in introducing the caravel — was great, and he mustered around him a collection of seamen, navigators and explorers until his court resembled a maritime convention.

Henry the Navigator instigated nautical research into ocean currents and tides, into the winds, into navigation by calculating the distance of the stars

Most intelligent people in the late 15th century accepted that the world was round. Martin Behaim produced the first terrestrial globe in 1492. Models like this one were engraved with Columbus's New World discoveries. They could be found throughout Europe's palaces and libraries.

and geographical latitude. He established a school of navigation near Sagres, and despatched expeditions in the course of which Madeira and Porto Santo were discovered.

Navigators in Henry's lifetime began to appreciate his helpful contributions to their science. They employed 'tables of declination which could help fix, in the ocean as in the southern hemisphere, the parallels and meridians of routes'.* The southernmost part of known Africa then was Bojador, the western Sahara, south of the Canaries. Henry became obsessed with Africa and dreamed of Portuguese seamen discovering this magical world.

Time saw the boundaries of knowledge spread further south along this inhospitable, burning desert coast — to Cape Blanc, to Cape Verde, to the mouth of the Gambia river. Henry hoped to discover the whole of Africa, to reach Prester John's legendary Ethiopia and the fabled lands of the Guinea.

Christopher Columbus would have been a lad of nine when Henry the Navigator died. He would soon become aware of the tremendous contributions the prince had made to Afro-Atlantic explorations, and when he landed after the shipwreck only a few miles from Henry's temple of navigational research at Sagres Columbus might have been aware of it. But by the time of the

* Paolo Taviani, p.67.

shipwreck, the prince's observatory and school had been wrecked and laid waste, and even if Columbus visited the site it is unlikely he could have found much inspiration there.

Still more questions about Columbus arise: there are not many clues as to why he determined to visit Lisbon. His son Ferdinand simply states, with almost dismissive unconcern, 'Finding himself near Lisbon, and knowing that many of his Genoese countrymen lived in that city, he went there as soon as he could . . .'*

It would have made more sense if Columbus had returned to Genoa after such an experience. Lisbon lay a week's walk away to the north, perhaps two days by horse, and where would he have acquired a horse having been left virtually naked after the shipwreck?

The consensus of opinion is that he continued to Lisbon by sea, travelling with other shipwrecked mariners to Cádiz first, before boarding a ship probably owned by the Spinolas or Di Negros. It is also probable that the Spinola galleon and the Di Negro *Bettinella*, which escaped destruction, fled back to Cádiz to effect repairs and that one or both of these ships transported the survivors to Lisbon.

Perhaps the clue to Columbus's determination to reach Lisbon comes in a statement that his brother Bartholomew was in that city carrying on the business of bookseller and chart maker. Las Casas wrote of him:

> To judge by the books and the nautical charts annotated and commented upon in his hand, which must have been his or the Admiral's, I believe that he was so skilled in that art that the Admiral himself could not far surpass him.

What is unknown, however, is whether it was the younger brother Bartholomew who settled in Lisbon first, or whether it was Christopher who induced the younger man to join him in Portugal's exciting capital.

Thus it was that Columbus journeyed to Lisbon, having experienced for the first time the broad wastes of the North Atlantic rollers and breakers that spent their majestic power along the coast of Portugal. Gone were the experiences in the protected waters of the Mediterranean: new, measureless visions of unexplored horizons opened up before him. His two main interests in life — his devout Catholicism and his intense desire to explore the oceans — were beginning to coalesce into a towering, stubborn, unassailable belief in his own destiny. Yet the reality was, he was a penniless survivor of a shipwreck.

In Lisbon there were to be found agents of Spinola and Di Negro whom Columbus would have known or to whom he could have secured an introduction. It is certain that one of them re-employed him. It is believed that either a second expedition of theirs set out from Genoa, which then stopped at Lisbon where Columbus was taken aboard one of the ships, or that he joined one of the two surviving ships of the corsair engagement, northbound to England and Flanders. Whatever the circumstances, it was at the end of this same fateful year of 1476 — or at the very beginning of 1477 — that Columbus visited London.

By the time he visited England's capital it was already the biggest and most thriving city in the country, its wealth firmly based on profitable commerce,

*Ferdinand Columbus, p.39.

The Thames and the Tower of London at the time of Columbus's visit to the city in 1476–77.

principally due to the wool industry, a trade conducted with the ports of France, Spain, Portugal, the Low Countries, Denmark and other Baltic states. The huge port area of London, straddling the wide Thames, made it an attraction to commercial traders, though Columbus would not have enjoyed the chilling showers and bitter winds of so northerly a country.

From London, he sailed to Bristol, a port forever linked with the explorations of John and Sebastian Cabot, lying snugly seven or eight miles from the Severn estuary, protected from pirates and invaders by the twisting river passing between gorges, difficult to navigate and subjected to tides of mammoth proportions.

There is no doubt about Columbus's visit to Bristol. But a lot of contentious doubt surrounds the question of his visit to Iceland. These northern waters – *Il Mare Tenebroso* or the Dark Sea as they were called – must have intrigued Columbus if only because much of their wastes had never been explored. He determined to visit Thule, where the English traded from Bristol.

THE NORSEMEN: SQUANDERED DISCOVERIES

THE NORSEMEN arrived in Iceland in 874, some years behind the Irish. In the fourth century BC the Greeks had described the island as a place six days sailing from Britain 'where land, water and air are all mixed together'. The Norsemen's rediscovery of Iceland has been regarded by some historians as one of the greatest seafaring exploits.

Incredibly their frail craft were stout enough to withstand the savagery of winter storms in the northern seas.

The Norsemen were the standard-bearers of Christianity to the Arctic regions. A thousand years ago Europe's first parliament — Iceland's Althing — adopted Catholicism as the country's religion.

In 982 Eric the Red crossed the sea leading to Greenland, where the lichen-covered rocks gave rise to the country's name, a geographical misnomer matching that of the Pacific Ocean.

Around the year 1000 the Norsemen ventured west, discovered the coast of Labrador and the island of rocks and ice we know as Newfoundland. Further south they came upon more promising land — Markland, the land of woods — which was almost certainly Nova Scotia.

In 1070 a chronicler refers to a land called Vinland, a land yielding wild grapes of the finest quality. Further evidence of this region is fragmentary and unsafe. Vinland disappears from the pages of history as a shadowy, unclaimed discovery of the vast continent of North America. There is mention of a Vinland map, but today this map is regarded as a forgery. Although these Norsemen were brave, pioneering, pragmatic people, they were unimaginative, with limited horizons, and they let slip the treasures of the New World.

They were not colonists. Even Iceland and Greenland slumbered in an ill-defined, non-colonial type of self-rule. Their American discoveries slipped away into near oblivion. It took the pioneering efforts of the Portuguese, Spanish, English and Italian mariners some five centuries later to reawaken the age of exploration and reap the rewards of discovery with all its measureless riches and benefits to man. It is possible that some fishermen of England may have sighted some part of the North American continent even as Columbus made his first voyage of discovery. It was John Cabot (1450–98), a Genoese who became a naturalised Venetian and finally settled in Bristol, who landed on Cape Breton Island off Nova Scotia in 1497 and planted the royal flag. His sons discovered Newfoundland and sailed as far south as Virginia.

Thule, or Ultima Thule, was the barren, bitterly cold and inhospitable island known today as Iceland. It was ruled at that time by Denmark but was dominated in effect by the English traders. If Columbus did in fact visit the island he would have found it depressingly unattractive. Its wild, harshly outlined beauty was cloaked in hours of semi- and full darkness, and by mists and snow. Volcanic mountains provided an overpowering presence, glacier-filled valleys and ravines brooded over the landscape: lava and ash littered the windswept plains. This environment coarsened the wretched populace which lived mostly underground for half the year when even the sea froze.

Columbus, through the words of his biographers Ferdinand and Las Casas, described his visit to this bleak place in terms capable of many interpretations:

> In February 1477, I sailed myself an hundred leagues beyond Thule Island whose northern part is 73 degrees distant from the Equinoctial and not 63 degrees as some will have it to be: nor does it lie upon the line where Ptolemy's west begins, but much more to the westward; and to this island which is as big as England, the English trade, especially from Bristol. At the time I was there the sea was not frozen but the tides were so great that in some places it swelled twenty-six fathoms and fell as much.

However, critics doubt that Columbus ever visited Thule and point to the inconsistencies in this passage: these deserve consideration. Let it be stated at the outset that some errors of transcription by biographers may have intruded. Columbus himself may have confused places and times, or he may have been lying or exaggerating in his statement — as he was wont to do.

Consider the reference to a tide rise of twenty-six fathoms. This is patently absurd when applied to Thule as Columbus does. There is no such tide rise in Iceland: the nearest to approach this is a mere quarter of Columbus's figure. But this figure of twenty-six fathoms is perfectly consistent with Bristol, and with the fact that a Genoese fathom equated to .578 metres. This would make Columbus's twenty-six fathoms equal to a little over fifteen metres, and this is not too excessive by the standards of Bristol and Avonmouth.* It thus becomes possible that Columbus got the figures right but wrongly remembered the place.

It is likely he also wrongly recalled the visit to Iceland as taking place in February 1477. Such a voyage from Bristol would have lasted twelve to fifteen days in the fifteenth century. Although research has shown that winter to have been exceptionally mild and the Icelandic waters relatively free of ice, trade between Iceland and England was not normally carried out during the bitter winter months. Columbus often made mistakes of dates and months, and this is likely to have been one such case.

What is less easily explained is his error in measurement of Iceland's latitude. His measurements do not conform with Ptolemy, and this is dismissed as a genuine error attributable to Columbus's relative inexperience at the time, and it was not for some years that he began to use the quadrant as a navigational aid. It has been observed that during this disputed voyage Columbus would have merely evaluated distances and positions by dead reckoning (basing his estimates on duration and direction of sailing).

Columbus's reference to having ventured a hundred leagues beyond Iceland

---

* Only Nova Scotia — not then discovered by John Cabot from Bristol — exceeds this figure.

— which is totally rejected by many historians as quite impossible — is given
an acceptable explanation if the transcription of the passage by Columbus is
re-transcribed. The one hundred leagues could be the reference to Iceland's
size — its circumference. One hundred leagues 'beyond Thule' is evidently
impossible if 'beyond Thule' is meant to indicate a north-north-eastern arc
embracing as it does the Arctic Circle and Jan Mayen Island.

Almost equally impossible to accept is 'west', for this would encompass
Greenland which would call for further comment from Columbus, possibly
including reports of attempted landings. And it is self evidently not 'south'.

It is only fair to chronicle a few observations in favour of accepting
Columbus's journey to Iceland. For example, the quoted statement came from
annotations. They were not addressed to anyone, so Columbus had no need to
exaggerate, no need to boast idly of his achievements; he could not be
enhancing his reputation nor be trying to influence anyone. In fact, there was
no need for him to lie or fantasise about the journey.

On balance, the consensus of historians is marginally in favour of accepting
that Columbus visited London, Bristol, Iceland, and even Galway, probably
visited on his return from Iceland. There — in Galway — he was told the tale
of two shipwrecked people, a man and a beautiful woman, each clinging to a
plank and each safely washed ashore. They bore distinct oriental characteristics
and it was claimed they came from Cathay — China. The story may have lost
something in translation — Columbus spoke Latin to the Irish — but the
thought remains that the story may in essence be true.

It would have fascinated Columbus that the Icelanders commonly accepted
that to the west of them lay Greenland and Labrador and possibly other lands.
To a dreamer like Columbus this would have been engrossing: it would have
captured his imagination. The need to delve deeper, to explore further, to seek
the unknown would have been compelling.

4 Lisbon: Gateway to the Atlantic

ONE can imagine Columbus returning to Lisbon from the Icelandic venture and mentally taking stock of his life and dreams. It is not easy to try to summarise his dreams: in this respect he was not a good communicator. Indeed, he adopted a ploy which is familiar to modern politicians who use it with success in the corridors of power: always to withhold information, never to divulge everything to anybody, for knowledge was power.

And knowledge Columbus was surely accumulating. His recent months of experiences since leaving the relative tranquillity of the Mediterranean had been nothing short of traumatic. There had been the battle with the corsairs when he was bloodied in battle. Then there was the miraculous discovery of an inner and a physical strength to swim two leagues (some six miles) to ensure survival. On a more general basis he had learned that the Atlantic Ocean contrasted violently with the gentler waters to which he was accustomed. The sea's awesome power in the northern waters around Iceland, the bitter coldness of the northern climes, the phenomenal tides of Bristol, all of these factors would have impressed Columbus and given him cause for contemplation, for wonder, even, at the fearsome majesty of the ocean.

It is believed that nothing in the northern wastes attracted Columbus to pursue discoveries in those harsh conditions where man found difficulty simply in surviving.

Nor did the south particularly attract him. Other navigators and explorers were already pushing forward the boundaries of discovery along the coast of Africa, though it was still to be another ten years before Bartholomew Dias would round the southern limits of the great African continent in 1487–8, naming it the Cape of Storms, which the king later renamed the Cape of Good Hope.

It was the west which fascinated Columbus. He had already shown a passion for knowledge about everything nautical and maritime, and in his adult life so far he had amassed a large amount of knowledge about seafaring in the Mediterranean. Now he had gained experience in the Atlantic, and it was to the west he looked: there lay his destiny.

Scholars, as has been said, regarded Columbus's time in Lisbon as a watershed, as a period of deep thinking when the bold, twin dreams of crossing the Atlantic and of discovering the Orient by sailing west began to form a single, compelling and all-consuming vision.

One biographer describes living in the Portuguese capital at this period as 'like a wild adventure'.* He continues:

*Christopher Columbus: The Dream and the Obsession, Gianni Granzotto, Collins, 1986, p.38.

Never before had a single geographical location bolted at such a dizzying pace to the forefront of human history. Everyone who had anything to do with the sea — sailors, scientists, astronomers, merchants — was involved in a kind of hand-to-hand combat with the ocean. For them too the best was yet to come, for the world was beginning to break out of its age-old insularity and take to the sea. The Portuguese and others living there were the first to believe that somewhere beyond the ocean, unknown lands existed. In Lisbon, this was all anyone talked about . . . among all the excitement, Columbus's imagination thrived.

Evidently Columbus felt comfortable in such a thriving city. He settled there apparently quite happily. Much is known of this period of his life, although gaps in the story leave us tantalisingly unaware of some activities. How he earned his living is not clear. Apart from making occasional voyages — which will be described in a moment — it is thought by Las Casas that he might have compiled nautical charts, for which there must have been a good demand, for sale in his brother's shop. He was certainly skilled at this craft, but there is no evidence to support Las Casas's suggestion, although it seems perfectly reasonable. In his brother's shop Columbus would have met scholars, thinkers, astronomers and mathematicians as well as seafarers, men who had studied the writings of travellers such as Marco Polo.* There would have been lively discussions.

Columbus became an omnivorous reader, closely studying the writings of travellers and scientists. Some idea of the range of his interests can be gauged

*Marco Polo (1254–1324) A Venetian of noble birth who travelled extensively throughout the Orient. He visited the Kublai Khan in China in 1275. Returned to Venice in 1295. Wrote an account of his travels which was translated into many languages, including English.

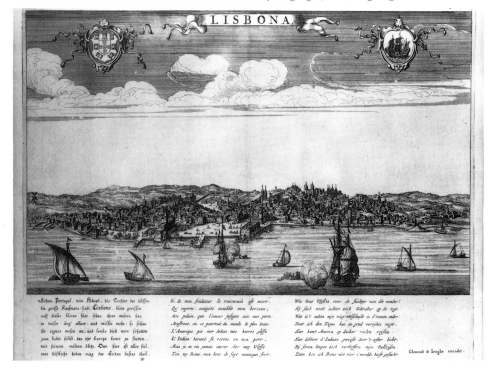

The Lisbon years helped Columbus prepare his plans for exploration. He would have recognised this engraving of the city.

IMAGO MUNDI

THIS priceless treasure is preserved in the Seville Archives. It is a volume in folio, bound in parchment, published soon after the invention of printing, owned by Columbus and heavily annotated in his own hand. It was written by a French cardinal, Pierre d'Ailly (sometimes Petrus de Aliaco), and published in 1480–83. The *Imago Mundi* (Image of the World) contains a wealth of astronomical and cosmographical information in Latin. Columbus was hugely influenced by it and scribbled annotations throughout the margins. The biographer Taviani has recorded that Columbus made no fewer than 898 marginal comments, known as postils, to this volume. These were all referred to by Las Casas when he compiled the Admiral's biography.

Columbus made more than 2,500 postils in incunabula, that is books printed at an early date, especially before 1501, and other volumes which have survived the centuries, almost all of which are written in corrupt Latin or in 'an impure Castilian'. Piccolomini's *Historia Rerum* contains 861 of them; a Castilian translation of Plutarch's *Parallel Lives* contains 437; there are 366 in the Latin translation of Marco Polo and just 24 in Pliny's *Historia Naturalis*.

The page shown here bears annotations by both Christopher and his brother Bartholomew Columbus. In the right hand margin the notes record the return of the explorer Bartholomew Diaz from his discovery of the Cape of Good Hope in 1488.

mundi

De quantitate terre habitabilis Capitulum octavum

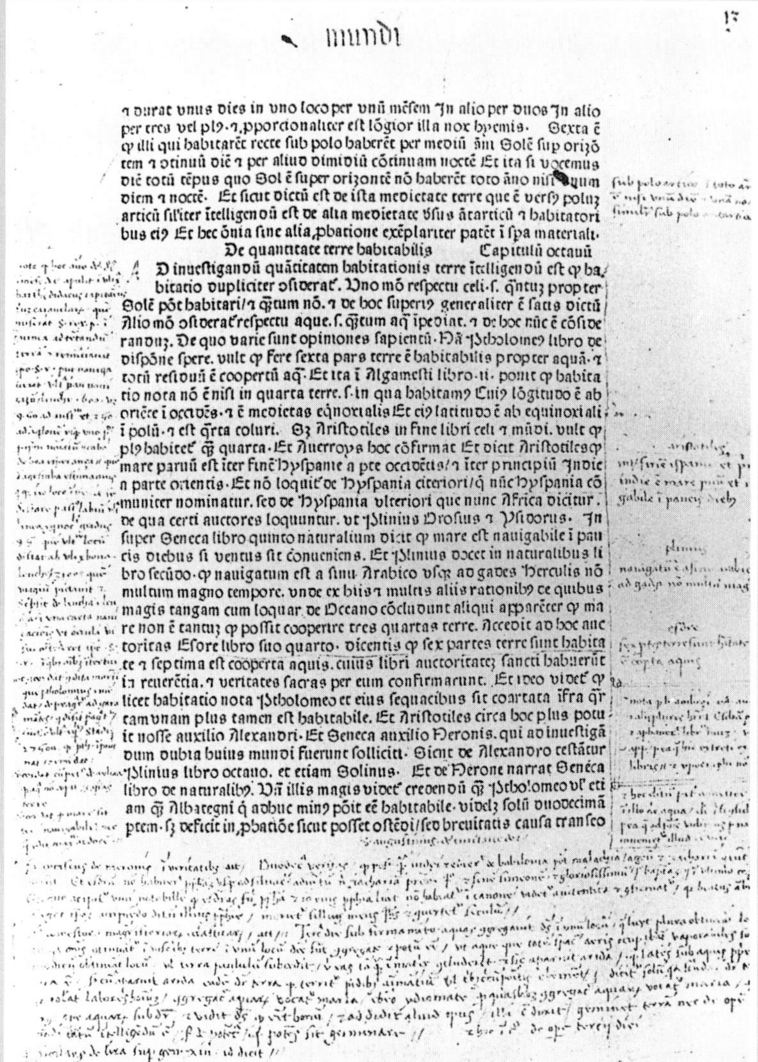

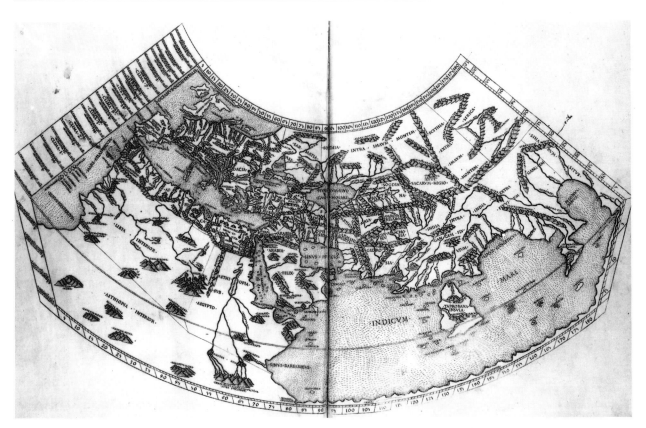

A map of the world according to Ptolemy from the 1478 edition of his *Geography*.

by many of the books which later formed part of Ferdinand's library and which are now preserved in the Columbian Archives in Seville, several of which bear Columbus's own annotations.

Among those which became his favourites, according to Granzotto, is believed to have been a copy of the Bible, compiled by a Spanish intellectual, which was a constant source of reference and reassurance to the Discoverer.

One of the most important secular volumes to which Columbus constantly referred was Cardinal D'Ailly's *Tractus de Imagine Mundi*, usually called *Imago Mundi* (Image of the World). Pierre D'Ailly, the one-time rector of the Sorbonne, had compiled a sort of digest of Greek and Latin writers' views on the world's geography, published in Louvain in 1480–83, which allowed Columbus to gain an insight into the works and thoughts of Plato, Aristotle, Cicero, Seneca, Macrobius and other great thinkers. Other volumes which became his constant companions, accompanying him even on his voyages of discovery, were the *Historia Rerum Ubique Gestarium*, an encyclopedia of cosmography and history with passages from classical writers on navigation, compiled by Cardinal Aeneas Piccolomini, printed in Vienna in 1477 (he later became Pope Pius II). Another favourite was the *Book of Marco Polo* or *Il Milione*, described as a Latin summary, by Francesco Pipino of Bologna, published in Antwerp in 1485. Pliny's *Historia Naturalis** was another

*Pliny the Elder (AD 23–79), the famous Roman writer on natural history.

†Claudius Ptolemaeus, astronomer and geographer, was born in Egypt and lived during the first half of the second century AD. His work on astronomy was the most authoritative for more than a millenium, until the brilliant work of Nicolaus Copernicus (1473–1543) arrived — too late for Columbus.

encyclopedic volume which was influential. It carried contributions on science, natural history and allied subjects.

Of all the books in his life, the one which influenced Columbus most was probably Ptolemy's† *Geographia*, published in eight volumes. The work summarised the geographical knowledge of the Greeks including a gazetteer with descriptions and locations.

Ptolemy also expounded the theory of latitude and longitude, the shape — spherical — and the size of planet earth, the extent of its seas and its central position in the universe with the heavenly bodies circling around it. He proposed means of projecting the spherical earth onto maps of a plane surface. He drew more than two dozen maps. His knowledge — as entrusted to his *Geographia* — held sway for more than a thousand years. Columbus was captivated by it. He did not necessarily believe all Ptolemy wrote, but he could not ignore him.

Carefully preserved to this day are clear marginal annotations Columbus made in his copy of D'Ailly's *Imago Mundi*. In his own handwriting he had noted *Mare totum navigabile* — all seas are navigable. Elsewhere he had added the postil *every country has its east and west*.

The Discoverer quaffed all this knowledge as if with an insatiable thirst until his search for knowledge became an obsession which drove him on and on, remorselessly seeking more and more information about the seas, the earth, about the stars, the sun and the moon.

While in Lisbon, Columbus attended church services, mass and vespers at the All Saints Church, in the course of which he met a young lady named Felipa Moniz (from her mother) Perestrello (from her father). They fell in love and married. The date of their wedding is unknown but researchers believe it to have occurred between 1479 and 1480. Little is known of the bride. She is described as 'of noble birth and a superior of the Convent of Saints'. She certainly possessed an aristocratic name. The Perestrellos had arrived in Portugal from Piacenza in Italy a century earlier. Felipa's father was one of Henry the Navigator's young students at the famous school at Sagres Castle. The sea was in his blood and he had taken part in the discovery of the Madeira archipelago and had personally captured the island of Porto Santo. Ferdinand describes the venture:*

> He and two other captains had gone with licence from the King of Portugal to discover new lands, agreeing to divide all they discovered into three parts and cast lots for the share that should fall to each. Sailing to the south-west they discovered the islands of Madeira and Porto Santo. Since the island of Madeira was the larger of the two, they made two parts of it, the third being the island of Porto Santo which fell to the share of . . . Perestrello.

Felipa's father was rewarded with the title of Governor of the island, but it proved to be a worthless post and the island of little use to anyone. Bartholomew Perestrello, a gentleman of the house of Prince John of Portugal, tried desperately hard to colonise and settle the island. He introduced seeds and plants but nothing flourished. He even used a rabbit to try a different form

---

* Ferdinand Columbus, pp. 39–40.

The house at Porto Santo where it is believed Columbus's
eldest and legitimate son, Diego, was born about 1475.

of colonisation, but this failed too. The soil was infertile and fresh water was difficult to find. Perestrello's family gradually descended into poverty. When Bartholomew died in 1467, the governorship of the island passed to Pedro Correa de Cunha, son-in-law of the widow, Isabella Moniz. He was the governor at the time of Columbus's marriage to Felipa.

The marriage lasted only a few years, five or six at the most, with Diego, described as his 'legitimate' son, their only child. Felipa died about 1485 in circumstances which are not recorded. It was a few years later, probably 1486 or '87, that Columbus met Beatrice Enriquez de Harana. She became his mistress and bore him another son, Ferdinand, described as his 'natural' son.

It was Diego who would come to inherit all Christopher's titles and privileges and wealth. The baby was conceived on Porto Santo. The newlyweds journeyed there at the invitation of Felipa's brother-in-law, the governor, and there they stayed for two years, the intention being that Columbus would set up as a trader, thus helping to ease the family's financial strains. After two years of no measurable success, the young family left the island and sought richer pickings in Funchal. But Columbus was never a trader. He was a born seafarer, and this aspect of his life earned rewards while he was in Madeira.

The archipelago, like the Canaries and the Azores, provided a listening post. It was an important base for all the Portuguese discoveries in the Atlantic. It became a port of call, a centre for the exchange of information, of seafaring activity and knowledge. Columbus wallowed in it.

Columbus was rewarded too by his mother-in-law, who accompanied the young couple to the archipelago. She gave him all her late husband's maritime documents — drawings, charts, log books, pilot books and handwritten notes of Atlantic and African routes, and notes to Madeira and the Azores: all of them of considerable worth to Columbus.

His years in Lisbon and the Madeira archipelago were not all devoted to marriage and the setting up of an agency, nor to dreaming, fantasising and studying. He also made some voyages, including one to Genoa, the last occasion he is known to have visited his town of birth. The evidence for this visit comes in a document which refers specifically to a visit made by Columbus from Lisbon to Madeira as a business agent for a Genoese firm in July 1478; and another cites that he gave testimony on 25 August 1479 in a court in Genoa.

The business trip to his native town would have given Columbus an opportunity to see his father and mother, undoubtedly for the last time, for he must have known by then that Genoa could give him no more in his dreams of discovery.

Lisbon was the gateway to the Atlantic — and Lisbon became his adoptive home town. Oviedo* relates that Columbus resided in Lisbon but 'like a grateful son he always came to the assistance of his aged father with a part of

---

* Gonzalo Fernandez de Oviedo y Valdes (1478–1557) was an indefatigable writer, part-journalist, part-diarist who chronicled events at the time of Columbus. Although described as the first official historian of the Spanish empire, his later historical works are not highly regarded.

the fruits of his labour, leading a modest life and not enjoying many favours or fortune . . .'

We know that Columbus voyaged from Lisbon to Madeira (in 1478) trading in sugar and acting as business agent for the Di Negro family; to Porto Santo (after his marriage); to Genoa in 1479; to the Canaries, the Cape Verde Islands and the Azores. He was totally absorbed into the maritime life style of the Portuguese, 'as if he were of their nationality' as Las Casas put it.

The tides and the currents fascinated him. When in the Azores he noted the persistent westerly winds blowing off the Atlantic, while in the Canaries he noted the prevailing winds blew steadily from the east. The Canaries, he decided, would be the latitude from which to set out on his westward enterprise.

When in Porto Santo, Madeira and the Azores, Columbus listened to the intriguing tales of other seamen, tales of flotsam and jetsam that the Atlantic rollers brought to the shores. He either saw with his own eyes or collected evidence from eye-witnesses of plants and reeds, canes and sticks blown by winds and carried by currents from the west, the plants not indigenous to the islands, the sticks sometimes skilfully carved, indicating people aboard ships or inhabiting islands and lands to the west.

When stories like this abound there are normally apochryphal ones too, and they are related here simply because, however unlikely, there might just be a smidgen of truth attached to them. One concerns the most westerly of the Azores — Flores. The tides supposedly washed ashore two bodies, identified as orientals by their strangely wide faces, a shape very different from that of a Christian. This story is virtually identical to that already related about Galway.

A second story, first mentioned by Oviedo in 1535, was considered by him untrue; but it has survived the centuries and deserves re-telling if only to show how rumours and exaggeration can lead to pure invention. It is probably an embellishment of the first washed-ashore story.

It is reported that when Columbus was at Porto Santo, a storm-bound, dismasted vessel became wrecked on the shore and was pounded to destruction. Only one survivor reached the safety of the shore. He was a helmsman, barely alive. Columbus carried him home and tended him. The helmsman told of his ship being carried by hurricanes to lands beyond the oceans. Columbus is reported to have asked the dying helmsman to draw a map, which he did, after which he promptly expired. The story became elaborated into a fanciful romance by a poet. Further elaboration by Columbus's adversaries told how he extorted the map then killed the helmsman, a man identified as the navigator Alonso Sanchez, a native of Palos. Scholars seem to discount the story in its entirety.

At about this time — 1482–83 — Columbus made another voyage that was to influence his thinking quite profoundly. His destination was Guinea and his objective was gold. The visit made as deep an impression as did some of his earlier voyages to Chios, Bristol, Iceland and Porto Santo.

As we have already read, Henry the Navigator encouraged navigators to explore the coast of Africa southwards, until in 1443 the island of Arguin, a few miles south of Cape Blanc marking the southern limit of the desert, was reached. A few years later explorers discovered the fertile lands at the mouth of the Senegal River and Cape Verde. In 1471 the explorers Pedro Escobar and Joao de Santerem made a landfall at what was then called Guinea, east of the

Ivory Coast lagoons, now named Ghana. There they found gold dust in substantial quantities and they named the site La Mina — the Mine.

It is thought that it was gold that attracted Columbus. If so, it must have been a powerful attraction because his voyaging to Guinea for gold does not fit conveniently into the pattern of his life's ambition to search to the west for the Orient. Instead, we find him sailing south along the African coast almost to the equator, then east as the coastline runs roughly west-east along the five degrees North line of latitude.

It was not a voyage of discovery — he was ten to twelve years behind the discoverers — nor was he engaged in the slave trade as his detractors have tried to demonstrate. And nor was he intent on trading food, timber and spices. But gold held a special fascination for him, and it was to do so all his life.

When he arrived at La Mina, he found a modest but flourishing trade in the precious metal, with an average of 800 kg of gold being exported to Portugal each year. He investigated the means of production: there were two. The first consisted of merely sifting the river sand — panning, as it is called — to separate gold dust (and the occasional nugget) from the alluvial sand. The second method was to mine the veins of gold-bearing rock in tunnels in the hills and mountains, crushing the ore and extracting the gold.

This experience at La Mina impressed Columbus deeply. Thereafter, wherever he voyaged he always enquired for gold. Where, he was quick to ask, were the rivers and the mountains of gold?

When Columbus returned from Guinea in 1483, enriched by these golden experiences, he had also experienced the sighting of the southern cross (it was so named many years later), a rare and uplifting event for any seafarer from the northern hemisphere, even in modern times. He would have been one of a few hundred seamen who had ever done so.

North, south, east. Columbus had now voyaged in all these directions, but the west still remained the mystery; the west still held the key. As he had known all along, and as the years had impressed on his mind time and time again, the answer to the east lay in the west: *buscar el levante por el poniente*.

Perhaps Columbus knew intuitively that a land mass lay to the west; perhaps his intuition came from his study of nature, of the tides and currents, of the migratory flight of birds, the setting of the sun even. All these factors provided pieces in the giant jigsaw puzzle he was trying to solve.

He knew, when he lived at Porto Santo and watched the sun set over the ocean from his vantage point, and he could not help reminding himself constantly, that two hours previously the people of Genoa would have seen the sun dip down beyond the western hills of Liguria. Perhaps someone like him, thousands of miles out into the Atlantic Ocean, was watching the rising of the self same sun. The thought intrigued him.

Few intelligent people in Columbus's time doubted the roundness of the world. All scientists believed it. Kings, princes and leading scientists all owned globes in their libraries. Of course the information the globes imparted was flawed, but the measurements were based on those provided by eminent geographers, discoverers and travellers of the past.

Ptolemy had explained how he considered the surface area of the globe to consist half of land and half of oceans. He based these calculations on the accepted 360 degrees representing the globe's circumference, and the distance of the land mass from Cape St Vincent (Europe's westernmost extremity) to Cape Cattigara, Asia's easternmost extremity, being 180 degrees.

This view was not held by Marinus, a second-century Greek mathematician. He regarded the land mass as extending to 225 degrees, with the water mass reduced to 135 degrees. Pliny, Aristotle and Seneca also considered the water mass to correspond generally with Marinus's calculation.

Columbus provided his own calculations based on these ancient thoughts. He took Marinus's figures as his base; to the land surface of 225 degrees he added another 28 degrees to take account of Marco Polo's discoveries in the Asian continent. Columbus then added another 30 degrees representing the distance between Cathay (China) and Cipango (Japan). He then calculated that on the basis of his departing on a voyage to Cipango he would use the Canaries, allowing him to reduce the calculations by a further 9 degrees (their position west of Cape St Vincent). Thus, Ptolemy's calculation of 180 degrees for the water surface — the ocean crossing — from Cape St Vincent to the Orient's easternmost point was reduced to only 68 degrees. Columbus trimmed yet another 8 degrees from the figure on the basis that he thought Marinus had over-estimated the globe's actual size. Thus, Columbus calculated the ocean crossing to be 60 degrees.

Many of these calculations by Columbus are now considered to have been the product of a political shrewdness, as well as being a geographer's intelligence. It was evident to him that in order to secure financial sponsorship from the crown or other sources he would have to make a presentation which would demonstrate a profitable return on the monies invested. And it could be argued that the shorter the projected distance to be travelled, the greater the chances of success and the quicker the likely financial returns, if only by minimising the dangers.

This form of mild deception was not the only error or deception contrived by Columbus. There was the question of distance as measured by miles rather than degrees. Ptolemy had estimated the length of a degree — which we know to be sixty nautical miles at the equator — to be about fifty miles. Aristotle, with an accuracy almost beyond belief, estimated the correct length to within yards.

Columbus needed to keep the mileage for a degree as small as possible to enable him to present his project in the most favourable terms, and he selected a calculation by the Arabian cosmographer Alfraganus (sometimes Al-Farghani)* who gave a distance of forty-five miles at the equator: this would be considerably less at the latitude on which Columbus intended setting out on his voyage of discovery.

These grossly misleading and erroneous calculations amounted to a case sadly flawed in two respects: the earth's size was misrepresented as being much smaller than it actually was, and the estimated eastward extension of Asia was grossly over-estimated. They placed Cipango (Japan) where America lies, and made no allowance at all for the American land mass which was still to be discovered. These were irresponsible deceptions which served the purpose of

---

*The brilliant philosopher lived from 384–322 BC. He was a pupil of Plato for twenty years in Athens, married Hermias and had a daughter and son — the latter by a concubine. He tutored the future Alexander the Great and opened a school at the Lyceum.

deceiving not only his prospective sponsors and their advisers, but himself, too.

It could be argued that one could, in all charity, attribute to Columbus an honesty about the calculations, that he genuinely did believe the extremity of the eastern land mass lay as close to Spain as he was suggesting and that the earth surely was as small as he declared. If this was so, then it must be allowed that he was gravely wrong in his calculations — and this then throws into question much else that he propounded and projected.

It is only fair to say that the great Paolo Toscanelli also miscalculated to this extent: the earth's circumference on the Sagres parallel he calculated was 16,530 miles (actually 19,909 miles) and at the equator 20,692 miles (actually 24,856 miles). In effect, he thought the world to be one sixth smaller than it actually is.

It is necessary at this stage to cast a look back over the shoulder to consider an incident which sprang into prominence years after its beginning. It relates to Paolo del Pozzo Toscanelli, to whom we have just referred. He was born in Florence in 1397, the younger son of Domenico Toscanelli, a wealthy merchant trader whose fortune was made by the fifteenth-century explosion in demand for trade between the east and Europe.

Busy trade routes were formed from Europe to India and China via what became known as the 'Mongol route' from the Black Sea — by permission of the Great Khan. Cities such as Genoa and Venice flourished.

Paolo Toscanelli had a profound intelligence. He became a physician, and, as well as practising medicine, became an astronomer, a physicist, taught mathematics to architects, became an authority on geography, cosmography and even cartography. He was also a respected philosopher. He devoted a long life to all these studies until his death at the age of eighty-four or eighty-five.

During this exciting period of the Italian Renaissance, Toscanelli was arguably the most distinguished scholar and scientist in the country, but he was a reticent, modest man, and consequently much of his outstanding work became pigeon-holed and he failed to win the acclaim accorded to others.

He and Columbus never met although they corresponded, and it is the existence of this correspondence which became controversial.

Through his marriage to Felipa Moniz Perestrello, and her contacts at court, Columbus secured the friendship of Canon, later Cardinal, Fernando Martins* who probably had some tenuous blood ties with Felipa. In his youth he had visited Rome and Florence and had established contacts with the science community and formed a friendship with Toscanelli. They corresponded about the exploratory voyages being made to Guinea during the reign of King Alfonso V of Portugal and about the possibility of a voyage of discovery to the west.

Martins told the king about his discussions with Toscanelli and the philosopher's imaginative ideas on reaching the far east by travelling west. Alfonso asked Toscanelli for an explanation. He answered with a letter written in Latin and enclosed a map embellished with routes to Cathay and Cipango

*Variously known as Fernando Martinez, Fernam Martins and Fernam Martinz.

Paolo Toscanelli (1397 – 1482) was one of the world's greatest scientists, and a contemporary of Columbus. He was virtuous, devout and to all intents and purposes, a vegetarian. Like Columbus he never realised the land mass of America existed, but he confirmed Marco Polo's discoveries as valid and knew that to reach the east a discoverer needed to voyage across the western ocean.

expressing clearly that the shortest and best route to the east lay in crossing the ocean to the west.

Alfonso was closely embroiled with the African coast discoveries at the time and it was not timely for him to consider Toscanelli's exciting concepts: they were put to one side for practically a decade.

In 1483, when Columbus was preparing to make a presentation to the king seeking sponsorship, he wrote to the scientist through an intermediary in Lisbon and despatched a small globe on which he indicated some of his thoughts.

According to Ferdinand Columbus, Toscanelli replied enclosing a copy of his own letter which he wrote to Canon Martins on 26 June 1474 — 'Done in the city of Florence.' This letter displays a high clarity of thought, an evidently high degree of intelligence and a clear exposition of the possibility to *buscar el levante por el poniente*.

Toscanelli went on to explain that due west from the city of Lisbon there were marked on the map twenty-six spaces, each of which represented 250 miles, to Quinsay in China, the modern port of Hangchow, just south of Shanghai.

Toscanelli continued in his letter to describe in awesome terms the riches of the orient, the sizes of the Chinese cities, their number of marble bridges and gold-roofed palaces, most of which had already been reported by Marco Polo.

THE TOSCANELLI LETTERS

EXTRACT from a letter by Paolo Toscanelli to Canon Fernando Martins, dated 26 June 1474:

'I was glad to hear of your intimacy and friendship with your most serene and magnificent King. I have often before spoken of a sea route from here to the Indies, where the spices grow, a route shorter than the one which you are pursuing by way of Guinea. You tell me that His Highness desires from me some statement or demonstration that would make it easier to understand and take that route. I could do this by using a sphere shaped like the earth, but I decided that it would be easier and make the point clearer if I showed that route by means of a sea chart. I therefore send His Majesty a chart drawn by my own hand, upon which is laid out the western coast from Ireland on the north to the end of Guinea, and the islands which lie on that route, in front of which, directly to the west, is shown the beginning of the Indies, with the islands and places at which you are bound to arrive, and how far from the Arctic Pole or the Equator you ought to keep away, and how much space or how many leagues intervene before you reach those places most fertile in all sorts of spices, jewels and precious stones. And do not marvel at my calling 'west' the regions where the spices grow, although they are commonly called 'east'; because whoever sails westward will always find those lands in the west, while one who goes overland to the east will always find the same lands in the east.

The straight lines drawn lengthwise on this map show the distance from east to west; the transverse lines indicate distance from north to south. I have also drawn on the map various places in India to which one could go in case of a storm or contrary winds, or some other mishap . . .'

In 1483 Toscanelli wrote to Columbus a long letter of which the following is an extract:

'I have received your letters with the things you sent me, and took great pleasure in them. I perceive your grand and noble desire to sail from west to east by the route indicated on the map I sent you, a route which would still appear more plainly on a sphere. I am much pleased to see that I have been well understood and that the voyage has become not only possible but certain, fraught with inestimable honour and gain, and most lofty fame among Christians. But you cannot grasp all that it means without actual experience or without such accurate and copious information as I have had from eminent and learned men who have come from those places to the Roman court and from merchants who have traded for a long time in those parts and speak with great authority on such matters. When that voyage shall be made, it will be a voyage to powerful kingdoms and noble cities and rich provinces, abounding in all sorts of things that we greatly need, including all manner of spices and jewels in great abundance. It will also be a voyage to kings and princes who are very eager to have friendly dealings and speech with the Christians of our countries . . . For these reasons and many others that might be mentioned, I do not wonder that you, who are of great courage, and the whole Portuguese nation, which has always distinguished itself in all great enterprises, are now inflamed with desire to undertake this voyage.'

Paolo Toscanelli

The existence of these Toscanelli letters later gave rise to the accusation that Columbus had stolen the philosopher's ideas, his chosen routes, the fruits of his mathematical calculations. But this is evidently not so. Both geniuses' conclusions bore errors of substantial dimensions. Columbus, for example, placed Cipango 2,400 miles west of the island of Hierro in the Canaries: Toscanelli made it 3,000 miles. In fact, today's airline distance is 10,600 miles.

However, Columbus must have been much heartened by such powerful support for his plans and for such sound scientific support for his presentation to the Portuguese monarch.

By the time Columbus was ready to make his application to the crown — in 1483 — the king was Alfonso's eldest son, John II, who had recently ascended the throne.

King John II of Portugal
(1455–95): detail of a
painting in Lisbon's
Museu Nacional de Arte
Antiga.

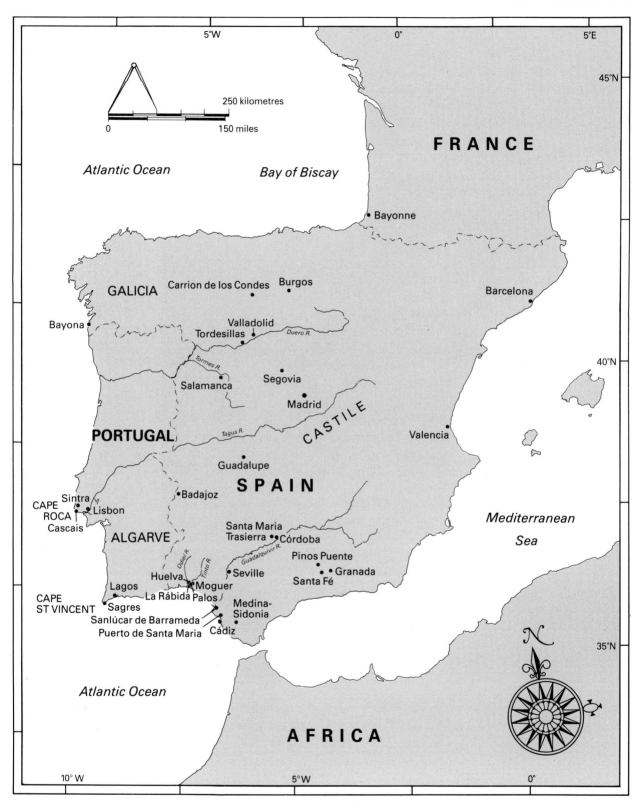

Iberian towns important in Columbus's life.

Either late in 1483 or early in 1484 — shortly before the death of his wife Felipa — Columbus made a clear, well-defined and scientifically based presentation of his projected voyage of discovery to the young king.

Columbus's aim was to secure from the king enough ships with all their victuals and paraphernalia to voyage westward through the western ocean to reach the island of Cipango. Although he made a persuasive and professional plea, and held out bewitching prospects of wealth and gold, the king does not seem to have been unduly impressed. He considered Columbus vainglorious, 'boasting his merits and full of fantasy and imagination'. Columbus was also described as 'a bit haughty . . . moreover he was rude and unruly'.

The king declined to give a decision at the audience. He sought instead the opinions of people whose views he respected, such as the Bishop of Cueta, Don Diego Ortiz, who was a cosmographer, and two Jewish scientists eminent in the field of nautical geography, José Vizinho and Master Rodrigo. All three declared Columbus's calculations faulty and his conclusions erroneous. They recommended rejection — and the king did just that.

Years later Columbus was to describe the encounter with the words, 'The Lord closed King John's eyes and ears, for I failed to make him understand what I was saying'.

It was now impossible for Columbus to stay any longer in Lisbon. On a professional score he had been humiliated by the king's refusal to grant his request to command a voyage of discovery: he would now no longer be employable by anyone in Lisbon in such a capacity. On a personal basis, he had now lost his wife and his bereavement left him with a young son, now four or five years old. Columbus decided to offer his enterprise to another maritime nation. The choice lay between those countries with an Atlantic coastline, powerful enough to be interested in and able to support a voyage of discovery of the magnitude Columbus proposed. There were three contenders — Spain, France and England. Columbus selected Spain. It was a sensible choice. He knew the country, knew the language and enjoyed the climate. Any of her southern ports would provide a fine starting point for the expedition. There was also an assurance of friendly northerly winds to the Canaries. Importantly, too, these islands lay on almost the same lines of latitude as Cipango, thousands of miles to the west. Once at the Canaries, Columbus knew he would be in the zone of prevailing north-east winds which would ensure a steady, unwavering westerly course leading him directly to his destination.

His destiny, it would seem, was to be bound up with Spain and it is on all matters Spanish that we must focus our attention.

5 The Principals: The Catholic Sovereigns: The Unknown Face of Columbus

IT SEEMS a perverse irony of history that in the very year that Columbus opened up measureless opportunities in the New World, King Ferdinand and Queen Isabella issued a decree expelling all Jews from Spain. Between 160,000 and 180,000 distraught and destitute Jews were driven from the country in a mini-holocaust reminiscent of the twentieth-century persecution.

The Spanish Inquisition, established in Castile in 1479, took this sinister turn in an evil display of intolerance, discrimination and torture throughout the kingdom. In a period spanning a quarter of a century about 350,000 converted Jews, Mohammedans and heretics were persecuted, cruelly tortured or maimed for life; 28,000 were condemned to death and about 12,000 of them were burned at the stake.

Pope Sixtus IV displayed some qualms of conscience as the accounts of the terrified Jews who fled to Germany, France and Italy spread like the plague, scandalising the moderates, and he was impelled to rebuke the Catholic Sovereigns. It was a gentle rebuke, more of a gesture than anything else. Within a few years he was inciting Isabella to greater endeavours in eradicating heresy. It makes hypocritical reading to learn that in 1494, with the Inquisition in full swing, the Pope conferred upon Ferdinand and Isabella the title of 'The Catholic Monarchs' or 'The Catholic Sovereigns' in recognition of − among other things − their zeal for the faith, and the purification of their dominions from the Jewish heresy.

These two young sovereigns who imposed such gross agonies upon their subjects and terrorised hundreds of thousands of people for their faith were a well-matched pair, nicely complementing each other. Their story is the story of Spain − its establishment as a united nation and the founding of the great Spanish Empire.

Isabella was born on 22 April 1451, the year of Columbus's birth, daughter of the amiable, intellectual King John II, with a remote family connection to John of Gaunt. Her idle, self-indulgent father married twice and had two sons, one of whom succeeded him as Henry IV, and Isabella.

She grew into a fine young lady: 'tall, demure, attractive . . . with a clear, fresh complexion, light blue eyes and auburn hair.' She was described as having '. . . a good face, fair hair . . . she used no paints nor washes, and had a singular modesty and gravity in her looks. She was very devout and a lover of learning: she bore her husband affection, but mixed with jealousy. She had some knowledge of the Latin tongue which her husband wanted . . .'*

* Quoted in John Boyd Thacher's *Christopher Columbus, His Life, His Works, His Remains*, A.M.S. Press, New York, 3 vols, 1967, Vol 3 p.7.

Ferdinand of Aragon and Isabella of Castile ascended the Spanish throne as the Catholic Sovereigns in 1474. The king is shown here with their son, Don Juan.

THE CATHOLIC SOVEREIGNS

THE MARRIAGE of the 18-year-old bride to her 17-year-old groom united the two most powerful kingdoms on the Iberian peninsula, Castile and Aragon. Together they battled for years against Granada, defeated the Moors, restored order and a strong royal rule. They initiated a new penal system, originating the famous *Guardia Civil*, reformed the civil service, influenced the Church and stabilised the kingdom.

But their devout Catholicism and aims of unity and purity of faith led to misplaced zeal — and to the dreaded Spanish Inquisition.

It was the more cultured Isabella rather than the womanising Ferdinand who influenced the sponsoring of Columbus's exploring enterprise.

Her devout, 'sweetly plump and chaste' character is difficult to reconcile with the rule of terror.

King Ferdinand V of Castile (from 1474) was also Ferdinand II of Aragon and III of Naples. He lived from 1452 to 1516.
Queen Isabella I of Castile (1474–1504) and of Aragon (1469–1504) was born in the same year as Columbus — in 1451.

Isabella became a very marriageable commodity. She was brought up in strict virginal circumstances by a pious mother who instilled into her daughter strong religious principles and standards of conduct. Evidently these did not include compassion.

In 1468 she became heiress to the throne of Castile, making her doubly attractive as a marriage partner. Castile was large, important and powerful, comprising much of Spain as we know it today save for the north-eastern region from the Pyrenees to south of Alicante.

Ruler over Aragon, this north-eastern region, was King John II and the heir to this throne was Ferdinand. He was born on 10 March 1452 and from the age of ten he accompanied his father in war and peace, following many pursuits which helped to develop him into a vigorous young man, battle-experienced, a tough horseman, athletic and muscular; well groomed, some would think, for the turbulent and violent life of a king in the Middle Ages. He had 'no learning given him in his youth: yet he learned to read history and converse with learned men'.

By the time he was just seventeen – when Isabella was eighteen – the youngsters were both ready for marriage. It is believed that the shrewd young lady selected the Aragon prince from her many admirers rather than having him thrust upon her. They married on 19 October 1469, but even before that – ten and a half months earlier when the articles of marriage were signed – she stamped her authority on the union. Perhaps rightly so; after all, she brought to the marriage far more than he did.

The dynastic union of Castile and Aragon bore all the signs of a prosperous future.

Within five years of the marriage Isabella ascended the Castilian throne on the death of her unlamented, corrupt and profligate brother, Henry IV. Ferdinand flaunted his true colours in a display of bullying bravado by claiming Isabella's crown of Castile as his own, denying a female's right of succession. His claim was rejected by an ecclesiastical court, and the claim petered out through lack of popular support. The Castilians wanted nothing of him: Isabella was their undoubted queen and in their minds Ferdinand was relegated to a minor role.

Ferdinand came into his own a few years later when his father died in 1479 and he inherited his own throne, the crown of Aragon. Castile and Aragon became united into one dynamic whole. The Spanish Empire had been born.

Ferdinand seems a not unpleasant character. He grew into a man 'of middle stature, limbs well-proportioned, countenance graceful and pleasing though grave; mien majestic, complex, somewhat swarthy – tanned with being always in the field; chestnut-coloured hair, and long: his beard trimmed after the manner of that time, his head balding, his mouth small . . . his back broad, his voice sharp, quick of speech, quick wit, sound judgement and courteous disposition.'

Isabella is considered to have been an enlightened monarch. She brought to her reign a Thatcher-like, single-minded reforming zeal which galvanised her court, the arts, the populace, the country as a whole. Corruption was, if not ousted, severely curtailed; justice reformed; the rule of law re-established. Wrong-doers were punished. A cultural revolution revitalised the hearts and minds of the intelligentsia. Trade, agriculture and businesses responded to her reforming authority. Castile prospered as never before.

But Isabella's character was flawed. She accepted that life for her poorer subjects was harsh, that cruelty was the norm, that so-called justice still dispensed the harshest of punishments, even torture and death: life was cheap in these circumstances, and Isabella accepted cruelty as did most others.

In religious matters she was a bigot. She regarded heresy as a mortal sin and determined to eradicate it from her realm. Spain was generously peopled with Jews and Moors who harboured religious beliefs totally alien to those of Catholics. Pope Sixtus IV granted a Papal bull — a little reluctantly — authorising Isabella to set up her own Inquisition, responsible to her, not the Pope, with the specific aim of dealing with Jews, the traditional enemies of Christianity. The evil Spanish Inquisition was set up in 1479.

In 1492, after nearly ten years of barbarous fighting with unbelievable atrocities on both sides, the Moors, Mohammedans to a man, surrendered their last refuge of Granada to the Catholic Sovereigns, barely months before Columbus departed on his first voyage of discovery.

It was against this backdrop of religious and racial persecution, of an authoritarian queen and a macho king, that Columbus struggled to get a sympathetic hearing for his plans. The attractive, demure, blue-eyed queen to whom he appealed was also, paradoxically, the instigator of the dreaded Inquisition, and she carried the blood of tens of thousands of non-Christians on her hands.

This then was the woman who finally gave Columbus support, pledging, if legend is to be believed, her crown jewels of Castile if need be.

Isabella enjoyed some empathy with the discoverer, even, if we are to believe some chroniclers, a sexual liaison. In time, she was taken ill and died on 26 November 1504, eighteen months before Columbus himself died. After her death it was to be another two years of unrest, of disputed claims for her vacated crown, before Ferdinand was to rule the whole of Spain in his own right. He did so then for the next ten years until his death in 1516.

There is an interesting postscript regarding English affairs. One of Isabella's daughters was the Infanta Doña Catalina, known to the English as Catherine of Aragon, for twenty years the wife of Henry VIII. The lack of a son and Henry's affection for Anne Boleyn brought about a divorce and Catherine retired with the title of Dowager Princess of Wales.

The Unknown Face of Columbus

There are known to be more than eighty portraits of Columbus in existence throughout the art galleries and collections of the world. As far as is known, none is painted from life. Perhaps the earliest is the Talleyrand — Figure 2 — painted by Piombo in 1519, thirteen years after the Admiral's death. Scholars have attempted to select from this mass of portraiture what they consider to be the nearest likeness to Columbus, taking into consideration all the varied descriptions of the man by his contemporaries. Even so, the belief can only be speculative. It is thought that the nearest likeness is probably Figure 5, the De Orchi portrait. It bears the Latin inscription *Columbus The Ligurian. Discoverer of the New World*. Liguria is the region around Genoa. The artist's name is not known.

Figure 1. It is believed that the Ferrari portrait of the discoverer was painted at the end of the sixteenth century. It depicts the Admiral in unaccustomed warrior's uniform, bearing a baton in his right hand. In the upper dexter corner there appears Columbus's mysterious signature and his arms over which is superscribed *cf Columb*. In the lower dexter corner is the top of a large terrestrial globe of the world. The portrait bears remarkable similarities to the Jovious characteristics.

Figure 2. This is known as the Talleyrand Portrait, the original of which is in the Metropolitan Museum of Art in New York. Art critics have pronounced it a genuine Sebastiano del Piombo (1485–1547). However, although contemporaneous, it is thought most unlikely to have been painted from life. Sebastiano would only have been twenty-one at the time of Columbus's death, and it is known that he took up painting late in life. It is believed to have been painted long after the Admiral's death. It was owned by the Duke of Valençay de Talleyrand de Sega.

Figure 3. Paulus Jovious or Paolo Giovio (1480–1552) wrote a history of the world and lived in splendour in a villa on Lake Como, where he founded a museum of art and a gallery of portraits of notable people: this was done under the patronage of Pope Leo X.* Jovious studied medicine in Rome before following the church and literature. He was made Canon of Como and later Bishop of Nocera de Pagani near Naples in 1527.

Jovious is believed to have preserved a portrait of Columbus — certainly it is known that such a portrait existed in the middle of the sixteenth century, though it is not claimed that this one was from life, or that the artist ever saw the Admiral: this is simply the first mention of such a painting.

The portrait was engraved by a skilled Swiss engraver, Tobias Stimmer, and some believe it to be the earliest known likeness. Jovious published his *Elogia Virorum bellica virtute illustrium* in Basle in 1551, but it was only in the second edition in 1575 that the Stimmer engraving of Columbus appeared.

*This extraordinary man — Pope from 1513–21 — was made a cardinal at the age of fourteen, though only admitted to the sacred college at the age of seventeen in 1492. He was the son of Lorenzo de' Medici, the Magnificent.

Figure 4. The Cevasco portrait belongs to the municipality of Genoa, the gift of an eminent sculptor, Giambattista Cevasco. It is believed to be a portrait of Columbus. It is described as 'a work of *cinquecento* [sixteenth century], most precious in expression and truth'.

Figure 5. The pedigree and circumstances surrounding the De Orchi are disputed in many quarters, but they are supported by many known facts and the story becomes intriguing. When the 400th anniversary of Columbus's discovery approached at the end of the last century, it was asserted that a Dr Allessandro de Orchi of Como possessed the original Columbus portrait alleged to have been in the Jovious collection in the mid-sixteenth century.

It is reported that at the beginning of the seventeenth century the villa and museum formerly owned by Jovious became the property of his nephew — Francisco Giovio. Some years later — about 1613 — the art collection was divided among the nephew's sons, the greater part being bequeathed to the eldest son. Thus the collection passed down through generations until in 1848 a female of the line inherited the estate and the collection. Antonia, the inheritor, married Flaminio de Orchi and in 1870 the portrait was inherited by their son, Allessandro. It is now preserved in the Museo Civico in Como.

Figure 6. The Theodore de Bry engraving of Columbus is the one most frequently reproduced, but it is decidedly suspect. It first appeared in De Bry's *Collection of Voyages*, published in 1595. De Bry wrote of his engraving: '. . . Columbus was a sagacious man of great mind and soul, the King and Queen of Castile before that he should depart from them, commanded that his portrait should be painted from life by some renowned artist, in order that if he never came back from his expedition they might possess of him some memorial. And so to my great joy lately . . . I have had a copy of this from a friend of mine who had received it from the artist himself . . . I have caused this picture to be cut in metal by my son Jean de Bry . . . which I now offer thee in this present book.'

Experts believe all this to be totally untrue. There is no supporting evidence whatsoever — from Oviedo, Las Casas nor Ferdinand Columbus. Nor is the face considered a good likeness — it is not long as all reports quote; the cap is quite unfashionable; and the portrait shows a dimple and warts, neither of which are mentioned in other reports of Columbus's features.

6 Escape to Spain: Presentation at Court

PALOS stands today just as it did five hundred years ago when Columbus knew it intimately, barely thirty miles from the Portuguese border in the southernmost province of Andalusia, in the splendid Gulf of Cádiz. Fifty miles to the east of Palos the province's capital city, Seville, lies in the valley of the river Guadalquivir. It is dominated by the immense cathedral, acclaimed as one of the world's most beautiful, with unrivalled stained windows and exquisitely clustered columns. By following the coastline from Palos south-eastwards along the gulf towards Gibraltar, you come upon Cádiz, a sea port destined to make its mark not only for sustaining the voyages of discovery, but also a century later making the headlines when Francis Drake launched a pre-emptive strike there.

Huelva, another seafaring town, is separated from Palos by a stretch of water representing the confluence of the two rivers Odiel and Tinto. Also close by Huelva and Palos, as if rubbing shoulders, lies Moguer. It was from these three towns, drenched in both sunshine and their centuries-old maritime heritage, that Columbus was to recruit most of the seamen who accompanied him on his first voyage of discovery. The three towns were also conveniently close to Seville and Córdova where the Catholic Sovereigns frequently resided.

On a hill overlooking Palos, standing proud like a landmark, was the Franciscan monastery known as La Rábida. It stands there still.

When Columbus was rejected by the Portuguese monarch and his court at the end of 1484, after having lived in the country for eight years, it was to Palos he went and to the monastery of La Rábida in particular.

Columbus had relatives in the Palos area. Two brothers-in-law, men married to sisters of his late wife, Felipa, lived there. One of these was named Pedro Correa; he was the governor of Porto Santo in the Madeira archipelago. So unattractive and unrewarding was the post that he was content to live instead at Huelva. The other — named Muller or Muliar — also lived nearby. Columbus no doubt saw these as possible homes for his young son, Diego, for whose upbringing Columbus had been responsible since the death of his wife.

More than this, Columbus knew of the Franciscan monastery at La Rábida, and he knew that the friars would give sanctuary and might even be prepared to educate the boy. Furthermore, he knew that some of the friars were scholars of astronomy and one even had the ear of the queen.

Columbus had no hesitation in leaving Lisbon — and heading for La Rábida.

Detractors have suggested that the speed and secrecy of Columbus's departure in 1484 after the King of Portugal's rejection was due to other, more sinister, reasons. Some say he travelled clandestinely by road, whereas it is much more

COLUMBUS – BY HIS CONTEMPORARIES

'. . . a man of tall and lofty stature, of ruddy complexion, of great intelligence and with a long face.'

The opening passage in the Libretto by Peter Martyn, in the San Marco Library, Venice: probably an interjection by the translator Angelo Trivigiano, 1504.

'He was of good stature and appearance, of more than medium height and with strong limbs, his eyes bright and his other features of good proportions: his hair very red and his face somewhat burned and freckled.'

Fernandez de Oviedo y Valdes, *Historia General y Natural de las Indias*, 1535 (1851 edition). As a youth he knew Columbus.

'There was a man from the country of Genoa called Christopher Columbus, a dealer in printed books who traded in the country of Andalusia, a man of very great intelligence without being very learned. He came to Castile in the month of June 1496 and because of his devotion he was dressed in robes of the colour of the ancient habits of the brothers of St Francis, made almost like a habit, and wearing a cord of St Francis . . .'

Andrés Bernáldez, *Historia de los Reyes Católicos D. Fernando y Doña Isabel*, 1869–75 edition. He was curate of Los Palacios, a village near Seville, from 1488 till 1513. He knew Columbus well.

'His form was tall, above the medium: his face long, his countenance imposing: his nose aquiline: his eyes clear blue: his complexion light, tending towards decided red: his beard and hair were red when he was young but which cares then had turned early white.'

Bartolomé de Las Casas, *Historia de Las Indias*, 1550 (1875 edition). He was a preacher, later a bishop, who knew Columbus and became the greatest curator of Columbian documentation.

Bartolomé de Las Casas was a meticulous biographer of Columbus.

Columbus found much spiritual and intellectual comfort in La Rábida monastery at Palos. This is today's modernised monastery.

universally believed now that he journeyed quite openly from Lisbon to Palos by sea, a voyage probably arranged by some of his Genoese friends.

Others claim he 'fled' Lisbon because he was bankrupt and thus managed to escape his creditors. There is no documentary evidence to suggest any such thing, although it is probably quite true that he was short of funds.

Others point to an even more sinister reason: it relates to the Toscanelli documents. It will be remembered that Toscanelli's letters and chart were of tremendous scientific importance. They were carefully housed in the national archives. It is alleged that Columbus got access to them and either made copies or even stole the originals. Again, there is no evidence to support this allegation.

Indeed, there is no foundation in the theory that Columbus left Portugal under any sort of cloud, let alone that he was escaping charges of dishonesty and stealing. It is true to say that Ferdinand Columbus recorded that his father left Portugal secretly for fear the king might restrain him. Las Casas, too, referred to the secrecy of Columbus's departure 'fearing the king would send after him and hold him'.

Different sources give differing accounts of Columbus's and Diego's stay at Palos. Some say they stayed with relatives then moved to the monastery: others say they arrived at the monastery first then made arrangements for the boy to stay with one of his aunts and for him to be educated, giving Columbus freedom of movement. Pictures of the arrival of the two travellers at the monastery depict them travel-worn and at the end of their tethers, seeking sanctuary. This is believed to have been a case of artistic licence. It is much more likely that they arrived by ship, refreshed by the sea air, and on arrival at the monastery were given the customary free admission accorded to pilgrims, and were allocated spartan cells.

At La Rábida in 1485 Columbus met Father Antonio de Marchena, the priest who was to exert a great influence on his life, and who became his friend and mentor through his next seven years in Spain.

Marchena was a pious churchman of high regard who introduced financiers, politicians and other men of influence to Columbus and converted them to his cause.

Marchena was a man of science as well as a priest. He had studied astronomy

This unattributed and undated painting from La Rábida shows Columbus and his young son, Diego, arriving at the monastery outside Palos in the early 1480s.

and cosmography, so his conversations with Columbus were profound and meaningful. Columbus had found a supporter, one to whom he could open his heart. Taviani commented on the friendship:*

> Columbus told Marchena of all his seagoing experiences — of Galway, of Iceland, of the Atlantic islands, of Guinea. He spoke of his stay on Porto Santo and of what he had learned of the Perestrello family. He described his negotiations with the Portuguese court. He produced the letter of Toscanelli whom he believed to be alive in Florence. He explained his theory of sea currents and winds, particularly the constant winds along the parallel of the Canaries. And he declared his absolute certainty that beyond the Sea of Darkness lay Asia — Cipango and Cathay: immense, rich lands populated by infidels awaiting Christian redemption.

Perhaps more importantly, it was Marchena who introduced Columbus to the Spanish court and to another priest, Father Juan Perez, the monastery's prior, who furthered Columbus's cause especially with Isabella. Perez had been an employee of the queen in the accounting office, then as a page. He left her service to become a friar then later became the queen's personal confessor, an honorary position but one of prestige and influence which Perez with his talent for politics was able to indulge to advantage.

Both these men were impressed by Columbus's evident devout belief in divine predestination and his determination to convert the natives of the lands still to be discovered to Christianity.

They agreed to help Columbus finalise his plans and to use whatever influence they could to secure support for the dreams of this charismatic Genoese. They were unable to help him make his presentation to the Catholic Sovereigns, but a royal council was convened to hear his case.

Isabella and Ferdinand were well occupied with war against Granada and rated no priority to this foreigner's grandiose plans of securing wealth from the Indies. Marchena's influence is evident inasmuch as the royal councillors granted Columbus's submission a deep and serious consideration. But after long debate the council recommended rejection of the plans.

Marchena then advised Columbus to approach the Sovereigns directly. This would not necessarily provide a private and personal audience, but it could lead to the Sovereigns delegating the submission to further examination by a commission of men of greater experience and expertise than the original council.

Marchena's influence proved greater than could have been wished. On 20 January 1486 Columbus was given an audience with the Sovereigns at Alcalá de Henares near Madrid.

It seems that Columbus only had himself to blame for the outcome of the audience. His presentation included the displaying of the world map his brother Bartholomew and he had drawn, depicting the lands Columbus believed existed and which he intended to discover. He spoke with passion and conviction, he quoted texts in support of his views, he received the support of Father Marchena, but he failed to convince the monarchs. A Spanish

* Paolo Taviani, p.169.

The University of Salamanca with its platersque frontage was one of the
four great universities of Europe with Paris, Oxford and Bologna. The Royal
Council met here in 1486–87 to debate Columbus's enterprise. Columbus
lodged in a nearby Dominican cell and fed in the friars' refectory.

historian, Gomera, dismissed his submission in these terms:* 'Since he was a foreigner, and was poorly dressed, and with no greater support than a friar, he was not believed or listened to by anyone . . .'

Nevertheless, the matter was delegated to a learned commission which seemed to approach its duty sluggishly. It was many months before it even undertook to begin its examination. It then debated the presentation for several more months.

Andrés Bernáldez, the historian and contemporary of Columbus, recalled the navigator's audience with the Catholic Sovereigns in May 1486 in the Alcázar which served as a royal palace in Córdova:

> He told them his dream, but they remained sceptical. He spoke with
> them and said that what he was saying was true. Then he showed
> them a map of the world. In this way he aroused their desire to hear
> more about those lands.

However, Columbus failed to impress the king to any great extent, although the more imaginative Isabella was seduced by his eloquence and enthusiasm, by his dreams of extending the horizons of Christianity to a New World. She arranged for Columbus to be given 15,000 maravedis immediately and virtually took him into service with the crown, giving him retainers for a year.

She also set up the committee assigned to give further consideration to Columbus's enterprise. Father Fernando de Talavera† was a private confessor of the queen and a man of great piety and learning. He was the prime choice to act as president of the council or committee. The members comprised men of letters, theologians, jurists, philosophers and scientists. There is no record of how many there were nor who they were, except for two names — Rodrigo Maldonado, a literary man, and Andrés de Villaton.

The council met for the first time towards the end of 1486 at Córdova and thereafter wherever the court was in residence — at Seville or Salamanca or elsewhere. Columbus held himself in readiness to attend whenever called upon. He followed the royal entourage, spending weeks and months in travelling throughout the kingdom. It was a soul-destroying experience, draining of energy and boring in the extreme as the council adjourned for long spells while some members fulfilled their lecturing or other clerical duties.

While in Salamanca, Columbus was befriended by Father Diego Deza, professor of theology at the city's university, who later became the tutor of the prince Don Juan. It was to be a useful assocation two or three years later when Deza became more influential at court.

It became evident to Columbus that the council members thought on an intellectual plane far higher than he could possibly cope with. His more imaginative concept of the enterprise left the council unimpressed. Ferdinand Columbus summarised the position:‡

> Some [of the council] argued this way. In all the thousands of years
> since God created the world, those lands had remained unknown to

---

* Quoted by Paolo Taviani, p.172.

† Later Archbishop of Granada who lived 1428–1507. He was a friar of the Order of St Jerome and prior of the monastery of Nuestra Señora del Prado near Valladolid.

‡ Ferdinand Columbus, p.61.

innumerable men and experts in navigation, and it was most unlikely that the Admiral should know more than all other men, past and present. Others, who based themselves on geography, claimed the world so large that to reach the end of Asia, whither the Admiral wished to sail, would take three years. For support they cited Seneca, who in one of his books debates the question, saying that many learned men were in disagreement on the question whether the ocean was infinite and doubted that it could ever be navigated; and even if it could be, they questioned whether habitable lands existed at the other end . . . Others argued, as some Portuguese had done about the navigation to Guinea, saying that if one were to set out and travel due west, as the Admiral proposed, one would be able to return to Spain because the world was round. These men were absolutely certain that one who left the hemisphere known to Ptolemy would be going downhill and so could not return: for that would be like sailing a ship to the top of a mountain: a thing that ships could not do even with the aid of the strongest wind.

It is thought that the council's deliberations ended in the spring of 1487 and its findings:*

considered the foreigner's promises and offers 'impossible, vain and worthy of complete rejection' and that 'it was not befitting the authority of the Sovereigns to favour an enterprise with such fragile foundations, which appeared so uncertain, even impossible to anyone, whether he was learned or ignorant, so all the sums invested in it would be lost'.

The Sovereigns relayed this decision to Columbus in August 1487 at the camp outside the city of Malaga where they had won a military victory. They couched it in rather neutral terms, giving the council's negative conclusion, but while not approving Columbus's proposition, nor did they positively reject it out of hand. Ferdinand and Isabella indicated that their first priority was the war in Granada and until its drain on their resources was resolved they were unable to support Columbus's enterprise.

It was rejection, certainly, but cloaked in qualified deferment: the hope of eventual support was implicit.

The Admiral's Mistress

In 1486–87, when the court rested for some months at Córdova, Columbus met and fell in love with Beatrice Enríquez de Harana. It was to prove an enduring relationship and the young girl — at twenty she was a good fifteen years his junior — brought him love and tranquillity during the years of torment he was to experience while endeavouring to secure sponsorship for his enterprise.

Although Beatrice came of a fairly well-to-do family of wine producers with lands at Santa María de Trasierra about twenty kilometres from Córdova, her circumstances were straitened and some reports even describe her as a peasant girl.

*Paolo Taviani, p.191.

SONS OF COLUMBUS

CHRISTOPHER Columbus is shown in this family group with his mistress, Beatrice Enríquez de Harana. Their son, Ferdinand, is shown in the centre, and Diego, his first-born son by his deceased wife Felipa Moniz Perestrello is seated on the left. No portrait of Felipa is known to exist.

Diego Columbus (*c.*1480–1526) was the eldest and legitimate son of Christopher Columbus and Felipa Moniz Perestrello. He was probably born at Porto Santo on the island of Madeira. His mother died when he was still a child. From the age of about five he was brought up by the friars of La Rábida monastery at Palos. His life is far less well-documented than his younger, illegitimate stepbrother, Ferdinand. As a late teenager he became a page for the prince Don Juan, son and heir of King Ferdinand and Queen Isabella. He married the well-placed María de Toledo, niece of the king and a descendant of the greatest grandee of Spain, the Duke of Alba. They had five or more children of which the eldest son, Luis, became the third Admiral of the Ocean Sea.

Diego was the inheritor of all the titles, honours and privileges of his famous father, though he preferred the title Viceroy to that of Admiral of the Ocean Sea. He became governor or Admiral of Santo Domingo. He embarked on years of litigation following the death of his father, but even his vast experience at court failed to stem its increasing disenchantment with everything related to the name Columbus. The squabbling was still going on many decades after his death.

Ferdinand Columbus (1487 or 1488–1539) was born at Córdova, the illegitimate son of Christopher Columbus and Beatrice Enríquez de Harana. His birth is given as 28 September 1488 (according to his epitaph) or 29 August 1487 (according to original papers in the Seville cathedral library). On the early death of the young Don Juan to whom the step-brothers acted as pages, Queen Isabella retained the Columbus boys as pages.

In 1502 Ferdinand accompanied his father on the fourth voyage of discovery. It is believed he made two more voyages after Columbus's death.

He served the Emperor Charles V in Italy, Flanders and Germany. Further travels took him to Africa and even Asia.

He was a passionate bibliophile and assembled perhaps the finest private collection of books in Europe, 15,370 volumes and manuscripts. According to the inscription on his tomb he wrote four books, the titles of which, like the books themselves, have not survived the centuries. His most important work was the biography of his father, written in Spanish. It was translated into Italian, appearing in Venice in 1571: all other translations stem from this edition. The work suffered from many mistakes and the early years were glossed over. He painted a somewhat distorted picture of his father and cloaked rather than cleared many incidents.

His knowledge of the sciences was considerable: navigation, geography and cosmography were his specialities, and he published an index of tables of the planet's longitudes and latitudes. He established an academy of mathematics in Seville.

He died prematurely on 12 July 1539, his epitaph giving his age as fifty years, nine months and fourteen days. He never married and left no children.

The only known likeness of Columbus's mistress, Beatrice Enríquez de Harana. Their son, Ferdinand, was the Adelantado or Governor of Hispaniola, and his father's biographer.

At a time when the masses were illiterate, she could both read and write. At a young age she was orphaned and taken into the care of her paternal uncle, Rodrígo Enríquez de Harana, and it was through his son that she was introduced to Columbus at a dinner party — hardly a setting for the peasantry.

Curiously, and this is one of the greatest unexplained mysteries about the navigator, Columbus never married Beatrice. They lived together quite openly, seemingly shrugging off any shame and the scorn of the public, the court and the church. True, it was an age of great liberality in such sexual matters — even a pope kept mistresses quite blatantly. But the image sits unhappily with Columbus. He was not unprincipled in religion: he was a devout Catholic and observed religious customs quite strictly.

It has even been said in explanation that Columbus's wife, Felipa, was still alive, but we know this was not so.

One explanation begins to have the ring of truth about it — but it is sheer speculation. Columbus was a dreamer, and his lofty intelligence could see a future for himself decorated with titles of nobility and of colonial viceroyalty. How then could he contemplate marriage to a girl half his age and someone little better than a peasant girl? The idea was preposterous. Better the shame and disgrace of living in sin with the young mistress.

In 1488* Beatrice bore Columbus a son, Ferdinand, who became a fine scholar, an aristocrat, a courtier of immense wealth, creator of a library of Spanish incunabula of rare distinction. He was his father's biographer† and in his book he never once mentioned his mother's name.

Perhaps she really was a peasant girl and the snobbish Ferdinand could not bring himself to admit such a lowly family connection. Conversely, he made many references to his father's higher-born Portuguese wife, Felipa. Beatrice slips away into the shadows of history, as mysteriously as she stepped into the limelight. There is no accounting for the fact that Beatrice's disappearance from records was so complete that she did not attend Columbus's funeral, although she is known to have been alive at the time.

Estrangement should not be read into this because Columbus's instructions in his will or its codicils were insistent. His son, Diego, was exhorted to 'take good care of Beatrice Enríquez, for she weighs heavily on my conscience, though I am at present unable to tell you why.'

One sentence with two tantalising mysteries! *Why* was he conscience-stricken? Was it quite simply that he had not married her?

'. . . though I am at present unable to tell you why . . .' What an extraordinary statement to include in the last will of a dying man: when, then, would he ever reveal the reason?

We cannot leave this subject without a brief glance at Columbus's other possible mistresses. One source refers to his affair with the Marchioness de Moya and provides, incidentally, a reason for not marrying Beatrice, because of his fear of upsetting the Marchioness and thus losing a valuable ear at court. Just how influential she was is indicated by a seventeenth-century report about her:‡

> Her intelligence was so lofty that she dealt with matters of the greatest importance: her advice was sought and accepted by the Catholic Sovereigns on many occasions. And when Columbus presented his proposals to them offering the discovery of the Indies, it is certain that [the Marchioness,] finding the queen confused and dubious . . . encouraged her and persuaded her so that . . . the navigator could undertake that remarkable venture.

It is believed more likely that Columbus had a relationship with the young and much more vivacious Beatrice de Peraza y Bobadilla, widowed with two young children, whom Columbus visited whenever calling at the Canaries. He is described by a friend as being 'fired with love' for her.

It has been suggested that Columbus even enjoyed a daring romantic attachment to Queen Isabella herself. True, they were of a similar age, with

---

*Either August or September 1488, but the preferred date is 15 August, in Córdova.

†*The Life of the Admiral Christopher Columbus.* See the bibliography.

‡ Paolo Taviani p.483 quoting Pinel de Monroy, Madrid, 1677.

similar characteristics, and there is no denying that she was sympathetic to this dreamer of a New World, and was influential in giving him the sponsorship he wanted. However, it would have been a dangerous liaison and it seems unlikely that both of them would have risked all else that they cherished for such a capricious relationship.

A friend of Columbus, Michele da Cuneo, reported the Admiral as being 'fired with love' ('tincto d'amore') for the wide-eyed Beatriz de Peraza y Bobadilla, pictured in this rare engraving. King Ferdinand also seems to have been captivated by her, and Queen Isabella removed her from the court by arranging her marriage with the governor of La Gomera in the Canaries.

7 The Royal Court: The Capitulations

I T WAS NOW, after his second rejection, that Columbus displayed the one quality that men of vision seem to possess above all others — persistence. After receiving the Sovereigns' rejection in August 1487 he lost no time in seeking another sponsor.

Brother Bartholomew was sent back to Portugal to re-open negotiations with King John II, and while in Lisbon he witnessed the arrival of the great explorer Bartholomew Diaz, discoverer of the Cape of Storms, the southernmost tip of Africa. The Portuguese Diaz had evidently discovered a route to India by sailing south and east, the very lands Columbus hoped to reach by sailing west. This alarming news threw Columbus's plans into confusion. He determined to visit Lisbon himself to seek an audience with the king. He wrote to John seeking a safe conduct against any danger of arrest. John wrote back in most generous terms, referring to him as 'our special friend', and acclaiming his 'art and good talent'. The king urged Columbus to visit Lisbon and guaranteed complete immunity. It is possible that the visit was made, but there is no record of it.

Columbus also considered visiting Charles VIII in Paris and Henry VII in London to seek support, but brother Bartholomew went instead. He had no success with either monarch.

It is possible that Columbus postponed his projected visits to England and France on the advice of Antonio de Marchena. Columbus was at a low ebb emotionally, and the support and advice from Marchena gave comfort and strength. Marchena suggested an approach to Spain's wealthiest citizen, no less a grandee than the 2nd Duke of Medina-Sidonia, ancestor of the 7th duke who, a century later, led the ill-fated Armada on its great enterprise against England.

Don Enrique de Guzman, Duke of Medina-Sidonia, had also been in Malaga when Ferdinand and Isabella rejected Columbus's proposals, and he was aware of the detailed examination to which they had been subjected. So when an approach was made to him by Marchena he had little hesitation in declining to give it support. A footnote to this item is that while these negotiations were proceeding the duke had become embroiled in a brawl with a fellow grandee and the Catholic Sovereigns had banished him from court.

Marchena and Columbus approached another powerful and wealthy duke, Don Luis de la Cerda Medina Celi, whose expansive estates were conveniently close to Palos at Puerto de Santa Maria, practically adjoining Cádiz.

Medina Celi was hugely impressed by Columbus and his plans, and immediately agreed to support the navigator. What had seemed to Columbus as great financial barriers appeared as nothing of the sort to Medina Celi.

The duke offered up to three or four thousand ducats to enable Columbus to be given all that he needed — three ships or caravels, supplies for a year, seamen and all necessary provisions. The ships were to be built in the port of Santa Maria, and the work was to proceed without interruption 'until it was done'.

Prudently, the duke informed the Catholic Sovereigns of his decision to support the venture and urged them to approve the favours and assistance that he and his family intended to give Columbus. It is not recorded what reaction the duke expected from the monarchs, but when Isabella expressed some interest in the project Medina Celi quietly and diplomatically withdrew to await developments.

Las Casas faithfully noted Isabella's response. She indicated quite clearly that if the enterprise was to go ahead then it should be under the auspices of the crown, that she herself would assume responsibility and that the royal council would be responsible for incidental expenses. Further, she wrote politely to Columbus inviting him to visit the court immediately. Some say she also sent 'a purse of florins . . . so that he could dress himself decently, buy a horse and present himself to Her Highness.'

Meanwhile, the friars of La Rábida and other friends of Columbus had been working in the background, while yet more friends at court came out in support. Father Diego Deza, whom Columbus had befriended a couple of years earlier at the university at Salamanca, was able to exercise some influence at court where he now tutored the infant prince.

Alfonso de Quintanilla was the court treasurer, and Columbus had made a point of cultivating a friendship with him. Quintanilla and Cardinal Mendoza, primate of Spain, who also looked kindly upon the navigator, were instrumental in encouraging Isabella to invite Columbus to an audience, which she did, in the summer of 1489, at Jaén, a few miles from Córdova. She was alone because Ferdinand was sixty miles away to the south-east at the siege of Bara. She made it clear to Columbus that while she would not give a firm decision to support the enterprise she gave him 'certain hope' that once the present Granada war was over, his problems would be solved. Meanwhile, she cautioned patience and invited him to live at court. It effectively overruled the duke's offer of financial help, but it was the best deal he could secure — and he was content.

After years of seemingly interminable waiting, Columbus now had success almost within his grasp. The war appeared to be in its closing stages, and with its ending would come the 'certain hope' of royal sponsorship. But the war did not end quickly, it dragged on for month after month, for another two years. Columbus had little option but to bide his time.

At the end of 1491 the war with the Saracens took a dramatic turn and early in the new year, on 2 January, the Moors capitulated.

Now that the war had ended Queen Isabella would be expected by Columbus to honour her promise given to him two and a half years previously, and to her credit this was the main reason she summoned him to the royal encampment at Santa Fé.

On arrival, Columbus discovered to his dismay he was to be subjected to yet another trial by interrogation.

In celebration of the Moorish surrender, Santa Fé was teeming with a great number of VIPs from whom the queen selected an awesome council. When

THE 1492 COUNCIL

QUEEN Isabella joined her husband King Ferdinand in accepting the surrender of the last Moorish king in all Spain, the young Boabdil. He kissed Isabella's hand in token of surrender on 2 January 1492. From the many eminent scientists, philosophers, intellectuals, cosmographers and nobles visiting the court the queen selected a council to evaluate Columbus's proposals. The full constitution of the council is not known but its size and importance can be imagined from the following known names:

President Father Hernando de Talavera, an exemplary churchman, a saint, spiritually modest.

Archbishops (3) of Toledo, Seville, Santiago.

Bishops (14) of Burgos, Valencia, Avila, Coria, Córdova, Léon, Oviedo, Astorga, Segovia, Zamora, Mondonedo, Lugo, Orense, Cádiz.

Dukes (9) of Villahermosa, Béjar, Medina-Sidonia, Medina Celi, Infantado, Alba, Nájero, Alburquerque, Cádiz.

Marquesses (4) of Villena, Astorga, Moyar, Aguíler.

Counts (10) of Modica, Ureña, Salinas, Bonavente, Cabra, Luna, Santisteban, Casteñeda, Haro and one other.

Others known to have served on the Council were:
Monsignor Pedro Antonio Geraldini, a friend of Columbus.
Don Pedro Gonzales de Mendoza, Cardinal Primate of Spain, known as 'the third king'.

Columbus appeared before the great assembly of eminent persons he must have looked long and hard for friendly faces. There were some, but not many. And even fewer spoke up in his support.

Six years earlier Columbus had appeared before the king and queen as a supplicant. Now, grown in stature, both physical and mental, he appeared because they had summoned him. He adopted a bolder stance. Perhaps those years of failure and rejection, and the intimidating aspect of the council, caused him to give the appearance of being arrogant. It was an attitude which did not endear him to the council; indeed, it antagonised many members and jeopardised his chances.

He insisted upon five conditions, or 'capitulations' as they were called, and when he expounded them he alienated even further those opposed to him, and also shocked his supporters. When he finished he was formally rejected, and was sent packing. He knew that this had been his last throw: he had risked all and had lost.

Or had he? Even as Columbus rode away from Santa Fé on his mule bound for Córdova and thence to France to try to interest the court in Paris, his friends at court were still pressing stoically and courageously for his cause. Two simple arguments were put forward which when explored seriously proved weighty and compelling.

Among these friends were Pérez, Deza, Quintanilla, the Marquise de Moya, Beatrice Bobadilla and Luis de Santángel. The last was the shrewdest. He was the administrator of the court's exchequer; a banker, a man of riches, inheritor of a businessman father's wealth derived from duties levied in Valencia, the duchy of Milan and the republic of Genoa. He was shrewd enough to sense the wealth to be gained from Columbus's explorations and discoveries. Santángel saw the merit of giving sanction to Columbus's capitulations. After all, they were post-dated inasmuch as the promissory note would only be called in once Columbus had actually made the discovery. If he made the discoveries he believed in and reaped a harvest of riches from the Indies, he and the crown would benefit to an enormous extent: the prizes were glittering. If he did not make the discoveries, then the question of many of the articles comprising his capitulations would simply not arise.

PAWNING THE QUEEN'S JEWELS

STATEMENTS have persisted for five centuries that Queen Isabella pawned her jewels to help finance the Columbus enterprise. This is discounted and explained in the narrative. What is not generally known is that some years earlier Isabella genuinely had pawned her jewels. The incident is well documented. In August 1488, at the height of the Moorish war, the monarchs' coffers were much depleted. Every means had been taken of raising money by imposing loans on cities and by offering life incomes against voluntary individual loans. More was needed. Isabella pawned some of her most precious jewels which included a ruby necklace, a wedding present from King Ferdinand, and the jewel-encrusted crown of Castile. She raised 60,000 gold florins, equivalent to 9,315,551 maravedis. The ruby necklace raised 20,000 gold florins and the Castile crown 35,000. Interest on the loans became payable from 10 September 1489.

It is interesting to compare these values with those for outfitting the entire Columbus expedition (about two million maravedis), even though it is not possible to give modern day equivalent values.

The second point Santángel put to his monarchs was his preparedness to lend them the necessary investment money to finance the expedition — or at least to raise the necessary backing with sponsors and patrons.

This incident, hedged about by much dispute as to who paid what, has never been satisfactorily resolved to this day five centuries later. What it appeared to do was to give the monarchs a 'no-loss situation' with the prospect of great riches.

It also gave rise to a celebrated story about the queen being prepared to pawn her jewels in order to raise capital to help finance the enterprise. Las Casas and Ferdinand Columbus give a broadly similar account. They relate that the queen told Santángel 'that she was willing that, against the jewels of her bedchamber, they should seek a loan of the amount of money necessary to fit out the fleet.' Santángel is reported to have replied that 'it was not necessary to pawn the jewels, for he would do a little service to Her Majesty by lending her his own money.'

Santángel's offer of financial wizardry and his common-sense, fresh look at the capitulations put a different complexion on the monarchs' view of the enterprise. It now became possible to effect a political about-turn and reject the council's recommendation to refuse support for the enterprise. King Ferdinand was persuaded. Isabella, one senses, had hoped all along to find a way of helping the tall, fair Genoese navigator. Together, they agreed to recall him.

A messenger was despatched by horseback with all speed. He caught up with Columbus on his mule at the bridge of Pinos, about four miles from Santa Fé on the way to Córdova, as Las Casas declared, 'with the determination to go on to France.'

It had been a very close run thing.

8 Preparations for Discovery

W HEN Columbus rejoined the court it was to embark on a series of negotiations to formalise and document all the agreements and what today we would call the small print. The first of these was the Capitulations.

The document was brief – its five articles occupied a little over one page. It was a strange document, too; one of intent rather than a legally binding one. But it represented an astonishing achievement for Columbus. Only a few weeks earlier he had been rejected, his dreams, hopes and visions of discovery cast aside by the royal council. Downcast, disconsolate, embittered even, he had cut his losses and was on his way to France. Now here he was with a document granting him every single thing he sought, without dispute or acrimonious squabbling – he, the persistent foreigner of lowly birth.

A few days after the signing of the Capitulations, signatures were applied to a document called the 'Titulo of 30 April 1492'. It defined more precisely the question of titles. A successful enterprise would be rewarded with the greatest title – created specially for him and his successors – Almirante Mayor del Mar Océano, with honours and privileges equal to those accorded to the Admiral of Castile, Don Alfonso Enríquez.

Don Alfonso was nobility of the highest order, an uncle of King Ferdinand, and he enjoyed precedence, privilege and dignities unmatched at court. The title of Admiral of the Ocean Sea went a long way towards satisfying Columbus's yearning for titles and honours. Viceroy and Governor would be very acceptable, but the naval rank dwarfed them in importance and honour. Columbus knew he was pitching his demands high, but he did not let them rest there. Along with this resounding title – such was his pride and vanity – he insisted that it should pass to his descendants in perpetuity: he was laying all the foundations for establishing a noble family and he aimed to see that Castile should maintain him and his successors in the manner befitting their rank.

His pride must have been palpable when the Catholic Sovereigns addressed him as *Don* Christopher Columbus, and later when they lauded him as Admiral and Viceroy. But with pride came arrogance, an objectionable attitude which he adopted before the intelligentsia sitting in council to hear his appeals for support.

Columbus was also successful in his demands under Articles 3 and 5. He scored heavily with their commercial implications and they became celebrated as the 'tenth' and 'eighth' articles. They were shrewd demands which helped establish Columbus and his family's wealth and fortunes.

Yet the articles were never properly honoured by the crown. Columbus was to spend the rest of his life persistently trying to secure settlement of what he understood the articles made due to him. He read into the clauses impossible

THE SANTA FÉ CAPITULATIONS

IN THIS sense a capitulation is a transaction or agreement on privileges to be granted: the more common meaning of a surrender seems equally applicable in this instance.

Columbus submitted a series of five high-handed articles which astounded and shocked everyone by their despotism. These were embodied in a document dated 17 April 1492: less than a fortnight later King Ferdinand and Queen Isabella conceded all Columbus's demands, and thus set in train the discovery of the New World — *Mundus Novus*.

This is a page of the Santa Fé Capitulations, each paragraph of which was signed by the royal secretary, Juan de Cólona. Columbus had sought and won an incredible series of concessions:

1. That Columbus should have for himself during his life and his heirs and successors forever, the office and title of Admiral of the Ocean Sea, in all the lands and continents which he might discover ... with similar honours and privileges as those of the High Admiral of Castile.

2. That he should be Viceroy and Governor General over all the said lands and continents with the right of nominating three candidates for the government of each island or province, only one of whom should be appointed by the crown.

3. That Columbus should be entitled to reserve for himself one tenth of all pearls, precious stones, gold, silver, spices and all other articles and merchandise in whatever manner found, bought, bartered or gained within his admiralty, the costs being first deducted.

4. That he or his nominees should be the sole judges in all disputes arising out of traffic between Spain and those countries he discovers.

5. That he might then, and his heirs in perpetuity, have the right to contribute one eighth part of the expenses in fitting out vessels for this enterprise, and receive an eighth part of the profits.

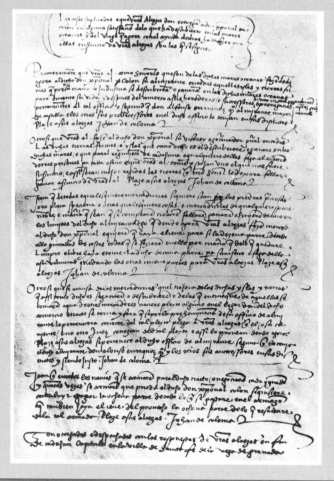

claims, and the wrangling over their meanings and the claims and counter-claims seemed never-ending. And when at last death relieved Columbus of these trials, his son Diego took up the cause and fought through the courts for what he thought were just claims. King Ferdinand wearied of these tiresome things and offered land and other riches for a renunciation of Columbus's claims, but the Admiral was irascible and adamant and fought like a cat to defend what he thought were his just rights. Death, as ever, brought a solution and by then Columbus was a very wealthy landowner despite everything.

The fact remains that Columbus sought and secured a form of contract with the crown, and troublesome though it may all have proved, it also brought to him and his family rich rewards.

Rich rewards also accrued to the Catholic Sovereigns. Exactly how great cannot ever be computed. Indeed, the whole costing of the expedition, the subscribers to the investment and the returns have been the subject of much dispute, and numerous attempts have been made to try to reconcile the apparent inconsistencies; but no one has provided a satisfactory resolution to the financial settlements.

We have already touched upon Santángel's having persuaded the monarchs to participate in the enterprise. 'All Columbus asks at present,' he argued persuasively, 'is a cuento.' A cuento or quento was a million maravedis.

Columbus is recorded as having commented that their Highnesses did not wish to contribute more than a million, '. . . so it was necessary to produce another half cuento, since that sum was not sufficient for the enterprise.'

However, records in the Simancas Archives show that Santángel was reimbursed one cuento and 140,000 maravedis [1,140,000 ms] for the money he lent, via bankers and financiers, to the Sovereigns.

Elsewhere it is recorded that Columbus found sponsorship and contributed not one eighth of the expedition's costs but 500,000 ms, considerably more than in Article 5 of the Capitulations.

If two sources are to be believed — both Paolo Taviani and Samuel Eliot Morison are virtually agreed on this point — then further investment sums brought the grand total to 2,000,000 ms. This exceeds by a considerable margin the total arrived at by John Boyd Thacher, regarded for long as the authority on the subject.

The balance sheet is further complicated by the costs attributable to Palos by an outstanding obligation of the town and its inhabitants 'sentenced by the Royal Council to supply the Sovereigns with two caravels fitted out at their own expense, for the duration of two months'. There is more to this story as shall be seen in a moment.

Meanwhile, we can tabulate the following figures and draw whatever conclusions one may care to.

It is virtually impossible to calculate a true comparative of the costs in Columbus's time to those of today. Changes in currencies and standards of living, in human behaviour, and the addition of inflation, purchasing power of currencies and a host of other factors all nullify comparisons.

COST OF THE ENTERPRISE[1]

Subscribers	Sources		
	Thacher	Taviani	Morison
Crown of Castile[2]	1,000,000	1,140,000	1,400,000
Columbus	167,542[3]	500,000[4]	250,000
Palos subscribed in kind: for *Pinta* 115,200 for *Nĩna* 57,600	172,800	360,000[5]	350,000[5]
TOTALS	1,340,342	2,000,000	2,000,000

Expenditure:[6]	
Salaries (Officers)	268,000
Wages (Men)	252,000
Maintenance	319,680
Rent of *Santa Maria*	172,800
Furniture, arms, trading supplies etc	155,062
	1,167,542[6]

Notes:
1. Three reliable sources are quoted. It is impossible to reconcile them. Thacher seems too plausible. Sums are expressed in maravedis.
2. Money provided by bankers and financiers on behalf of the Crown.
3. This is a convenient one eighth of the total.
4. Bankers and financiers are thought to have backed Columbus.
5. These two sums seem to be balancing items.
6. Thacher again conveniently balances the Crown and Columbus's subscriptions with these expenses.

For what it is worth, Morison reports that the maravedi was a small copper coin, 375 of which equated to the gold excelente of Granada. And this excelente had a value of $6.05 in pre-1934 US dollars.

Thacher concludes (after spending a chapter on trying to unravel this puzzle) with this comment: 'We may regard it as the most fortunate outlay of money since gold and silver were minted into coin.'

One other observation on this subject is worth recording, even though it must be purely speculative and uttered a little tongue-in-cheek: a Frenchman, Jean-Baptiste Charcot, more in fun perhaps than with mathematical precision, calculated that the court of Spain, in the century following Columbus's discovery, received *in respect of precious metals alone* 1,733,000 maravedis for every single maravedi invested in the Columbus enterprise.

In commercial terms Columbus's discovery of the New World, although not the Indies he had expected and hoped for, had proved the investment of the century.

In addition to the documentation already referred to — the Capitulations and the Titulo — there were two others of interest. One was a letter of introduction establishing Columbus's credentials to the Great Khan, whose kingdom Columbus genuinely expected to visit: the letter served also to introduce him to sundry other minor kings and princes he might encounter on the way.

Another document comprised a number of ordinances or orders directed at the people of Palos regarding the provisioning and outfitting of ships. It appears that sometime in the past Palos vessels had been implicated in a case of piracy, smuggling or importation of goods from Africa or some islands without having paid the necessary dues. A trial was held and Palos and its citizenry were found guilty. The court imposed a pay-later sentence. It was now proposed that this sentence should be called in. Granzotto captures the scene well:*

> This order, signed by Ferdinand and Isabella, was solemnly read in the parish church of St George on 23 May by the Palos notary, Francisco Fernández. This church still stands, next to the old castle ruins. It is made of *piedra caliza*, a yellow and brown sandstone . . . If you enter the nave you can still see in the shadow of arches supported by strong pillars the wrought iron pulpit from which the ordinance was read. Columbus was present for the reading. He himself had handed the document to the mayor of Palos who then turned it over to the notary . . .
>
> The church was swarming . . . many of them had to stand inside the doors, one of which faces a mountain, the other a valley.This latter was and still is called *la puerta d'embarcadero*, the door to the pier. A little red dirt road runs from the door down to the Rio Tinto . . . The seamen of Palos crowded this door . . . The royal decree demanded that the caravels be fully rigged 'within ten days of receipt of this order'.

At a stroke the parsimonious Sovereigns had solved two-thirds of the expedition's shipping requirements. Further, Palos would provide the port from which to launch the voyage of the century.

The two caravels which Palos provided were the *Niña* and the *Pinta*. The third vessel, the flagship *Santa Maria*, was described as a *nao*, a ship. Ships of this class could be as large as 750 tons but the *Santa Maria* is thought to have been about 100 tons. She was a round ship as opposed to a long ship. Vessels of the fifteenth century were described like this because of the ratios of their lengths and breadths. The classic example of a long ship was the Mediterranean oared galley. Long ships' ratios were about eight to one, while a round ship was about three or four to one. The round ship was propelled by sails alone, while the long ships carried banks of oars in addition to their sails.

Nothing is known for certain about the *Santa Maria*. No contemporary drawings, sketches or documents which would tell us exactly what she looked like have survived the centuries. Furthermore, she was sunk by shipwreck off Hispaniola as we shall see in due course. But we know that a *nao* was a bulky cargo vessel which needed a lot of canvas to propel her at any speed. She was rigged with square sails on the fore and main masts, with a lateen on the mizzen (or stern-most) mast. A spritsail or 'civada' could also be rigged under

* Gianni Granzotto, p.98.

This woodcut is said to have represented the *Santa Maria* but this cannot be so. It's first appearance pre-dated Columbus's discoveries.

MONTHLY SALARIES AND WAGES[1]

Rank	Ship	Name	Monthly salary 1492 in maravedis
Admiral[2]	*Santa Maria*	Christopher Columbus	
Captain	*Pinta*	Martín Alonso Pinzón	2500
Captain	*Niña*	Vicente Yáñez Pinzón	2500
Master	*Santa Maria*	Juan de la Cosa	2500
Master	*Pinta*	Francisco Martín Pinzón	1666
Master	*Niña*	Juan Niño	1666
Pilot	*Santa Maria*	Sancho Ruiz	1666
Pilot	*Pinta*	Cristobal Garcia Xalmiento	1666
Pilot	*Niña*	Pedro Alonso Niño	1666
Pilot[3]	*Niña*	Bartolomé Roldán	1666
Alguazil Mayor	*Santa Maria*	Diego de Harana	2500
Lawyer	? *Santa Maria*	Bombardino de Tapia	2000
Physician[4]	*Niña*	Maestre Alonzo	2000
Assayist	? *Santa Maria*	Castille	1000
Officer of the Royal Household	*Santa Maria*	Pedro Gutiérrez	1083
Inspector	*Santa Maria*	Rodrigo Sanchez	1083
Inspector	*Santa Maria*	Rodrigo de Escobedo	1000
Interpreter	*Santa Maria*	Luis de Torres	833
Steward	*Santa Maria*	Terreros	750
Steward	*Pinta*	Garcia Fernandez	750
Boatswain	*Pinta*	Maestre Diego	750
Boatswain	*Niña*	Bartolomé Garcia	750
Caulker	*Santa Maria*	Juan Perez Viscaino	750
Barber[4]	*Santa Maria*	Maestre Juan Sanchez	750
Sailor[5]	All three		500

Notes:

1. Most of these figures are based on a document dated July 1493 relating to an African expedition.
2. The Admiral received no pay — just the Eighths and Tenths payable under the Capitulations.
3. Roldán did not live to receive his pay.
4. Not to be confused with a surgeon, who only rated the same as a barber — see later entry in this column.
5. This is a typical entry to give a comparative between officers and sailors.

the bowsprit and even more canvas could be carried aloft as a topsail above the crow's nest. Yet, for all this sail area, she was prone to wallowing in anything of a sea and she was never an easy ship to handle.

Maritime scholars have been able to interpret certain facts and speculate to a high degree of accuracy about the ship's design. It is thought that the *Santa Maria* had a length of about 77 ft (23.5 m), a breadth of 26 ft (nearly 8 m) — a ratio of about 3:1 — and a draught of just under 7 ft (2.1 m).

She was owned by Juan de la Cosa, about whom a mystery has developed only in the past few decades.

TWO OF A KIND? THE MYSTERY OF JUAN DE LA COSA

SOME leading Columbian scholars, including Alice Bache Gould and Samuel Eliot Morison, are reconciled to the belief there may well have been two men by the name of Juan de la Cosa, even though such a coincidence stretches credulity rather far. Both were close associates of the great discoverer.

It was commonly supposed that the master and owner of the *Santa Maria*, Juan de la Cosa, a Basque from a Santoña parish named Santa Maria de la Puerto, was the same man who made the world famous map and who later explored the Spanish Main. But this was not necessarily so — even though the similarities go even further.

The cartographer was also a Basque, though he had moved to a small town in the Bay of Cádiz called Puerto Santa Maria.

Juan de la Cosa, the master of the *Santa Maria*, was responsible for the loss of the flagship when she was wrecked. He became disgraced and he was never mentioned by Columbus again. It is inconceivable that Columbus would have re-employed the disgraced mariner for a second voyage: this seems a compelling argument.

The cartographer, by contrast, was more competent and worked closely with Columbus. He shipped aboard the *Niña* in 1493 and made the Cuban voyage with him and later, in 1499, accompanied Amerigo Vespucci on his great expedition. This de la Cosa (c.1460–1509) is best remembered however for his skilled cartography. He was the first map-maker to record all the discoveries of the New World onto a chart.

He is portrayed here clutching one of his famous charts. The large hand-drawn map made in 1500 embodying all the recent discoveries is preserved in the Naval Museum in Madrid. Tragically, de la Cosa was attacked and killed by natives in Panama in 1509.

The other two vessels of the fleet were caravels, smaller and handier vessels than the flagship. The caravel was the pioneer vessel of discovery during the fifteenth and sixteenth centuries. She was a light, swift lateener with a shallow draught, ideal for explorers like Columbus and Vasco da Gama. The caravel derived from the fishing craft of the western Mediterranean, with a typical lateen or triangular rig combined with a vertical sternpost suspending the rudder, common to northern Europe. A caravel was readily converted to square rigging: it was then called a *caravela redonda* and carried square sails on the fore and main mast with a lateen on the mizzen mast, like the *Santa Maria*.

The *Niña*, in fact, set out as a lateen caravel, but before leaving the Canaries Columbus had her converted to match the *Pinta*.

The caravel was constructed to a traditional three-two-one (*tres, dos y as*) formula: the maximum length of the hull should be three times the breadth and the breadth twice the height between decks. Both caravels were a little under sixty tons. The ton in question was a *tonel*, a Seville measure equal to 1,267.81 lbs. It is supposed to be the weight of 1.66 wine casks containing 45.15 *arrobas* of wine, plus the weight of the casks. A pipe or *pipa* of wine contains 27.5 *arrobas* of wine, 25.356 lbs each. This seems too contrived to be acceptable. A less demanding definition is the space required to store two pipes of wine − roughly 60 cu ft (1.7 sq m). A pipe was a cask containing about 110 Imperial gallons.

The *Niña* was Columbus's favourite. He never liked the *Santa Maria*, but the *Niña* was certainly a smart little ship capable of carrying a cargo of about fifty tons. When the *Santa Maria* was shipwrecked it was to the *Niña* that Columbus turned and spent the rest of the voyage of discovery in her. Quite a lot is known about her. Her hull planks were 2½ inches thick (over 6 cms), secured with wooden pegs, the planks caulked with oakum and pitch. Large iron bolts gave added strength. Her main deck was also planked and pegged and caulked with a slightly arched effect, giving it a camber like a modern road. Right up forward was the anchor and its cable, and on the centre line a capstan for working the anchor. The main mast was forward of the main hatch and close by was stowage space for spars and the ship's boat. The wood-burning firebox − which served as the galley or kitchen − was also stowed amidships. No cook was carried aboard, probably the gromets − ordinary seamen or ship's boys − did the cooking.

The ship's heads were of the simplest design, comprising seats hung over the rails, one forward, another aft, where everyone from the loftiest to the lowliest performed his daily functions with total lack of privacy. They were called *jardines*, probably named after the gardens in which most privies at home were located. Good-humoured banter accompanied each visit. More often than not a wave would unkindly slap an unsuspecting performer. Many men of rank complained of the indecency of exposing themselves to all and sundry. *Jardines* were a great leveller.

The stern deck or quarterdeck gave the caravel her high-sterned profile. When Columbus was aboard he used the tiny cabin perched far aft on the quarterdeck, almost all its space being taken up by his bunk. Even so he was better off than the master and pilot who shared a 'cabin' not much larger than a cupboard below the quarterdeck.

Nearby the helmsman kept watch at the wheel, steering the ship by the compass. The captain of the watch kept his station on the quarterdeck, striding up and down watching the binnacle to check the helmsman was keeping course. The latter was on the deck below and was unable to see the ship's sails: he steered with skill by the feel of the ship.

During each watch a lookout was posted forward and another in the round top. The rest of the duty watch was responsible for the running and maintenance of the ship: decks had to be scrubbed and washed, sails needed constant attention, all gear such as ropes, sheets and braces needed trimming, tightening or loosening.

Below decks almost every foot of space was occupied for stowage, with just about enough space for the men to get their heads down. They slept clothed. The stench below decks was sickening. Water seeped into the ship's bilges and the wooden hand pumps had to be regularly manned to keep the leaks in check. It was the carpenter's or the caulker's job to prime the pump and ensure its efficient operation. But everywhere was dark, lit only by oil lamps, and dank and cramped beyond description.

It would have been a delight to get up top with fresh breezes blowing, helping to dispel the more evil smells.

Apart from the enormous quantity of stores for sustaining the crews throughout the coming months, each ship stowed cargoes of trinkets, like glass beads, hawks' bells, knives and brightly coloured cloth, to use as gifts to natives, such as had proved useful in African expeditions.

The total numbers of men carried aboard these ships is generally agreed to have been about ninety (perhaps forty aboard the flagship, twenty-six aboard the *Pinta* and twenty-four in *Niña*), but there is still confusion about their names. The acknowledged sources are Thacher and Morison*, who quotes the

* Morison details Miss Gould's sources: see p. 183 and note 16 to his *Christopher Columbus: Admiral of the Ocean Sea*. He calls it the most important piece of original Columbian research this century.

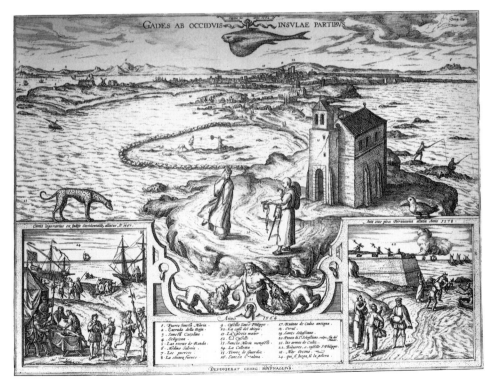

Cádiz, major sea port of Andalusia, saw much of the comings and goings of Columbus's fleets.

work of Alice Bache Gould. It is not possible, therefore, to list the first roll call of those who served in this historic voyage. It must await the work of another researcher.

What can be drawn from all this research is that there were a few men from northern Spanish towns but the preponderance of men came from the traditional seafaring towns of Andalusia, such as Cádiz, Seville, Córdova, Jerez and Puerta Santa Maria, and many more from Palos, Huelva, Moguer and Lepe. Further, it can be said with confidence that they were among the best of Spanish seamen, a far cry from the jailbird myth.

No priest served aboard any ships of the squadron. At first glance this seems suspicious or mysterious. The reason is plausible enough. Priests, monks, missionaries or churchmen of any sort did not take part in voyages of discovery as a general rule, but they did in voyages of what might be called consolidation, when they set out to meet the needs of the European colonists and to try to convert the local unbelievers. This they subsequently did in large numbers and spread the word of the gospel throughout the New World. The point is also made that it would have been singularly tactless on meeting kings and princes for the first time to introduce Spanish priests intent on converting them to Catholicism.

The absence of priests aboard the three ships should not imply a lack of religious observances. Far from it! These would start every day at daybreak with a gromet intoning a chant and then the mustered ship's company reciting the Lord's Prayer and the *Ave Maria*. Throughout the day seamen would recite chants to accompany their duties. Every half hour when a gromet turned the sand-glass a chant would be taken up. At sunset, too, as a boy lit the binnacle lamp the mustered hands saluted the Blessed Virgin with her ancient canticle, *Salve Regina*.

CRIMINALS IN THE CREWS

FOR CENTURIES the claim has been sustained that Columbus's ships contained a good percentage of criminals among the crews; after all it was not uncommon in the late Middle Ages for ships of war to be manned by men recruited from prisons and other places of known criminal associations.

Careful research, however, has revealed that in Columbus's first voyage of discovery only four men have been documented unquestionably as criminals. This is not to say there were no others; perhaps a few escaped the documentation process — but such a number would have been very few. Certainly there is no evidence of a 'horde' or large numbers being involved. The four known criminals were:

Bartolomé de Torres
Pedro Izquierdo
Juan de Moguer
Alfonso Clavijo

It appears that Torres was the real criminal: he killed a man in Palos. The other three managed to aid his escape from detention and all were subsequently sentenced to death. The four men offered themselves to Columbus under a royal safe conduct or amnesty: 'And by these presents we grant security to all and any persons who shall go in the said caravels with the said Christopher Columbus . . .'

In due course, when the men returned to Palos, they were pardoned. Torres benefited from his experiences and made good after his pardon. He accompanied Columbus on the second voyage as a crossbowman. Juan de Moguer also joined the second voyage, aboard the flagship as an able seaman. Years later he had progressed to become a pilot.

Before leaving this section we need to focus for a moment on two leading figures in the first voyage of discovery. They were the brothers Pinzón. The Pinzón family of Palos was both an asset and a handicap to Columbus. The affection with which the people of Palos remember Martín Alonso Pinzón is exemplified by the statue in the town centre: it is not of Columbus, it is of Martín Alonso Pinzón. He was a man of such local eminence, of such repute as a navigator and seaman, that there is no denying he was judged by Andalusians as the greater man. Columbus by comparison was an intruding foreigner.

Pinzón's importance was underlined when Columbus turned to him, the man with local knowledge, to assist in the fitting out of the ships for the enterprise, an enterprise which was entrusted to Columbus but which many considered should have been awarded to Pinzón. There is little doubt that he tried assiduously to snatch from Columbus's grasp, or to claim by stealth and subterfuge, the rewards he considered more rightly his.

Why, his supporters claimed, Pinzón was researching the enterprise to the Indies quite independently of Columbus, and indeed in 1492 before the fleet sailed Martín was in Rome visiting the Pope's library, researching ancient volumes and writings on the lands to be discovered in the Sea of Darkness. Others, less captivated by this sneaky, untrustworthy man, say the Rome visit was nothing of the sort, just his annual visit to the Tiber with a shipment of sardines.

Martín Alonso Pinzón captained the *Pinta*. He sought personal glory by usurping Columbus's claims. Columbus criticised him in mild terms: 'he has by language and actions occasioned me many troubles.'

Vicente Yáñez Pinzón was Martín's younger brother and a great explorer in his own right. He is portrayed holding a quadrant, identical with the navigational instrument used by Columbus for taking sights.

However, Pinzón played a notable part in the expedition. He had many attributes and much to offer Columbus. He was a seaman *par excellence*, and in years of sailing the seas of the Mediterranean, the Canaries and Africa's Guinea, he had accumulated a small fortune, including his own ship. By 1492 he was a man of some substance, authority and power.

Columbus was introduced to Pinzón by a mutual friend, Father Marchena. It must have been a memorable meeting: two men with great knowledge of the seas and of ships and navigation. If there was envy on Pinzón's part, he would also have displayed great respect because Columbus's knowledge of these matters was incomparable.

Columbus recruited Pinzón as captain of the *Pinta*. Enthusiastically, Pinzón recruited his younger brother, Vicente Yáñez Pinzón, promising him captaincy of the *Niña*. The two of them started recruiting crew members from all over the region. A contemporary noted how he saw:

> Martin Pinzón going in search of people saying: friends, come along, make this voyage with us. Why do you live here pinching pennies? Make this voyage. We should discover lands with the help of God and . . . we should find houses with roofs of gold and all riches and good fortune . . . many people were found in the cities of Palos, Huelva and Moguer.

Another chronicler reports he saw:

> Martín Alonso Pinzón well determined to make the discovery in the company of Christopher Columbus and he took with him on his ships his brothers and many relations and friends; and it was known . . . if [he] had not decided to make this voyage and had not taken part in it personally, no one would have dared go, for many of those who went were going to their death and they had little hope of coming back.

Columbus had found a great ally in Pinzón: one who later would not hesitate to stab him, metaphorically, in the back. For the time being Columbus was well content, the ships were fitted out, the crews mustered and the enterprise was about to be launched.

9 Columbus's Journal: Dalliance in the Canaries

CHRISTOPHER Columbus sailed from Palos on 3 August 1492. His squadron — grandly named 'fleet' — comprised the *Santa Maria*, *Niña* and *Pinta*. It was his first and most momentous voyage of discovery.

The fleet's daily occurrences and experiences were recorded by Columbus in his *Journal*, the original title of which was *Book of the First Navigation and Discovery of the Indies*. It was his log or *diario*, but for convenience is always referred to in English as his *Journal*.

Columbus wrote every word of it in his own hand. It became a long, discursive volume full of his thoughts, dreams, hopes and feelings as well as all the seafaring items about weather and sea conditions. The *Journal* is regarded in maritime circles as perhaps the most important document in maritime history.

Alas, the original holograph copy has long since disappeared: a tragic loss, rendered less so by Columbus's contemporary, the meticulous historian Bartholomew de las Casas. He transcribed it into the document which has survived the centuries. However, there is a danger with transcriptions. How closely do they follow the original work and reflect the author's thoughts — and nuances? We know that Las Casas considered Columbus's *Journal* too rambling and in need of editing. He abridged the work, exactly to what extent we shall never know, and added his own commentaries. The final result was a work of great worth and merit, flawed by some errors (though not of great consequence) and diminished, of course, by its not being the original holograph. Sometimes Las Casas used the first person when quoting Columbus direct, and at others the third person when they were his comments. But whatever its faults, it remains one of history's most fascinating works.

The loss of the original came about in this fashion: on returning to court from his first great voyage Columbus handed his documents, including the *Journal*, into the safekeeping of the king and queen so they could have them analysed and assessed by their expert advisers. Copies were supposedly transcribed and the original retained by Isabella, Columbus himself receiving a copy.

It is believed that Columbus's son Diego acquired a copy and took it with him to Santo Domingo when he was installed as governor there. It is this copy — Diego's — which Las Casas consulted and transcribed into the *Journal* we know today. Diego's copy has failed to survive the centuries. Nor is there any trace of the original Columbus work. Sadly, there is no trace either of any journals relating to the second, third or fourth voyages. Thus, Las Casas's transcription becomes a rare and valuable document indeed.

It was a time of extensive exploration by men like Vasco da Gama,

Magellan, Cabot and Dias. All kept journals, but none matched Columbus's for detail. He recorded the minutiae of the voyage, not only the wind direction, sea conditions and the distances covered by each ship during each day, but all that had been sighted such as fish, birds and any floating matter, every day of the voyage. Of course, it was often tediously repetitive.

On Thursday evening, 2 August 1492, all the officers and men, gentlemen volunteers and gromets from Columbus's three vessels attended mass at the Church of St George in Palos. The church stood but a short distance from where their vessels lay. Those families who were able to attend also thronged the church, praying for the blessing of the Virgin upon their menfolk who were about to embark on an enterprise of unknown and unimaginable dangers. They all received a short blessing and then exited by the 'door to the pier' to board their ships in readiness for departure in the morning.

The next day dawned clear with an almost motionless sea, a Mediterranean-like sky and the promise of fierce heat. But of wind there was hardly a breath. Friday was portending ill luck even before they started. Setting sail on a Friday

The Flemish engraver Jean de Bry depicted scenes from his father Theodore's *Collectiones Peregrinationum in Indian Orientalum et Indiam Occidentalem* (1590–1634). This scene shows Columbus taking leave of the Catholic Sovereigns at Palos before embarking on his first voyage.

was a curious choice for Columbus. He knew that to superstitious persons — and seamen often are superstitious — Friday, the day of the Lord's crucifixion, was an unlucky day. Other biblical references point to Adam and Eve eating the forbidden fruit on a Friday and to Adam dying on a Friday. As it turned out, Fridays were anything but unlucky for Columbus during his first voyage of discovery. Not only did he sail on a Friday, he made his first New World landfall on Friday 12 October, he sailed from Hispaniola for Spain on Friday 4 January 1493, and he anchored *Niña* in Palos harbour on his return to Spain on Friday 14 March.

Before dawn on the morning of 3 August Columbus ordered the anchor to be weighed 'in the name of Jesus'. His Captain-General's banner — a dark green cross on a white ground — was hoisted to the masthead, but it hung limply, like the sails. When unfurled they hung empty, wrinkled and creased. Columbus's *Journal* described the departure briefly and inadequately for such a momentous occasion:

> Friday 3 August 1492. We set sail from the bar of Saltes [in the harbour of Palos] at eight o'clock and sailed with a strong breeze till sunset, sixty miles or fifteen leagues. [Italian: four miles to the league.] South, afterwards South-West and South quarter by South-West which was the course for the Canaries.

Columbus failed to capture the scene, the three ships with barely any movement on them sailing slowly from their river anchorages, passing beneath the walls of the monastery where friars were reciting their canonical prayers. Columbus knelt in prayer as the *Santa Maria* passed by, many of the crews following suit, snatching off their red woollen caps to bare their heads.

It was a leisurely passage. It took two hours for the ships to clear the Saltes bar which marked the beginning of the open sea. Once freed from the land, a breeze began to fill the sails, the ships gathered speed and the southerly course was set.

By evening a south-westerly course towards the Canaries was maintained and the mainland of Europe was lost to sight. A sense of loneliness pervaded the crews. The great venture into the unknown was really and truly under way.

The very next day an emergency occurred with the rudder aboard *Pinta*. It became unshipped through either jumping its gudgeons or a pintle shearing. She was forced to strike sails and was evidently in difficulties. A heavy sea was running at the time and it was difficult to effect even temporary repairs. Columbus ordered the ships to Grand Canary, the largest of the thirteen Canary islands, but strong winds dispersed them. Nevertheless the *Pinta* managed to press on and reach Grand Canary with its shipyard facilities where the rudder could be repaired, failing which, Columbus had ordered Pinzón to try to buy another ship. Columbus allowed the winds to take the other two ships to Gomera, a smaller island to the west of the group, the greenest and most fertile of them all, where he could replenish supplies of food and water.

There was another reason. On arrival there it was learned that 'the mistress of the island', Doña Beatrice de Perara y Bobadilla, was expected hourly to return from a visit to Grand Canary. After several days of waiting, neither the beautiful lady nor the repaired caravel had put in an appearance. Columbus sailed for Grand Canary to try to locate Pinzón only to find it had taken *Pinta* twelve days to make harbour. While repairs were in hand, Columbus ordered

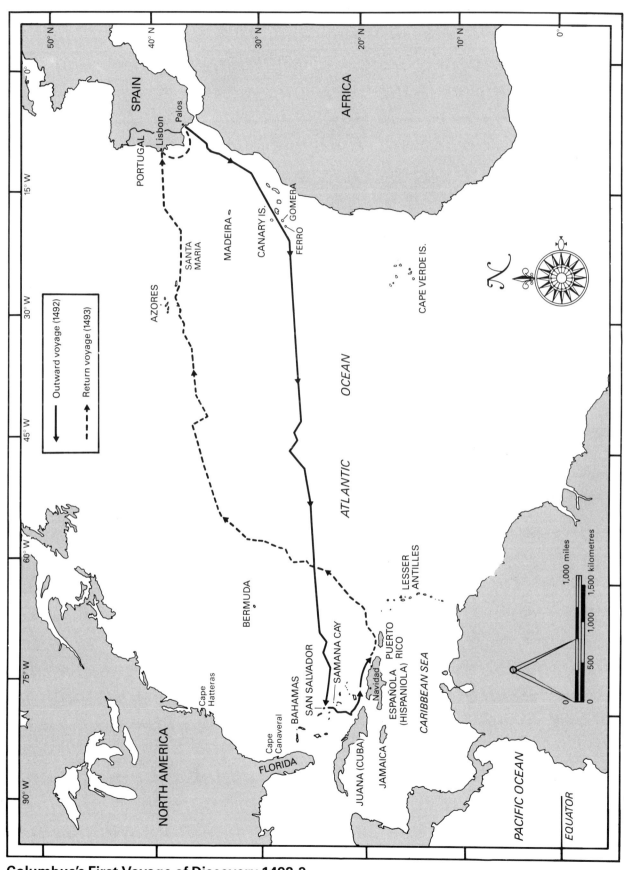

Columbus's First Voyage of Discovery 1492-3.

On all four voyages of discovery Columbus visited the Canary Islands to re-provision his ships. This monument stands at Las Palmas in Gran Canaria.

the *Niña*'s lateen rig to be changed to square to improve her sailing characteristics. He judged she would perform better in the belt of the easterlies, where he knew the winds blew steadily every day from the east or north-east and where a square-rigged ship had every advantage. He also knew that in latitudes further north the prevailing winds blew equally steadily and reliably from the west; winds which would sail his fleet home from the Indies.

It was not until 1 September, almost three weeks after departing Palos, that the three ships, being in all respects ready for sea, hoisted sails and departed

SHIPS OF THE DISCOVERY AND A MODERN CRUISE LINER

SHIPS OF THE CARIBBEAN

Ship	Crown Princess	Santa Maria	Pinta	Niña
Tonnage	70,000	about 100	55–60	58–60
Length	804ft (245m)	80ft (24.5m)		67ft (20.2m)
Breadth	106ft (32.3m)	26ft (7.9m)	25ft (7.6m)	21ft (6.4m)
Passengers/ Crew	1590/671	40	24–26	24
Speed	22.5 kn	6.5 kn	8 kn	8 kn

The recent discovery of a 400-page bundle of documents named the *Libro de Armadas* in the Seville Archives has revealed new information about Columbus's favourite ship, the *Niña*. For example, she had four masts, not two or three as had been believed. She was probably used on three of the Admiral's voyages. She was probably fifty-eight to sixty tons, had a length of sixty-seven feet, a beam of twenty-one feet and drew just under seven feet. She was equipped with a two hundred-pound anchor and carried eighteen tons of wheat, seventeen tons of wine, seven tons of sea biscuits, two tons of flour, over two thousand pounds of cheese, a ton of salt pork and eleven butts of water. She was armed with ten breech-loading swivel bombards and carried eighty lead balls, one hundred pounds of gunpowder and seventy-four lances. She also had three smaller anchors and one ship's boat.

Source: National Geographic Society.

Grand Canary. They arrived at Gomera and found safe anchorages. Beatrice Bobadilla had now returned home and it is reported that she received Columbus warmly.

One biographer goes this far in commenting upon their relationship:*

> And Beatrice of Gomera? Much has been made of her relationship to Columbus, the subject of whispers even at the time and fertile ground for invention in the centuries that followed. There may have been something between them. It is possible that the lady governor and the explorer did more than exchange polite smiles. Perhaps it wasn't until this second visit that they finally dropped all inhibitions. Beatrice was an energetic, impetuous woman. She always knew what she wanted. Columbus was no womaniser, but neither was he accustomed to saying no . . . One may speculate as one likes: there are no documents . . .

Four days were spent provisioning ships with water from the freshwater river, meat, flour and cheeses, and timber from the woods.

On the evening before departure the crews gathered for a mass and to confess their sins in the Church of the Assumption close by the port. They returned to

* Gianni Granzotto, pp.120–21.

their ships by the light of a moon just one day from being full. They had been refreshed, were well fed and now they were expectant at the knowledge they were on the brink of a dangerously exciting enterprise.

On the morning of Thursday 6 September the fleet weighed anchor, hoisted sails and met the same wind conditions that had prevailed at Palos, so light that the sails hung limp and creased. This Thursday is generally regarded as th day marking the beginning of this first voyage of discovery. Course was held resolutely to the west.

TEN CONTEMPORARY EXPLORERS

It may prove salutary to pause a while as Columbus sets out on this westerly course to take a brief look at his exploring contemporaries who were also pushing horizons further and further from Europe.

CABOT, John (1450–c.1499) Discoverer of Newfoundland. He was born Giovanni Caboto in Genoa and became a naturalised Venetian, but moved to London before settling as a merchant in Bristol with his family in 1484 or thereabouts. He was encouraged by Columbus's discoveries to set out in 1497 on a northerly voyage of exploration. After fifty-two days at sea in the *Matthew* he discovered Cape Breton Island, thinking he had reached Asia. The following year, with the backing of King Henry VII, he discovered Newfoundland and Nova Scotia and sailed along the eastern seaboard of North America from Labrador to Virginia, possibly reaching Chesapeake Bay. He remained baffled by his failure to locate Cipango.

CABOT, Sebastian (c.1476–1557) Navigator and cartographer. He was the son of John Cabot and was born either in Genoa or Bristol. Possibly accompanied his father in 1497–8 on the expedition to Newfoundland and Nova Scotia. In 1508–9 he sailed to Hudson Bay in search of Asia. It is known that he sailed as far south as the River Plate in South America while in the service of King Charles V of Spain as pilot-major. He failed to colonise Brazil and Paraguay, was imprisoned and exiled from Spain. He was welcomed back to England. Edward VI appointed him his inspector of the English navy and a governor of the Company of Merchant Adventurers. A copy of his famous map of the world (1504) is carefully preserved in the Bibliotheque Nationale, Paris.

DIAS (or DIAZ, NOVAIS or NOVAES), Bartholomew (c.1450–1500) Portuguese navigator and discoverer of the Cape of Good Hope, which he rounded in 1488, naming it Cabo Torment**ó**so (Cape of Storms), which King John then renamed Good Hope. In 1497 he sailed with Vasco da Gama to the Cape Verde Islands. He sailed to the Gold Coast (Ghana) and in 1500 sailed with Cabril to Brazil. Ironically he was drowned when his ship and three others foundered in a storm off the Cape of Good Hope. He is universally accepted as the greatest of the Portuguese pioneers who explored the Atlantic in the fifteenth century. There is no known portrait of him. He had a son, Antonio. His grandson Paulo Dias de Novais gave his name to São Paulo, Brazil in 1576.

GAMA, Vasco da (1460 or 1469–1524) Portuguese navigator and fearless sailor. He heralded a new era in world history with his pioneering voyages to India in 1497–9, 1502–3 and 1524. He was raised to the nobility as the First Count of Vidigueira for his reaching Calicut via the Cape of Good Hope and pioneering the eastern route to the sub-continent by way of Mossel Bay (Natal), Mozambique and Mombasa. In Calicut he experienced much native hostility. He was despatched there time and time again to help quell riots. On one occasion he burned a ship carrying Moslem pilgrims, and on another bombarded Calicut. On his way back from his third venture in 1524 he died at Cochin. His portrait, 'Knight of the Order of Christ', hangs in the Museu Nacional de Arte Antiga, Lisbon.

MAGELLAN, Ferdinand (1480–1521) Celebrated Portuguese navigator. He was born in Sabrosa or Porto, Portugal. He served both Portugal (1505–12) and Spain (1519–21) in the East Indies, taking part in the conquest of Malacca in 1511. Later King Charles V of Spain welcomed him and sponsored a squadron of five ships to find a westward route to India. After stopping at several points along the South American coast, including Rio de Janeiro, Magellan found the strait leading from the Atlantic to the Pacific, now bearing his name. He was the first navigator of the Pacific, which he named. He discovered the Philippines, where he was killed in a skirmish with natives. The only ship of the five to return to Spain was the *Vittoria* (or *Victoria*) of eighty-five tons, to which goes the honour of being the first ship to circumnavigate the world. She was captained by Elcano and brought back seventeen men and four natives plus incontrovertible evidence that the earth was round. The date was 8 September 1522.

OJEDA, Alonso de (c.1465–1515) Spanish navigator who sailed with Columbus on his second voyage of discovery, 1493–6, and took part in the setting up of the colony on Hispaniola. In 1499 Amerigo Vespucci accompanied him on a voyage of discovery which included the sighting of the mainland of South America. He explored the northern coastline from French Guiana to the Gulf of Venezuela.

PINZON, Martín Alonso (c.1441–93) Spanish navigator. He was born in Palos, Seville. He commanded the *Pinta* on Columbus's first voyage of discovery, 1492–3. He became separated from Columbus, reached Hispaniola and returned to Palos, planning to reach Spain earlier than Columbus in order to claim the credits and honours due to the Admiral. Incredibly, both ships arrived home the same day. Some historians credit him with great intelligence and skill in navigation. He was envious of the honours and rewards heaped upon Columbus. He died within days of his return to Spain in 1493. Some say he was worn out by his labours, others that he died of a broken heart.

PINZON, Vicente Yáñez (c.1460–1524) Spanish navigator and brother of Martín Alonso Pinzón. He too was born in Palos. He commanded the *Niña* ('Little Girl'), third and favourite ship of Columbus's squadron on the first voyage of discovery, 1492–3. In 1500 Vicente sailed west across the Atlantic, sighting Cape St Roque on the eastern shoulder of Brazil, then sailing north-west along the coast to the mouth of the Amazon and finally as far as Costa

Rica. In 1508—9 he carried out further exploration along the coast of Central America. Historians are still unclear whether he explored Honduras and Yucatán, or went south to Venezuela and Brazil.

VELASQUEZ, Diego (1465—1524) Spanish conquistador and navigator who sailed with Columbus to Hispaniola on the second voyage of discovery, 1493—6. He was born at Cuellar in Spain. In 1511 he led the expedition which conquered Cuba and established the first Spanish colony there. He became the first Spanish governor of the island. In 1514 he founded the city of Santiago in Cuba, and a year later Havana. He despatched expeditions in 1517 and 1518 to explore further the coasts of Mexico and Central America beyond the Yucatán peninsula. In 1519 he despatched Cortés to conquer the Mexican mainland. He died at Santiago de Cuba.

VESPUCCI, Amerigo (1454—1512) Florentine explorer who became a naturalised Spaniard. He was a contractor for Columbus at Seville. In 1499—1500 he sailed with Ojeda to the northern coast of South America (French Guiana). He went south-eastwards towards the Amazon estuary before sailing north-west to the Gulf of Venezuela. In 1501 Vespucci served the Portuguese crown and sailed for the eastern seaboard of South America again. He claimed to have sailed as far south as 50 degrees (almost its entire length), nearly as far as the Falklands or the Magellan Strait, but it is believed he only reached a little south of the River Plate. Documentation of Vespucci's voyages is still fiercely contested, although his voyage with Ojeda is thought to be authentic. He is regarded by some as a usurper, but this is not to deny his undoubted scientific and navigational skills and knowledge.

10 The Outward Voyage of Discovery

A T THE end of the fifteenth century, navigating at sea was hardly an exact science. Nearly all maritime voyaging was done by 'coasting' — keeping within sight of land with the ability to identify landmarks such as promontories, rivers, church steeples, headlands and other prominent features. To voyage out of sight of land was to navigate by dead reckoning or by celestial navigation — navigating with a knowledge of the stars, the moon, their angles above the horizon and a mastery of the instruments for measuring these angles.

The problems of navigating had only partially been solved at the time of Columbus's voyages. What instruments there were available were clumsy to handle and inaccurate in use. King John II of Portugal was aware of this problem and had summoned a commission of scientists and maths experts in 1484 to report on the matter. Some of their findings were published as *Regimiento do Astrolabio e do Quadrante*, a manual for the use of the astrolabe and quadrant.

What instruments, then, did Columbus have at his command? Those which were available were rudimentary and even crude. He determined his course by use of the mariner's compass, the most reliable navigation instrument obtainable in those days. The compass comprised a circular card decorated with designs of diamonds, lozenges and lines which marked the thirty-two compass points (each of 11.25 degrees). The card was suspended on a pivot in a circular bowl so that it could rotate freely with the motion of the ship. A magnetised needle was fixed to the underside in line with the north-south marks on the card.

The fore end of the bowl was marked with a line (known as the lubber line) and represented the direction in which the ship's head pointed. As the magnetised needle always sought magnetic north, the point on the floating compass card opposite the lubber line indicated the ship's head or course.

The compass was mounted in a fixed position in a tall binnacle or wooden box which carried a small hood to protect it from the elements, and a small lamp to illuminate it in the dark. One compass would be provided for the captain and pilot and another would be sited close to the helmsman to enable him to steer the ship on a particular course.

In order to navigate by dead reckoning Columbus needed to know — in addition to the ship's course — the ship's speed and the time. This would enable him to draw on a chart a track of the direction shown by the compass and the distance he reckoned the ship had travelled in a given time.

Time aboard Columbus's ships was measured by the half-hour sand glass or *ampoletta*. It dominated the ship. Every half-hour a duty gromet would turn the

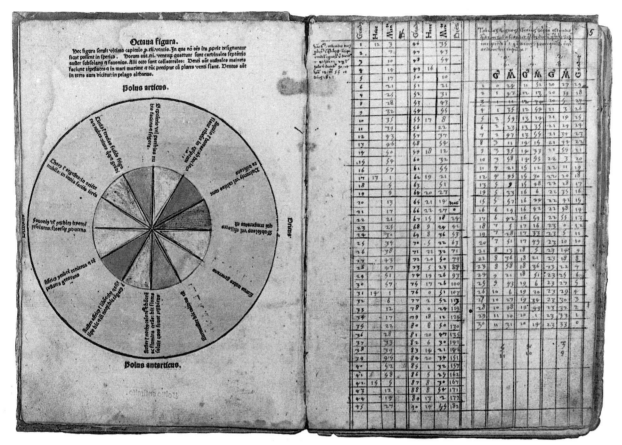

It is possible that Columbus took this navigational aid on his first voyage of discovery. The compass is coloured and the tables of winds and light hours at different latitudes appear to have been calculated by Columbus himself.

sand glass and sing out a call or chant heralding the fact. After eight turns — just as in modern days — the watch would change.

Rudimentary though this form of navigation was, Columbus had developed it into an art form. It is reported that he had a finely developed sense of the sea; an example of this will be given in a later chapter when he foretold the arrival of a hurricane. He could also estimate the speed of a ship by watching the bow wave moving down the side of the ship and passing astern. Perhaps more accurately, a ship's speed was judged by what was called a *corredera*, a small weighted piece of wood, towed on a thin line, knotted at intervals — rather like a leadsman's line — the number of knots passing through the hand in a given time giving the speed of the ship. It gave rise to the term 'knot' describing the speed of a ship.

Navigation by observing the position of the heavenly bodies (astro- or celestial navigation) was used by Columbus just as it had been used by navigators for centuries, though it is only fair to say the instruments were rough and ready and the results correspondingly inaccurate.

Nor is it by all means certain that Columbus was a good astro-navigator, although the evidence shows he gained some egotistical satisfaction from being thought so. He had often observed the sense of admiration others had shown when he was engrossed in measuring the altitude of the Pole Star to determine the ship's latitude. There is little doubt that Columbus perpetuated this aura of wonderment and mystery which to the uninitiated seemed mystical.

Columbus employed a quadrant, which was a lightweight version of the astrolabe. The *Journal* records Columbus using the quadrant four or five times before he discarded it, believing it to be working wrongly. This is not altogether surprising. A quadrant, in effect a crude early sextant, had no optics. It had five scales (in addition to the regular degree scale it had sine, cosine, tangent and cotangent). It was nearly impossible to use at sea in anything other than a dead calm because it had to be suspended, pendulum style, to measure the angle between the vertical and the line of sight to the celestial body.

The most accurate navigational aid during Columbus's era was a sound knowledge of the stars, particularly, in the northern hemisphere, of the Pole Star. The angular distance of the star above the horizon had been measured since the earliest of mariners by the crudest — almost literal — rule of thumb. The pilot's hand sufficed: a finger's thickness between the horizon and the Pole Star equalled two degrees, the wrist about eight degrees and the span of a hand about eighteen degrees.

Although this astrolabe postdates Columbus, it typifies the mariner's instrument for taking sights in the 15th century. Columbus preferred the simpler quadrant.

Columbus would have known that the stars at night were excellent indicators of time. All stars and constellations move fifteen degrees every hour from rising to dawn, as does the sun during the day. Further, Columbus would have known that a star's setting position is always the angle of the rise point plus 270 degrees. For example, a star which rises at 60 degrees in the east would set at 330 degrees in the west (60+270=330).

The chart Columbus used would have been large pieces of sheepskin onto which were sketched with a fair degree of accuracy the coasts of Spain, Portugal and North Africa, and perhaps a little less accurately the islands of the Azores, Madeira and the Canaries. Less accurately, indeed grossly inaccurately, other hypothetical islands were sketched in, while far to the west Cipango and Cathay were drawn by guesswork, ignoring totally the unknown vast continents of the Americas barring the way to the east via a western route.

Longitude, of course, was the trouble. Without an accurate chronometer Columbus employed Ptolemy's calculations, not without success. In place of lines of longitude Columbus marked lines on his chart representing 'hours' west of Cádiz, to correspond with the movement of the sun, stars and constellations, again allowing fifteen degrees for every hour: twenty-four hours equalling the 360 degrees of the globe.

It was not until Saturday 8 September that the helmsman felt a light north-easterly wind on his right shoulder and Columbus was able to set a westerly course. But the *Santa Maria* took in so much water that progress for the day was poor — a mere twenty-seven miles.

When, on the following day, the last trace of the westernmost island of the Canaries archipelago, Hierro, dropped below the horizon astern, Columbus was impelled to comfort the men, many of whom wept for fear they would not see land again. 'As Hierro disappeared,' Ferdinand Columbus wrote, 'so did the rest of the world.'

Columbus determined upon a subtle deception which he maintained for the whole of the voyage west. To dispel the crew's fears of a long voyage he decided to announce fewer leagues than were actually covered each day, allowing the men to think they were not so far from home as they actually were. He kept a separate, secret record of the true figures. For example, on Monday 10 September the *Santa Maria* actually sailed 180 miles, but Columbus reported this as 144 miles.

By now Columbus and his tiny fleet had encountered the trade winds, those unvarying winds which blow continuously each day from the east to the west.

'Whatever Columbus might have known about the trade winds he learned first hand,' wrote Gianni Granzotto who, like Morison before him and Robin Knox-Johnston after him, sailed Columbus's route to the Indies.*

> During his long sojourn in Madeira and during his voyage to Guinea,
> both being places on the Atlantic within the tropical region where
> the trade winds blow . . . Columbus had noticed . . . the wind was
> always blowing from the east and slightly east-north-east, and never
> from anywhere else. Clearly, such winds would be propitious for sailing

* Gianni Granzotto, p.124–6.

westward, towards the sunset . . . Columbus made great efforts to understand the true nature of the trade winds.

Granzotto went on to discuss cloud formations:

> [Columbus] didn't merely encounter the trade winds, but actually 'saw' them . . . It is true of the trade winds. They are always accompanied by a procession of clouds large and small and all in a line like soldiers . . . Whenever the trade winds finally do appear, these grey, amusing vapours will without fail materialise in the tropical sky astern . . . Together with them the wind blows straight into the sails, the good trade wind blowing westward . . .

Columbus's intention clearly was to sail due west along the twenty-eighth parallel, for this, he believed, was the latitude of Cipango. The distance he had estimated as about 750 leagues, or a little more than 2,000 nautical miles, and he expected to make his landfall in three or four weeks.

The first ten days out of Gomera were a delight, the warm, mild days prompting Columbus to make the comparison: 'It was like April in Andalusia. The beautiful mornings were a source of great pleasure for all, and lacked nothing to make them more enchanting, except perhaps a song of nightingales.'

If nightingales were lacking, then other birds made up for their absence. Practically every sighting is recorded by Columbus in his log. Each sighting caused a stir among the crew as everyone associated a sighting with the nearness of land. Herons were the first to be seen, and someone recalled being told they never flew more than thirty miles from land. Huge, grey albatrosses were seen, as were petrels, wheatears, aerobatic swallows and a ringtail, a white bird with a long, plumed tail, unused to sleeping on the sea.

Another creature was caught by one of the crew — a live crab, described in the log as an indication of the nearness of land because crabs are not found 240 miles from land.

It was not land but sargasso weed which had provided a home for the crab: the small fleet had entered the Sargasso Sea, an alarming experience for the sailors. It all began mildly enough, with large patches of the green weed which grew larger and larger until the sea seemed covered to the horizon with 'great banks of very green grass that looks as though it was just recently cut from the earth. We all reckoned that we must be near an island.' Some of the sailors feared the weed was so thick it would engulf their ships: it was altogether a frightening experience of the unknown.

Columbus logged the sargasso phenomenon with care and precision, noting the various aspects of the 'sea of grass' with descriptions of the form of the weeds, the animals inhabiting the grass, describing the mixture of dead and live weeds, the berry-like globules which he mistook for fruit but which proved to be filled with air thus keeping the weed afloat. The weed propagates by partition, constantly growing greenish shoots at one end blending to a brown at the other. Columbus was the first to dare sail through the weeds and the first to give accurate information about this great natural phenomenon.

It was at about this time — 17 September — that another anxiety arose. It was noticed that when the ships' navigators took bearings of the Pole Star the compasses declined to the north-west a full point. Columbus correctly interpreted this phenomenon as a magnetic variation away from the Pole Star 'towards some other fixed but invisible point.' The fact is that variation in Europe at this time was so small that it escaped detection, so the discovery of an error in mid-Atlantic rather alarmed Columbus. However, quite rightly he realised that it was the movement of the Pole Star that caused the variation and not an error in the compass. He managed to placate the apprehensive pilots and the frightened crews.

On Monday 17 September Columbus reported that they had sailed 165 miles (though he only admitted to 144 to the crew) and that the sea was as placid as the river at Seville. He also recorded a hint of disturbance about Martín Alonso Pinzón in the *Pinta*. The previous day the *Pinta* − 'a swift sailer' − had run on ahead of the flagship, then lay-to waiting for the larger ship to come up. Columbus had found her, and Pinzón reported having seen a great flock of birds the previous day moving west. He had followed their direction hoping to sight land that night. He didn't. Columbus was impelled to record his opinion of Martín Alonso:*

> He is a fine captain and very resourceful, but his independence disturbs me somewhat. I trust that this tendency to strike out on his own does not continue, for we can ill-afford to become separated this far from home.

Pinzón reported to Columbus that in the darkness he had seen land covered by cloud forty-five miles to the north. Members of the flagship's crew tried to persuade Columbus to alter course to the north to search for this land: ' . . . my calculations do not indicate that land is in that direction, and I am not going to waste time with it.'

Columbus's early fears of Pinzón's behaviour were well founded. He had good reason to distrust the man. As we shall see, but for the grace of God, at the end of the voyage Pinzón might well have robbed Columbus of much of his glory.

Pinzón continued to press Columbus to alter course to the north, but the Captain-General resolutely refused:†

According to my charts there are islands in that direction, and also to the south, and I am sailing between them. It is my desire to go directly to the Indies and not get side-tracked with islands that I shall see on the return passage.

There seems no substance to the report of the islands. At the time of this incident the fleet was in mid-Atlantic, and on this same day the captains of the ships recorded the following distances west of the Canaries: Juan Niño reckoned 1,320 miles; Cristobal Garcia Xalmiento of the *Pinta* recorded 1,260 miles; and Columbus's own pilot, Sancho Ruiz, calculated 1,200 miles.

The following day, Thursday 20 September, a fortnight after departing Gomera, Columbus changed course for the first time to take advantage of a variable wind. This day, too, was one of increasing bird activity. Pelicans had recently landed on the ships, and other birds had been identified − a turtle dove, a water-wagtail, a ring-tail and other land species. A bird like a tern was actually caught − a black bird with a white tuft on its head and webbed feet.

† Robert Fuson, p.64.
† Robert Fuson, p.64.

These birds sleep ashore and search for food each morning at sea, venturing no further than sixty miles. Other indications of the nearness of land were the sighting of a whale, and the passage of singing land birds.

The morale of the crews rose and fell like the tides, high when birds were sighted, presaging land, then low when the ships were almost becalmed in smooth, unruffled waters. Columbus reports: 'my crew had grown much alarmed dreading that they should never meet in these seas with a fair wind to return to Spain.' At other times great apprehension was felt by the presence of weeds so thick and matted as to impede the ships' progress, arousing the fear that they might become trapped as if in ice.

The volatile attitude of the crews is understandable even though it must have seemed perverse to Columbus. When the wind blew constantly at their backs they were scared they would never find a wind to return them to Spain. When a suitable wind blew the men complained it was inconstant, or it created no heavy seas which proved to their minds it would never blow hard enough to return them to Spain. Columbus allayed their fears: the nearness of land, he assured them, kept the seas smooth. Soon after, on Sunday 23 September, a wind arose from the west-north-west with a rough sea, and the men were astonished. Columbus saw this as a sign from the Almighty. Ferdinand Columbus recorded:*

> . . . he stood in need of God's aid, such as Moses had when he was leading the Jews out of Egypt and they dared not lay violent hands upon him on account of the miracles that God wrought by His own means.

On the following day — Monday the 24th — Columbus confided his fears to his *Journal*:†

> I am having serious trouble with the crew, despite the signs of land that we have and those given to us by Almighty God. In fact, the more God shows the men manifest signs that we are near land, the more their patience and inconstancy increases, and the more indignant they become against me. All day long and all night long those who are awake and able to get together never cease to talk to each other in circles, complaining that they will never be able to return home. They have said that it is insanity and suicidal on their part to risk their lives following the madness of a foreigner. They have said that not only am I willing to risk my life to become a great lord, but that I have deceived them to further my ambition.

Columbus noted the spreading disloyalty of the majority of his crew who judged they had done more than could reasonably have been expected of them — they had gone where others had never dared to sail. He continues with this Monday entry:

> I am told by a few trusted men (and these are few in number!) that if I persist in going onward, the best course of action will be to throw me

---

* Ferdinand Columbus, p.71.
† Robert Fuson, pp.66–7.

into the sea some night. They will then affirm that I fell overboard while taking the position of the North Star with my quadrant. Since I am a foreigner, little or no account will be asked of the matter, but rather, there will be a great many who will swear that God had given me my just deserts on account of my rashness.

In this significant entry Columbus reverted to his distrust of the Pinzóns whom he believed were siding with the near-mutinous crews, most of whom, like the Pinzóns, came from Palos:*

I know that Martín Alonso cannot be trusted. He is a skilled mariner, but he wants the rewards and honours of this enterprise for himself. He is always running ahead of the fleet, seeking to be the first to sight land. But I am fully aware that I must use him, for his support is too great among the men. I am also confident that if I lose command, the fleet will never reach the Indies and will probably never get back to Spain.

The very next day at about sunset Pinzón demonstrated the accuracy of Columbus's beliefs. Pinzón had brought the *Pinta* close alongside *Santa Maria* to send across a map on a line. Pinzón mounted the *Pinta's* stern and excitedly shouted across to Columbus 'Land! Land, sir! I claim the reward!'

Pinzón was pointing to what appeared to be a land mass about twenty-five leagues [*sic*] distant.† Columbus fell to his knees to give thanks to the Almighty and recited *Gloria in excelsis Deo* with his crew and companions. Pinzón did likewise aboard the *Pinta* while the crew of the *Niña* clambered up the rigging to get a better view of the land. Columbus estimated that it lay about seventy-five miles to the south-west. He altered course towards it and sailed through the night.

Sighting land at seventy-five miles is highly unlikely. From the *Santa Maria's* crow's nest to the horizon was about ten nautical miles and from Columbus's position on the sterncastle only about seven. Fairly low-lying islands could be seen from his vantage point at a distance of about twenty nautical miles. Seventy-five seems impossibly wrong.

At sunrise the so-called land was discovered to be squall clouds and in the afternoon Columbus continued his westerly course. The mood aboard the ships can be imagined. The sea, Columbus recorded, 'was like a river' and the air was 'sweet and balmy'.

The days' events continued in a repetitive fashion for nearly a fortnight with Columbus logging each day's correct mileage and the mileage he told the crew, together with his recordings of birds sighted.

During this period there was another false alarm. Columbus had warned all ships' crews that if anyone made a claim to sighting land and that after three days sailing it should prove to be false, the reward of an annuity of 10,000 maravedis promised by the Catholic Sovereigns would be forfeited. Under these instructions all lookouts proved reticent, reluctant to hazard their likely reward.

At the morning rendezvous on Sunday 7 October (the dawn and sunset assemblies were to take advantage of the times when there was least haze and the best visibility) Captain Vicente Yáñez Pinzón in *Niña* ran ahead of the

---

* Robert Fuson, p.67.

†Ferdinand Columbus, pp.72–3.

other vessels, then fired a cannon and ran up a flag to announce he had
sighted land. Course was altered, but as the day progressed it became obvious
that this was another illusory cloud formation. Spirits aboard all ships sank and
even Columbus was impelled to take some remedial action rather than simply
to sail steadfastly to the west.

Many large flocks of birds flew over, coming from the north and speeding to
the west-south-west. Before sunset, course was shaped for the west-south-west to
follow the birds for two days. Twelve vari-coloured birds, 'of the kind that sing
in the fields', landed on the flagship, rested themselves then flew off.

That evening tunny fish were sighted and in the following morning more
birds — a pelican, ducks, a pigeon, and many little birds. Columbus used the
same metaphor he had used before: the air was as fresh and fragrant as April in
Seville.

Yet all these indicators gave no sign of land. Grumblings and complaints
filled the air. Columbus reproved the men: having exhausted all his
exhortations and explanations, he told them bluntly, for better or worse, they
had to complete the enterprise. He reminded them that he had set out to
discover the Indies and he had no intention whatsoever of abandoning the
idea. Discover them he would — with the help of God.

11 Landfall in the New World

THURSDAY 11 October 1492 was a momentous day. Signs were given to the adventurers that undeniably indicated the nearness of land. Spirits rose and morale noticeably improved. Men cheered when a green branch passed by the *Santa Maria*, and a large, greenish fish heralded a nearby reef. Men aboard the *Pinta* sighted a cane and some sticks, one deftly carved by an iron tool. A small plank or board and an abundance of seashore weeds and reeds were seen, and the *Niña's* crew saw a freshly cut thorn branch loaded with red berries.

Early that evening Columbus and his crew — as was their daily custom — sang the *Ave Maria* at vespers. He took the opportunity to remind the crew of the favour Our Lord had bestowed on them by 'conducting them so safely and prosperously with fair winds and a clear course, and by comforting them with signs that daily grew more abundant.'*

He also reminded the crew that once they had reached a point 700 leagues from the Canaries (which they had considerably exceeded) no night sailing would be permitted for fear of running aground in the dark. However, he intended to overrule that restriction for this night. The crew therefore must be ever vigilant, lookouts doubled and, as an additional reward to the Catholic Sovereigns' annuity of 10,000 maravedis to the first man to sight land, he, Columbus, would give a velvet doublet as a personal token.

At ten o'clock that night Columbus was on the sterncastle. He thought he saw a light like a wax candle bobbing up and down — perhaps a fisherman raising and lowering a lamp; or someone visiting house to house with a lantern. Pedro Gutiérrez† was summoned and after a few moments confirmed that he saw it, too. Rodrigo Sanchez, the fleet comptroller, was summoned but neither he nor anyone else could detect a light. Columbus agreed that it was so uncertain he would not claim it to be land.

Shortly before midnight the moon rose. The *Santa Maria* was running smartly before a westerly at about nine knots. The *Pinta*, a faster ship, lay well ahead.

At two o'clock — it was now the new day of Friday 12 October — the *Pinta* fired a cannon signifying the sighting of land. When the flagship caught up with her, Columbus learned that it was a seaman from Lepe named Rodrigo de Triana, who was the claimant to having sighted land.

Pandemonium broke out aboard the caravel, the noise of cheering, shouting, singing and praying drowned only by the cannon shot. Triana could scarcely believe his good fortune: a pension for life awaited him . . .

---

* Ferdinand Columbus, p.77.

† A gentleman volunteer: officially *repostero de estrados del rey*, butler of the king's dais.

But in fact he never received a copper maravedi for his sighting, let alone the velvet doublet. In an act of incredible meanness Columbus himself claimed the Sovereigns' reward, regarding the light he had seen four hours earlier as the first sighting, and his claim was adjudged by the Sovereigns to be the winner. Perhaps it was thought proper that it should be Columbus who had the honour of first sighting land rather than poor Triana. Columbus continued to receive the annuity till his death. Triana took it all badly. He was outraged at being robbed of what he thought was his just reward. He came to a bad end according to reports. One says he hanged himself from a ship's mast or yard. Another − even less credibly − says he defected from Christianity, converted to Islam and died in battle for the Moors.

For the rest of the hours of darkness of that early morning of the twelfth, the three ships lay to, sails furled, all the crews wide awake, expectant beyond description. By five o'clock the pale light of dawn began to reveal a white sandy beach fringed with a screen of green trees. As the light increased the great trees could be identified, pelicans were seen idly walking on the beach − but of other inhabitants, none. It was a spellbinding occasion. Then they appeared. From behind the trees there emerged the inhabitants. Columbus logged the greatest moment of his discovery with these words:*

> At dawn we saw naked people, and I went ashore in the ship's boat, armed, followed by Martín Alonso Pinzón, captain of the *Pinta*, and his brother Vicente Yáñez Pinzón, captain of the *Niña*. I unfurled the royal banner and the captains brought the flags which displayed a large green cross with the letters F and Y at the left and right side of the cross. Over each letter was the appropriate crown of that Sovereign. These flags were carried as a standard on all of the ships. After a prayer of thanksgiving I ordered the captains of the *Pinta* and *Niña* together with Rodrigo de Escobedo (secretary of the fleet) and Rodrigo Sánchez of Segovia (comptroller of the fleet) to bear faith and witness that I was taking possession of this island for the King and Queen. I made all the necessary declarations and had these testimonies carefully written down by the secretary. In addition to those named above, the entire company of the fleet bore witness to this act. To this island I gave the name San Salvador, in honour of our Blessed Lord.

No sooner had these formalities been completed than the islanders approached the beach and the landing party. Columbus described them − men and women − as being 'as naked as their mothers bore them'. They all appeared young, apparently under thirty, well built, tall, straight legs, well-proportioned bodies with an olive-coloured skin like Canary islanders, not black as expected. Their fine faces were marred by unpleasantly broad heads. They all had large eyes, straight, coarse black hair, like horse hair, which was worn cut short over the eyebrows, with a large hank grown down to their shoulders.

Some decorated themselves with paints − some black, others white and some red: some the whole body, others just the face, and still others just the eyes or nose.

* Robert Fuson, pp.75−6.

Discovery of the Bahamas: this crude woodcut of a forty-oared galley appeared in the first illustrated Latin edition of Columbus's first Letter to Santángel in 1493.

Las Casas captured it in these words:

> The Indians gazed dumbstruck at the Christians, looking with wonder at their beards, their clothes and the whiteness of their skins. They directed their attentions to the men with beards, but especially towards the Admiral, who they realised was the most important of the group, either from his imposing presence or from his scarlet clothing.

They touched the men's beards with their fingers and carefully examined the paleness of their hands and faces. Seeing that they were innocent, the Admiral and his men did not resist their actions.

These Indians, so called because Columbus believed he had reached the eastern regions of Asia or India, appeared peaceful and simple folk, evidently quite intelligent and quick to learn, easily repeating words they heard only once, though of a primitive simplicity.

They bore no arms and knew nothing of iron. When shown the discoverer's sword one man grasped it firmly and cut himself. Any darts, spears or javelins they possessed had had their sharp tips hardened in a fire, sometimes with the ends armed with sharp, pointed fish teeth.

Their canoes fascinated the Spanish seamen. They were made from the trunks of trees, the largest ones capable of holding forty to forty-five men, the smallest being one-man boats. They were all propelled by wooden paddles.

The Spaniards noticed that the Indians wore gold pendants hanging from a hole in the nostril. By sign language it was learnt that the gold came from the south of the island where a king lived who possessed many large vessels of gold. It was also learnt that to the south and the south-west there were many other islands and large countries.

During the day much trading went on, the Spaniards exchanging small trinkets like glass beads, hawks' bells (small round bronze bells, the size of a small coin, attached to hawks in falconry), sailors' red caps and even broken pieces of crockery or glass. In exchange the sailors received parrots, skeins of woven cotton, darts and other goods. The trading was one-sided, the Indians believing the visitors to have come from heaven and willing to trade all they had for a meaningless trifle.

The island of San Salvador on which Columbus had landed was described in the *Journal* as fairly large and very flat (that is, no mountains), densely wooded and with several bodies of water. Columbus specially mentioned a very large lagoon in the middle of the island: the word was lagoon (*laguna*) and not lake (*lago*), which has a special significance. The island was named Guanahani by the natives.

It might be thought a simple matter to identify Columbus's landfall using his *Journal* as abstracted by the meticulous Las Casas. Alas, this is not so. Apart from the fact that it was in the Bahamas, there is no firm, incontrovertible evidence to pinpoint the landfall, no co-ordinates, no dimensions, no identifying landmarks of any consequence other than the lagoon. As Fuson points out*, the Bahamas land areas, extending for some 750 miles, comprise 36 islands, 687 cays and 2,414 rocks. Discounting the rocks, this leaves 723 islands of varying sizes to choose from as the San Salvador landfall. Most of these islands and islets can be eliminated for a variety of reasons. For example, many are so evidently wrongly placed to be serious contenders. Many others lack a coral reef enclosing a harbour 'large enough for all the ships of Christendom', as Columbus described it.

The long list could be shortened further by eliminating islands without an

* Robert Fuson, p.199.

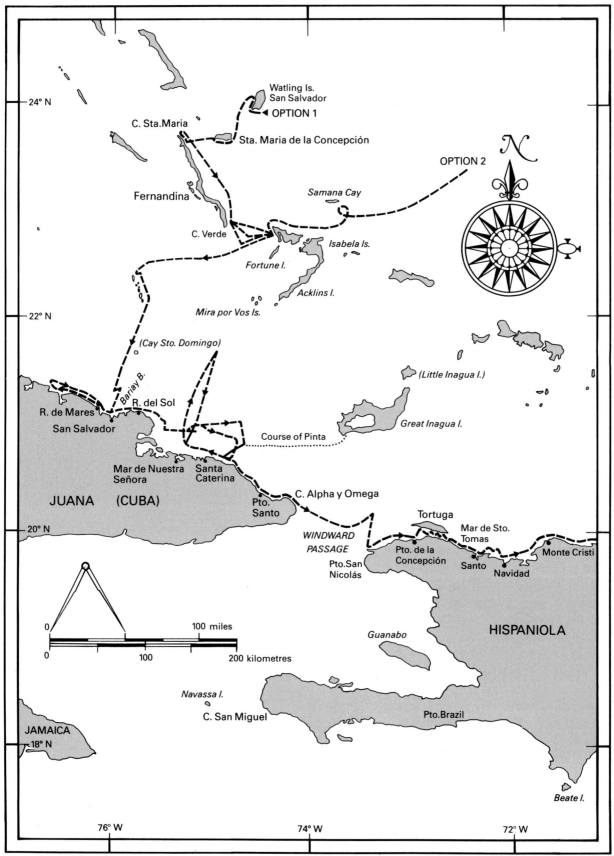

First Voyage: Samana Cay and Watlings Is. options. Track through the Bahamas to Cuba and Hispaniola.

interior lagoon, and others by not having a natural rock formation like an abandoned quarry. These criteria reduce the contenders to a mere handful. Nine, in fact, are serious ones. They are: Watlings, Cat, Grand Turk, Mayaguana, Samana, Conception, East Caicos, Plana Cays and Egg/Royal (north-west of Eleuthera Island).

Of these, two in particular have maintained serious support from scholars and historians, namely Watlings Island and Samana Cay. Watlings led the field for centuries and among its champions have been some of the world's finest Columbian scholars. The towering J.B. Thacher gave his seal of approval to Watlings in 1902. The masterly Samuel Eliot Morison, doyen of naval historians and one who sailed the Columbus routes in 1939–40, agreed with Thacher and thirty-two years later still – in 1972 – Taviani confirmed his choice of the same island. Their combined views gave compelling support for Watlings.

In 1881 the USN Captain Gustavus Vasa Fox published a report,* a persuasive and brilliant piece of investigative maritime research work, which gave support to the landfall being the obscure Samana Cay. Little came of it for about a century until the National Geographic Association published the findings of an impressive team of specialist investigators including a whole team of computer specialists, translators, archaeologists, navigators, mathematicians, cartographers, some scholarly consultants, photographers, a pilot, artists and camera technicians. They gave support to Fox's claim that Samana Cay and not Watlings Island was Columbus's first Bahamian landfall.

Samana is regarded as acceptable on account of its size, position and shape, and further arguments are based on eight points, many of which are abstruse navigational interpretations of Columbus's *Journal*.† Many scholars consider that these have not been convincingly explained, and still reserve judgement.

Columbus never said so, but the first landing must have been a let down. He had spent most of his adult life in search of a dream and had spent thirty-three days sailing into the unknown in search of Cipango and Cathay to be rewarded with a small wooded island inhabited by a handful of unclothed, primitive natives. The reality failed to match the dream. Instead of intelligent fifteenth-century beings, he had met tribesmen of an ancient age.

Worst of all, in some ways, was being blithely innocent of the fact that a huge intervening land mass barred the sea route to the East by sailing west. So convinced was Columbus and his senior colleagues of the closeness of Cathay and Cipango (he believed he had made a landfall on an outer fringe of islands to Asia) that he determined to leave San Salvador quickly to continue his search. He took with him six or seven natives who displayed an intelligence and a quickness to learn Spanish words. It was agreed policy that Indians should be kept aboard and eventually taken home to Spain; they were to learn the word of God, and ultimately return to their native lands to preach the gospel.

* Appendix 18, Coast and Geodic Survey Report for 1880: 'An Attempt to Solve the Problem of the First Landing Place of Columbus in the New World' by Captain G.V. Fox USN.

†See Robert Fuson, pp.199–221, where he presents the arguments for Samana in Appendix A, 'The Landfall Theories.'

SHIPBOARD VICTUALS – HARD TACK TO PINEAPPLES

COOKING aboard the caravels was a crude affair. Like everything else it was a cramped business. What else could one expect when comforts and conveniences were totally lacking for the lowliest seaman as well as the Admiral himself. Columbus and the master, Juan de la Cosa, had a primitive cabin each in the stern castle, but most men slept on deck, exposed to the elements as were the cooking arrangements. The galley furnace or firebox was protected from the winds by a hood of crude design.

The quantity of food available to the ships' companies rarely drew complaints, but the quality left much to be desired. It started with a modest breakfast, usually a ship's biscuit and some garlic cloves, a chunk of cheese and as often as not a pickled sardine.

The crews enjoyed only one hot meal a day and this was available at about eleven o'clock in the forenoon. This coincided with the change of watch.

Watchkeeping started with the seven o'clock trick, with four hours on and four hours off (watch and watch about: there is no evidence that a dog watch was introduced to change the daily watch sequence for the men, though this would almost certainly have been done). Those going on watch at eleven o'clock ate first, followed by the relieved watch.

The Spaniards' basic diet comprised salted meat, hard tack (biscuits) and soups which were made from chickpeas, lentils and beans. This was supplemented by cheese, sometimes a little rice and barrelled anchovies or sardines. For variety there were sometimes fresh fish caught by the off duty watch with trailed fishing lines. Fish as large as sharks were sometimes hoisted inboard. Food was eaten with fingers from a wooden bowl. Olive oil was carried in huge earthenware jars and used for cooking the fish, meat and legumes.

Once the ships made landfalls in the Indies water casks and emptied red wine casks were refilled with fresh water and depleted stores of food were replenished.

Curiously, the fresh foods we associate with the West Indies today were not the indigenous produce then: bananas, coconuts, breadfruit, sugar cane, almonds — and others — were introduced later, many of them by the intrepid Captain Bligh. Fresh shellfish abounded, plus the natives' staple diet of cassava. Pineapples were tasted for the very first time by Europeans.

The only drinks referred to were wine and water. Neither tea nor coffee had been introduced yet, and the Spaniards did not care for beer as did the English.

Food quality was often disgusting. Ferdinand Columbus described the horrifying deterioration of the ships' hard tack to a kind of porridge alive with worms:

> What with the heat and the dampness even the biscuit was so full of worms that, God help me, I saw many men wait till nightfall to eat the porridge, so as not to see the worms; others were so used to eating them that they did not bother to pick them out, for they might lose their supper by being too fastidious.

It is likely that a day's ration of food per man amounted to:

1¾ lb bread. (Salted flour could be made into unleavened bread and cooked in the fire's ashes.)
1½ *cuartillos* or pints of wine.
½ *azumbre* (equal to 1½ pints) of water.
¾ bushel of peas and/or beans for thirty men.
Undetermined amounts of meat, fish and oil.

Contemporary sketch of a pineapple from Oviedo's *La Historia General y Natural de las Indias*, 1547.

Columbus was obsessive about three things. The establishment of the Christian word and the conversion of unknown thousands of people to God's faith was the first. The second was his search for gold, and 'the place where gold is born'. He made constant references to the precious metal — 'I decided not to linger . . . for I saw there was no gold there'. Thirdly, of course, was his belief that he would reach China, Japan and India by sailing west.

He knew from his study of cartography that Japan was fringed to the north by an archipelago of islands. Guanahani (San Salvador), he was stubbornly convinced beyond any doubt whatsoever, formed part of this Asiatic or Indian archipelago. He judged therefore that Japan, his prime objective, lay in a south-westerly direction. If, in setting out in that direction, he should miss the island, he reassured himself he would inevitably come upon China, further to the west.

The three ships set off in a south-westerly direction, discovering 'so many islands that I could not decide where to go next'. Columbus came upon one not much different from San Salvador. 'To this island I gave the name Santa Maria de la Concepción,' he wrote; and a few days later, 'I named this island Fernandina' (now named Long Island). Another was named Isabella — after the queen (now Southern Crooked Island and probably then including Fortune Island).

Other islands were logged, landed upon, named, skirted around, but all the while Columbus was searching for the landfall that would confirm he had discovered the lands ruled by the Great Khan. Nor did he forget gold. On Sunday 21 October he logged his resolve to search for a king on Isabella Island who wore many gold decorations. He also confided his plan to sail for another — much larger — island which he firmly believed was Japan but which in fact turned out to be Cuba. From there he intended locating another large island called Bohio (Hispaniola). In between these islands, he would visit others he came across to seek gold and spices. Finally, he declared, his intention was to visit the mainland and search out the city of Quinsay (the modern Chinese city of Hangchow).

Columbus believed Cuba to be Japan partly because of the talk of its wealth and magnificence. On Sunday 28 October he made his landfall at Bahia Bariay, today's town of San Salvador on Cuba's northern coast. He thought he had never seen anything so beautiful as Cuba appeared. He especially admired the verdant, wooded areas, the clear deep waters off the coast, the sparkling waters of the many rivers, the soft breezes and pleasant temperatures. The trees had luxuriant foliage, the beautiful capes were covered in palms, and the hinterland rose to high mountains.

Columbus named the island in honour of the heir apparent to the crown of Castile — Juana.

There had been much talk ashore of gold and the Indians told Columbus of an island where the precious metal could be collected from the beaches by candlelight then pounded into bars. The island was called Babeque (modern Great Inagua Island) and it lay to the east. Columbus resolved to go there, but before doing so he wanted to continue his westward exploration. He took his fleet to sea but after a day's sail to the west the ships ran into contrary, and dangerous, onshore winds. The ships came about and put in at Puerto Gibara close by the original landfall on Cuba, and there they remained for eleven days.

During this time Columbus judged it timely to send an embassy of two Spaniards and an Indian from San Salvador with a local native to travel up country with the aim of meeting the Great Khan or the Emperor of China.

With the benefit of historical hindsight it can all be seen as pathetically useless, but it gives an insight into the mind of this cruelly deceived discoverer.

The deputation's Christians were Rodrigo de Jérez and Luis de Torres, the latter of whom had lived with the Adelantado of Murcia, was a converted Jew and had been selected for the voyage because of his knowledge of Hebrew, Chaldaic and Arabic: it was hoped he could act as interpreter when Columbus met the Great Khan.

These envoys travelled thirty-six miles inland to a large village of a thousand people living in fifty large houses. They were welcomed by the natives, carried shoulder high and treated like royalty. But it was a fruitless visit. No trace had been found of a great city, of buildings or palaces of any significance, of any culture other than primeval. However, the envoys had shown considerable courage in undertaking the trip in view of the rumours which abounded about men with one Cyclops-like eye and others with dog snouts who ate men. First, the Spaniards were cautioned, these men would behead their prey, then drink the blood and cut off the genitals: indeed, cannibalism was not just a rumour, as we shall see.

While the deputation was away the remainder of the crew rested, their ships careened by beaching so the hulls could be scraped clean and caulked where necessary, the depleted stores replenished as far as possible. The river area where the ships were anchored was explored. The men discovered the sweet potato (like carrots and tasting of chestnuts), beans (unlike the European variety) and what was called panic grass, which was corn (maize), all unfamiliar to Spaniards. Cotton abounded, covering the hillsides with its wild growth.

It was here in Cuba that we find the first reference to the use of tobacco.

Rodrigo de Jérez and Luis de Torres met countless people, the men always naked, the women wearing a small swatch to cover their private parts, the men with firebrands in their hands and herbs to smoke. Las Casas describes the custom:

> [the herbs] are dry, and fixed in a leaf, also dry after the manner of those paper tubes which the boys in Spain use at Whitsuntide: having lighted one end they draw the smoke by sucking at the other, this causes a drowsiness and a sort of intoxication, and according to their accounts relieves them from the sensation of fatigue. These tubes they call by the name *tabacos*.

Las Casas recalled knowing many Spanish colonists who were addicted to these tubes and on being reproached for the habit declared they were unable to give it up. 'I did not see what relish or benefit they could find in them.'

It is a quirk of history that had the winds been advantageous Columbus could have sailed north-west and in two days might well have discovered Florida. But other factors prevailed. After a few days resting at Puerto Gibara the deputation returned with stories of palm-thatched huts and naked Indians, a far cry from the marbled bridges and gold-leafed roofs of fine buildings which the Spaniards had hoped to find.

This 1493 woodcut shows Hispaniola and many of the islands Columbus discovered.

Columbus was anxious to put to sea again. He found the weather somewhat cold and in view of the contrary winds thought it inadvisable to prosecute his explorations any further northwards. He decided instead to seek out Babeque with its beaches of gold, and Bohio, described by the Indians as a large island to the south-east.

For the next several days the small squadron sailed east and south along Cuba's coast, Columbus noting and naming the capes and gulfs, the coves and headlands, glorying still in the verdant splendour of the island with its diamond-shaped mountains.

The enjoyment of this natural beauty was marred by an incident of treachery on behalf of Martín Alonso Pinzón, an incident which in other circumstances could have resulted in his execution for desertion or mutiny. It took place late in November when the small fleet was engaged in one of its forays in search of the island of Babeque while easting along the Cuban coast.

The fleet altered course for the mystical island in torrential rain with contrary winds 'until the hour of vespers'. As there was no sign of the island, course was altered back to the Cuban coast. It was while on this leg of the voyage that the *Pinta* was seen to draw away from the flagship towards the alleged direction of Babeque.

Columbus was furious with Pinzón. It was a deliberate act by the Palos man: Columbus called it an act of treachery and concluded that sheer greed had motivated him.

The remaining two ships held course to the south and exposed lights in the hopes Pinzón would see them and rejoin. The night was clear and bright with a fresh breeze which would allow the *Pinta* to come up. Others report the night was misty and dark, that the *Pinta* may well have confused courses and lost contact with the flagship. Deliberate desertion or confused communications? In his heart — and in his log — Columbus confided his thoughts: treachery and desertion, the Admiral had no doubts about it. Pinzón evidently wanted to gain glory for finding the wealth of gold which only needed to be picked up off the b

The remaining two ships made the Cuban coast and resumed course for Hispaniola. Columbus was impressed with the Cuban coastline, with its huge pine trees, straight as arrows, well suited for masts and ships' planking, enough to build as many ships as anyone could want.

He was entranced by the region and by everything he saw — the trees, plants, fruits, harbours — 'such marvellous beauty that it surpasses all others.' Such was his description of the place he named Puerto Santo. Here, too, he first saw canoes of great lengths cut from a single tree. One such decorated canoe was estimated to be sixty-three feet long, able to hold up to 150 people.

After several days rest, Columbus took the first opportunity of favourable winds to depart these delightful surroundings and set course for the cape he could see further to the east, beyond which was another large island, across a large bay, as Columbus called it. It was in fact the passage between the islands of Hispaniola and Cuba — the Windward Passage. After discovering 360 miles of the Cuban coastline he now set his sights on Bohio.

The Indians aboard the two ships made their feelings and fears very clear at the prospect of landing on this new island. Legend had it that the island housed people with one eye in their foreheads, and another tribe with the name *Canib* or *Carib*, people who ate humans. It is to this intriguing island that we must now turn our attention.

12 The Discovery of Cuba and Hispaniola: Wrecking of the Flagship

COLUMBUS saw so much similarity between the beauty of this new island and the Spanish countryside that he named it La Isla Española (The Spanish Island), corrupted in time to Hispaniola. It is now shared between Haiti and the Dominican Republic. Columbus noted that it appeared to be cultivated and 'the crops look like wheat in the month of May in the vicinity of Córdova'. The trees resembled those of Spain, and the fish caught in nets by the Spanish sailors — sole, skate, salmon, shad, dory, corvinas, sardines and crabs — all reminded them of home.

Columbus in *Santa Maria*, with the *Niña* in company, entered harbour at the hour of vespers and named it Puerto Maria. Almost immediately he changed his mind and called it Puerto de San Nicolás in honour of St Nicholas, whose feast day Thursday 6 December was.

If he was almost lyrical over Cuba, he was even more so over this countryside. The port was splendid, too, with deep, crystal-clear waters and good shelter from the sea.

He set out on an exploration of the island's northern coast, taking advantage of the off shore winds, discovering and naming dozens of landmarks. The ships dropped anchor on the eve of the day of the Immaculate Conception in a bay surrounded by hills which Columbus christened, with only the barest hint of imagination, El Puerto de la Concepción. Ashore, however, it was less than immaculate. Swarms of insects attacked the sailors, impelling Columbus to rename it Bahia de los Mosquitos — a name it retains to this day.

On another day the two ships sought shelter from rough seas and contrary winds in the mouth of a strong-flowing river, opening into a beautiful verdant valley which opened further into plains covered with trees and plants of every kind. Eschewing biblical connotations, Columbus named it Paradise Valley — Val Paraíso. Today it is the French-built city of Port-au-Paix.

It was onto the beach at Val Paraíso that natives emerged from the hinterland in their hundreds, natives of a more attractive appearance than the other islanders discovered so far. They were tall, slender and well-proportioned, naked as the day they were born and with light complexions, some — especially the women — with skins so light they might have come from Spain. Columbus's abstracted log for Annunciation Day, Sunday 16 December, read:

> Soon there came to the beach more than five hundred people, and, shortly after, their king, all gathered together near to where the ships were anchored close to land. Presently they approached one by one, and then they came onboard in crowds, but they brought nothing with them, except that a few wore nuggets of very fine gold in their ears and noses, and these they gave very readily to the Spaniards.

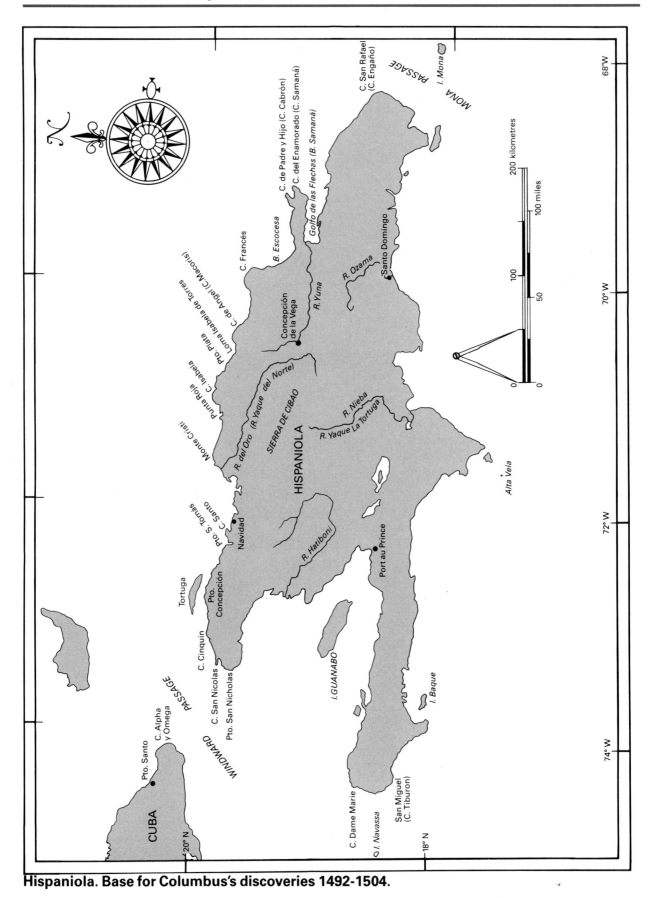

Hispaniola. Base for Columbus's discoveries 1492-1504.

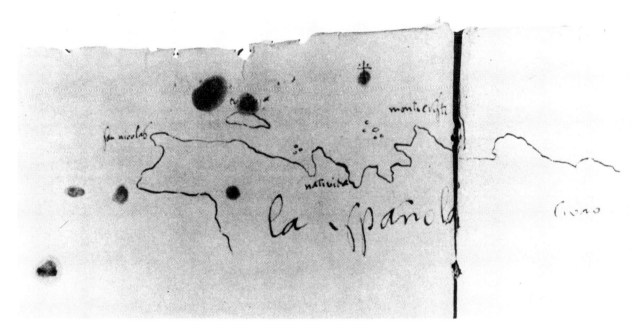

Time and time again Columbus had told his Spanish crews to treat all the natives with respect, always to give something, however modest, in return for gifts — even broken pieces of glass or pottery became exchangeable for small gold items such as ear and nose rings. What appears to have been a relatively minor problem — at least the number of incidents in the early days of discovery were few — were the sexual approaches of the Spaniards to the women, though it seems almost inconceivable that lusty men such as these sailors would manage to contain themselves after so many weeks and months of celibacy.

The Spaniards could see the native king on the beach and the natives offering him their respects. He lay on a sort of palanquin held shoulder-high by four natives. Columbus sent the young cacique a present, which was received with great ceremony.

The following day the king paid a ceremonial visit to the flagship with scores of his attendants, both male and female, all stark naked, including the king, and the women showing no signs of bashfulness.

The ships were decorated with banners and bunting in celebration of a feast day. Lombard shots were fired to herald the day and to mark the arrival of the king. Columbus was eating when the visitors arrived. The king would not allow Columbus to rise nor to interrupt his meal. The visitors were offered the food and drink of Castile. The king tasted morsels of each item out of politeness and passed the remainder over to his advisers.

The young king evidently admired a cover on the Admiral's bed: Columbus presented it to him, along with some other beads which Columbus was wearing and some red shoes. The king was delighted beyond description.

The expansive approach to Acul Bay was named by Columbus La Mar de Santo Tomás — the Sea of St Thomas — and the harbour was called El Puerto de la Mar de Santo Tomás. When Columbus attempted to describe these places he realised he had exhausted his supply of superlatives. Each newly discovered

For centuries it was thought that this sketch of north-west Hispaniola showing Cape San Nicolas and Monte Cristi was drawn by Columbus himself. Today this is disputed, if only because of the wrongly spelt Nativida, and La Espagñola, a spelling Columbus never used.

place seemed more splendid than the last. Of Santo Tomás, Columbus wrote: '. . . this is superior to them all, and large enough to contain all the ships of the world . . . From the entrance to the bottom of the harbour is a distance of five leagues.'*

But a beautiful environment came a poor second to Columbus's interest in finding rich deposits of gold. From one old counsellor he learned that within a radius of one hundred miles there were numerous islands producing gold from the earth. The old man mentioned 'an island made entirely of gold'. But it was all illusory. We know today that all these rich deposits of gold did not exist. Columbus was on a wild goose chase. The nearest deposits in any quantity were far away in as yet undiscovered Costa Rica in Central America. He beseeched the Almighty in his endeavours: 'Our Lord in His piety,' he prayed, 'guide me that I may find the gold.'

On Christmas Eve 1492 Columbus sailed his two ships (the *Pinta* was still missing) before a light wind from La Mar de Santo Tomás to Punta Santa, the high promontory (nowadays called Cape Haiti) down which huge boulders cascade to the shore, spilling into the sea. Columbus had some difficulty rounding the cape against contrary winds, but once round, the breezes fell away. The sea became calm 'as water in a dish', as Columbus aptly described it. The moon gave little light. Both ships — the *Niña* leading by half a league — barely had way on them, their sails hanging limply.

By eleven o'clock that night, at the change of watch when the gromet turned the half-hour glass, the two ships were in a position about three miles east of Punta Santa.

Everyone was exhausted. It had been a tough haul round the promontory with plenty of hard physical work. Columbus himself was flagging having had no sleep for two days and one night. He had a word with Juan de la Cosa who was in charge of the watch and went below to his cabin. All those not on watch settled down to sleep, but even those on watch succumbed. Juan de la Cosa, in an act of gross dereliction of duty, found a quiet spot and fell asleep after giving the helmsman a star to steer by. Finally, the helmsman roused the gromet watching the half-hour glass and gave him charge of the tiller. The lad coped as best he could, but it was a man-sized job, heavy and demanding, so much so that Columbus had expressly bidden in standing instructions never to allow a boy at the tiller.

The current took the *Santa Maria* and ran her aground on a bank — thankfully not a coral reef — where she stuck fast. Everyone was roused. Columbus made preparations for launching the small boat, intending it should take an anchor and kedge the ship off the bank. But Juan de la Cosa, the master, and others jumped into the boat intent on saving their lives by heading for the *Niña*, about a mile and a half to windward.

The *Niña*, quite rightly, refused to allow them aboard, and they returned, chastened, to the *Santa Maria*.

Juan de la Cosa's relationship with Columbus had never been of the best and, after this incident, they were daggers drawn. Columbus regarded De la Cosa's desertion as cowardice and treachery. In his defence the master explained he pulled the boat to *Niña* to seek help. After all, he argued, it was his ship — he owned the *Santa Maria* — and he had no wish to lose it.

* Error: five *miles*. Both Columbus and Las Casas erred many times over distances. Las Casas, in particular, often mistook leagues for miles and vice versa.

Furthermore, he felt a sense of responsibility for the ship's wrecking and sought to make amends by getting help.

While this charade was taking place Columbus gave orders for the mainmast to be cut down and cast adrift to lighten the ship, and all ballast to be jettisoned in the hope of being able to refloat the ship. But she was stuck fast. In due course her seams opened, she took in tons of water and was beyond salvage.

Columbus despatched Diego de Harana and Pedro Gutiérrez to the local king, Guacanagari, who lived about five miles away. Their plea for help in the form of large canoes brought an immediate response, and throughout Boxing Day everything movable was taken from the ship, carefully stacked ashore, and guarded against robbers by a squad of natives.

The *Santa Maria*, in one of history's most momentous shipwrecks, gradually disintegrated under the ebb and flow of the tides and the remorseless pressure of the currents over the bank on which she rested.

Several factors combined to convince Columbus of his future course of action. It was evident that all of the two crews could not be accommodated in the tiny *Niña*. It was certain — if only in Columbus's mind — that a gold mine existed on the island of Hispaniola, with rich, easy pickings. It was also a fact that the natives were friendly: they had displayed a brotherly love far beyond anything to be reasonably expected when the flagship sank. And finally, the wrecked ship had been stripped of anything usable — all the timber from the decks, planking from the hull, even the keel, masts, decking, and fore and stern castles. Columbus resolved to establish a small colony ashore. Forty-odd men would be left behind to build a fortress of all the salvaged timbers, 'as good a tower and fort as possible, and wide moat'. He resolved too that these men should discover 'the exact location of the mine from which the gold is extracted'.

To enable the men to survive, a year's supply of provisions was set aside — wine, bread, grain for growing, and other survival goods, all to be stored in cellars below ground.

Of the thirty-nine men who actually stayed behind most were volunteers, and many others also wished to stay in order to share in the golden spoils which everyone was certain existed.

In command of the colony Columbus nominated his friend and relation by marriage Diego de Harana from Córdova, and the two lieutenants were to be Pedro Gutiérrez (the king's major-domo) and Rodrigo de Escobedo, secretary of the fleet. Others in the party included a surgeon to deal with the inevitable tropical fevers and strange illnesses, a master-at-arms, a caulker, a carpenter, cooper, tailor and a gunner to look after the lombards and falconets salvaged from the wreck.

Columbus made much of a display of strength by firing these weapons, which frightened the natives almost to death. It also impressed on them that the sailors were not a group of castaways at the mercy of the natives but were powerful and well armed.

While Columbus carried on with his preparations for departure aboard *Niña* and the construction of the fortress — to be named Navidad — proceeded,

word reached him that some Indians had sighted another ship — evidently the *Pinta* — on 27 December, two days' sailing time away to the east.

Clearly, Columbus was much put out by *Pinta*'s absence. He wanted Pinzón to rejoin and remain in sight: no wandering off, probably discovering the gold mine then scuttling off to Spain to claim the glory. Columbus decided to make arrangements to go in search of Pinzón and to punish him for desertion.

On Friday 4 January 1493 Columbus addressed all the men remaining behind, said farewell to the cacique, boarded the *Niña* and prepared for sea. Anchor was weighed, *Niña* skirted the reefs and gained the open sea. She set an easterly course along the northern coast of the island (today's Dominican Republic) in search of the *Pinta*.

Columbus could discern a very high mountain on the horizon dead ahead, looking like an island, but in reality connected to the mainland by a low isthmus. He named it Monte Cristi. Beyond the mountain lay a beach twelve miles long. Inland there rose other mountains comparable to the beauty of the sierras of Córdova. The *Niña* anchored for the night and to his *Journal* Columbus confided that Japan was on the island, and that it abounded in gold, spices, mastic and — oddly — rhubarb. The following day an extraordinary meeting took place. Ferdinand Columbus described it:*

> After they had sailed with contrary winds farther to the east of Monte Cristi, on Sunday morning 6 January, a caulker sent aloft sighted the *Pinta* running westward before the wind. Coming up to the Admiral, Captain Martin Alonso Pinzón boarded the flagship and began to invent reasons and excuses for having separated from him, saying it had happened unavoidably, against his will. The Admiral well knew it was not true — being aware of Pinzón's hostility toward him and the insolence he had displayed at various times on the voyage; but he thought it best to pretend to believe him and dissemble everything lest the whole enterprise come to ruin — and this could have happened very easily, since the majority of the Admiral's crew were Pinzón's townspeople and many were his kinsmen.

There was no doubt in Columbus's mind, however, that Pinzón had deserted the fleet off Cuba on 21 November to gather up the gold which the Indians had assured him abounded on the island of Babeque. However, Pinzón had been dismayed to find no gold there and had turned towards Hispaniola where other natives told him there was plenty of gold. Ferdinand Columbus reports:

> On this voyage which had taken him twenty days, he had sailed no more than fifteen leagues west of Navidad, as far as a little river that the Admiral had named Rio de Gracia.† There, Martín Alonso tarried sixteen days and found much gold, which he obtained in exchange for objects of trifling worth. Half of this gold he had divided among the crew of his caravel in order to gain their consent to his keeping the rest by virtue of his title of captain. Yet he later sought to convince the Admiral he knew nothing of this gold.

Pinzón revealed to Columbus, as if cleansing his conscience, that natives had told him of another island to the south of Cuba, called by the natives Yamaye

The building of the ill-fated fortress of Navidad took place in 1493. This woodcut is taken from the illustrated edition of Columbus's Letter of the same year.

* Ferdinand Columbus, p.99.

THE MYSTERY OF COLUMBUS'S SIGNATURE

Of all the mysteries surrounding Columbus none is so intractable as the self-created puzzle of his signature. It has defied cryptanalysts who can only surmise his meaning and now — five hundred years later — still leaves the matter in dispute. One source unravels the monogram like this:

S alva	Save me
S A S	
X ristos M aria Y osephus	Christ Mary Joseph
Xpo FERENS	I come bearing Christ

Another historian explains:

Xpo FERENS means the Christ bearer, and [he] believes the initials mean, in Latin, 'Servant am I of the Most High Saviour, Son of Mary.'

After his first triumphant voyage of discovery and his adoption of the title Admiral of the Ocean Sea, Columbus added 'El Almirante' to his usual cryptic signature.

Curiously, he insisted in his will that his son, Diego, and his successors should adopt the same signature, but neither Diego nor his successors ever did.

There is only one certainty about the signature and that is that Columbus took the answer to the puzzle to the grave with him.

(Jamaica), where gold could be found in nuggets bigger than eggs. It was all a grand fantasy.

The relations between the Admiral and his senior captain continued mutually suspicious and as taut as a bowstring. Columbus was content to leave matters as they were. He could sense a feeling of impatience and irritability in the crews. They were beginning to get anxious to go home after four months at sea. He judged that it was about time to begin the homeward voyage. He continued for a few more days, coasting towards the east, naming all the capes, gulfs, rivers and possible ports along the way.

The last landfall in the Indies unfortunately proved to be an unhappy experience. The *Niña* and *Pinta* had coasted to a splendid natural harbour, where the two caravels anchored in twelve fathoms of crystal-clear water. The gulf in which this harbour lay was nearly at the eastern extremity of the island of Hispaniola.

A boatload of Spaniards went ashore to replenish stores and came upon some natives armed with bows and arrows. They were 'of a more unpleasing appearance.' Their faces were 'smutted all over with charcoal, though in all parts [i.e. all over] they are accustomed to paint themselves with a variety of colours.'

From one native brought aboard, Columbus learned of the island of Matinino, peopled only by women. At first this native was taken to be a Carib (the Indian name for the island of Puerto Rico which gave rise to the name Caribbean), one of the savage, man-eating tribe sometimes called Caniba. Other Indians stood in terror of these cannibals.

Later in the day another boatload of Spaniards went ashore and was met by a belligerent group of about fifty natives daubed with paint and wearing headdresses of parrot feathers. Otherwise, they were stark naked. Squabbling developed during the bartering of trinkets for bows and arrows, and in the ensuing fighting some Indians received crossbow and sword wounds. Although they numbered more than fifty against just seven Spaniards, the natives fled, discarding their bows and arrows on the beach. It was a brief but bloody encounter and a sorry note on which to end the voyage.

Columbus named this beautiful place Golfo de las Flechas. Three hours before dawn, on Wednesday 16 January 1493, Columbus sailed from the Gulf of Arrows with the *Niña* and *Pinta* on the homeward voyage.

13 The Voyage Home

THE LAST land Columbus saw as he turned for home was Cape Santelmo (the modern Cape Engaño). By now both caravels were leaking badly, and were in urgent need of refitting. A week after sailing, the *Niña* had to heave-to many times because the *Pinta* was sailing badly with an unsound mizzen mast. In the abstracted *Journal* Las Casas quoted Columbus, who could not resist a dig at Pinzón:

> The Admiral remarks that if the captain, Martín Alonso Pinzón, had taken as much care to provide himself with a new mast in the Indies, where there are so many fine trees, as he had exerted in running away from him in the hope of loading his vessel with gold, they would not have laboured under that inconvenience.

The homeward voyage was totally different from the outward one. There were no pleasant trade winds to take them comfortably to their destination. For the homeward run Columbus believed he would need to sail north and east, intersecting the westerly course he had held on the outward voyage, heading still northerly to pick up the west winds at about the latitude for Spain, then taking the ships almost due east. The voyage can be visualised if these degrees of latitude can be kept in mind: Columbus's departure point at the Gulf of Arrows was just over 19 degrees N and his destination was Cádiz at about 37 degrees N. The longitudes were from about 70 degrees W, to Cádiz at about 7 degrees W.

It was to be a long haul with two not very seaworthy ships, although both were to be subjected to enormous storms and would confound everyone by their ability to survive.

It was no easy task following an ENE course, as the prevailing wind direction compelled the captains to tack their ships constantly. This is exemplified by Columbus's log entry abstracted by Las Casas for Tuesday 22 January 1493:

> After sunset last evening they stood to the NNE, with the wind from E to SE, and sailed eight miles an hour for five glasses, adding three which were sailed before the watch, in all eight . . . Afterwards sailed NE and N, six glasses . . . then four glasses of the second watch to the NE . . . then till sunrise ENE, eleven glasses . . . till eleven o'clock in the forenoon . . . when it fell calm and they made no further progress. The Indians went into the sea to swim. Tropic birds and much weed were seen.

The homeward voyage presents us with one of the finest examples of navigation at sea ever undertaken. It also demonstrated Columbus's uncanny 'feel' for the sea, his ability to 'read' its signs to indicate the ships' position. On 10 February after more than three weeks at sea, averaging about one hundred miles a day on a variety of tacking courses, the plotted positions of the two caravels were discussed aboard the Admiral's ship. Las Casas recorded: '... reckonings were kept by Vicente Yáñez Pinzón, his two pilots Pedro Alonso Niño and Bartolomé Roldan, and the pilot from the *Niña*, Sancho Ruiz da Gama.'

All of them placed the ships in positions far beyond the Azores, to the east, in the general area of Madeira or Porto Santo.

> The Admiral was much behind them, finding himself that night south of the island of Flores and in the latitude of Nafe in Africa. Thus their accounts made them nearer Spain than his by 450 miles. He remarked that by the grace of God they shall find upon making land who is the most correct.

Admiral Samuel Eliot Morison, who replicated Columbus's voyage in a yacht, reckons that Columbus showed a remarkably accurate dead reckoning position − out by only a couple of dozen miles. Morison marvels, too, at the navigator who looked at the Pole Star with the naked eye, observed it to be at about the same height as at Cape St Vincent, which is at 37 degrees N, and expressed the view he was in a position about 34 to 35 degrees N − an incredible assessment.

But the voyage was not over yet − by a long chalk. Other matters of a serious nature were to intrude before the caravels made their long-awaited landfall.

The winter of early 1493 was a period of violent storms and bitter cold in the Atlantic. Winds at Lisbon kept ships storm-bound in the port for several weeks on end. Storms raged with particular intensity during the period 12−15 February. Morison calculated that the wind reached the equivalent of force eight on the Beaufort scale. On Tuesday the 12th Las Casas transcribed into the abstracted log:

> ... the wind began to blow furiously with a heavy sea, and if the caravel had not been a good vessel, and well prepared, they would have been in danger of perishing. During the day they sailed eleven or twelve leagues with much labour and hazard.

The entry for the following day, Wednesday the 13th, catches the mood of the situation and the sea conditions with frightening clarity:

> From sunset till day, they laboured exceedingly with a high wind and furious sea. It lightened three times in the NE which in the Admiral's opinion was a sign of a violent tempest from that or the opposite quarter. They scudded under bare poles most of the night, and afterwards set a little sail ... In the day the wind remitted somewhat, and then sprung up with more violence; the sea was terrible, running cross and causing the vessel to labour excessively ...

The next day the *Niña* tried to ride out the storm, which persisted with unabated strength. It was a most frightening experience. Both ships ran before the storm winds. The *Pinta* was unable to take the heavy seas well and she scudded due north before the southerly wind.

The *Niña* struggled to maintain a course to the north-east, towards Spain. Both ships carried flares and lamps to help them keep in touch with each other, but by daybreak contact between them had been lost and both believed the other had foundered in the storm.

Aboard *Niña* the crew struggled to keep the ship from broaching-to: lack of ballast and depleted provisions made her specially unhandy in anything of a sea, let alone such a storm. Empty casks were filled with sea-water to act as stabilising ballast to lessen the chances of capsizing. The storm raged. Men slumped to their knees in prayers and devotions, and drew lots to decide who should make a pilgrimage as an act of thanks for deliverance from the storm. Chick peas, one nicked with a cross by a knife, were placed in a cap and drawn by the crew. The fact that the crossed one was drawn by the Admiral himself makes one suspect he 'fiddled' the draw. The pilgrimage was to visit the shrine of Our Lady of Guadalupe in Estremadura, carrying a large wax candle.

A sailor named Pedro de la Villa from Santa Maria de Santoña drew the lot for a similar pilgrimage to Our Lady of Loreto in Italy. A third lot was drawn for a pilgrim to attend a one-night vigil at the church of Santa Clara de Moguer near Palos.

Columbus also drew this lot – and one becomes convinced that the draw was fixed.

As the fury of the storm battered the small ship, almost engulfing her, the crew vowed to go barefoot and in shirts to the first shrine of Our Lady they could find.

Columbus comforted himself with the belief that the good Lord could not allow everything that had been achieved and so laboriously fought for over the years to be squandered and himself destroyed in the tempest when it was largely 'for the exaltation of His church.'

So desperate for survival did Columbus become in the storm that he wrote on parchment a long description of events, of his discovery of new lands, of courses and routes, sealed and addressed to the Catholic Sovereigns, with the promise of a reward of a thousand ducats to whoever should deliver the letter to their Highnesses. The letter was sealed in wax and secured in a large wooden barrel, then cast overboard.

On Friday 15 February the skies showed signs of clearing, the winds abated slightly and the seas subsided a little. Soon after sunrise land was sighted to the ENE. It was an island of the Azores. 'My navigation,' the Admiral logged immodestly, 'has been very accurate and I have steered well.'

It took a few days of beating against the wind to reach an anchorage. It was the island of Santa Maria: the first landfall on the homeward voyage. Three men from ashore came aboard bringing with them gifts of fowl, fresh bread and other refreshments, together with greetings from the Portuguese captain of the island, João Casteneira (sometimes João de Castanheda).

In fulfilment of the vows made at the height of the storm – it still continued to rage – half the ship's company were sent ashore barefoot and in shirts with the ostensible approval of the Portuguese. The pilgrims walked to a hermitage dedicated to the Virgin. The three Portuguese also went ashore to request the chaplain who had the keys to the shrine to say a mass for them.

In a moment of treachery, the Spanish seamen were attacked by the Portuguese, taken prisoner and their boat seized. It is not clear what they expected to derive from this hostage-taking. It took days of parleying before the

Portuguese captain had a change of heart; until then he had maintained that a commission held by Columbus from the Catholic Sovereigns was worthless: the king and queen of Castile were not recognised in the Azores. Whatever the reason, Captain Casteneira relented, released the hostages and allowed the *Niña* to proceed after replenishing stores. She caught a fair wind for Spain.

Hardly had the great storm abated than another of equal proportions struck the battered ship. On Sunday 3 March a violent squall struck the *Niña* and split all the sails, placing her in imminent danger as the squall increased in intensity to a storm, with a rising cross sea and a violent wind which drove the *Niña* before it under bare poles. The crew resorted to drawing lots again, this time to send a pilgrim to Santa Maria de la Cinta in Huelva. It will come as no surprise that the lot fell upon Columbus.

Despite the thunder, lightning, torrential rain, running before the storm, and the crashing ferocity of the seas which pounded the little ship to near destruction, the *Niña* survived the fierce ordeal, although it was a close run thing. Signs of land were noticed by the crew. Columbus held off out to sea as best he could so as not to be run ashore.

When the sun rose it was to see land – the mainland landfall on the homeward voyage – which Columbus then recognised with dismay as the Rock

De Bry's engraving captures Columbus's return to Lisbon after his successful first voyage of discovery, 1493.

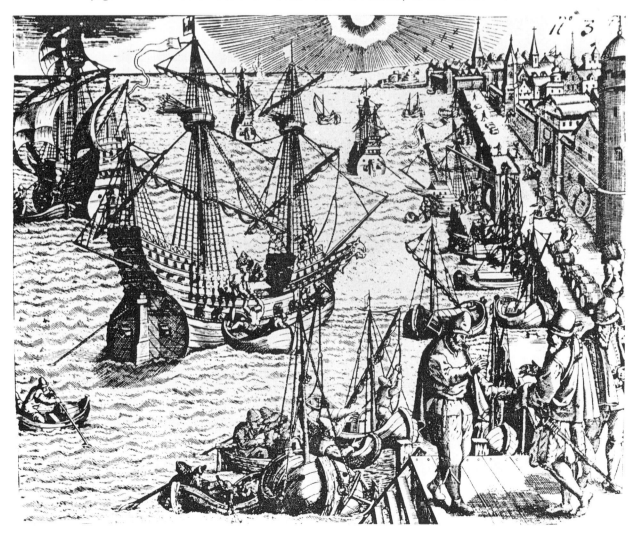

of Sintra at the Tagus estuary, close to Lisbon. It was the last place he wanted to visit. However, people ashore offered up prayers for the ship and her sailors, all in wonderment at the vessel's survival after such a period of violent storms which had wrecked dozens of vessels on Europe's coast. The *Niña* came close to destruction on the treacherous rocks overlooking Cascais but the Admiral's skill averted a wrecking. In the sanctuary of the river anchorage Columbus wrote to King John of Portugal seeking permission to take the *Niña* to the city of Lisbon rather than anchor in the remoter regions of the Tagus, where criminals might be tempted to raid a ship which rumour had it was loaded with gold. Further, the *Niña* could undergo some immediate repairs to keep her seaworthy.

Nearby in the anchorage lay a large warship bearing more weaponry than any ship Columbus had ever seen before. An armed boat pulled away from the warship and approached. A man hailed the *Niña*. He was the master of the ship and no less a person than Bartholomew Dias, one of the world's greatest explorers, who had met Columbus in Lisbon back in 1488.

He demanded that Columbus should get aboard the boat and give an explanation of himself to the stewards of the king and to the warship's captain. Columbus haughtily announced that he was the Admiral of the Ocean Sea to the Catholic Sovereigns and would render no such account to anyone and would only leave his ship under force of arms. Dias, described as the patron of the warship, replied that Columbus might send in his place the master of the *Niña*, an offer which was totally rejected by Columbus, who added that it was the custom for the Admirals of the Sovereigns of Castile to die rather than surrender their people. Dias asked to examine Columbus's papers. The Admiral was happy to comply and Dias must have wondered at the story he heard from Columbus. Dias returned to the warship and shortly afterwards the captain, Alvaro Dama, colourfully dressed, and with full ceremony and pomp accompanied by drums and pipes and trumpets, climbed aboard the *Niña* and offered to serve Columbus in any way he wished.

The story of Columbus's triumph spread like wildfire. For two days the *Niña* attracted large crowds of people clamouring to see the vessel which had discovered a new world; they also wanted to catch a glimpse of the Indians. The 'vast multitude' of visitors included knights and two stewards of the king.

On Friday 8 March Don Martin de Noronha (or Noroña) arrived with an invitation for Columbus to visit the king then staying at Valle de Paraíso about twenty-seven miles away. The king was taking refuge there in a monastery in order to keep clear of a plague epidemic raging in the capital. Columbus was escorted there through dense pine forests to see the 38-year-old king. He was accompanied by one of the handsomest of the Indians he had brought home with him.

There was much tension between King John and the Admiral. Both must have been well aware of their previous meeting when Columbus the supplicant had been rejected, whereas now, in a sense, the roles were reversed. It was the rejected man who now held all the court cards while the king who had rejected him had to listen to a catalogue of successes.

In the event, the king dealt with the situation with due decorum. Despite his expressed view that Columbus was 'very vainglorious in boasting his merits', the king and his court showed courtesy, kindness and the highest honour — sitting in the royal presence with his head covered. Columbus was offered everything he wanted and all the facilities of the Lisbon dockyards.

After hearing of Columbus's successes, the king expressed the opinion that he understood — according to a capitulation or agreement between Portugal and the Catholic Sovereigns — that Columbus's acquisitions belonged to the Portuguese crown.*

Columbus countered this with a complete denial of any knowledge of such a capitulation. He was, of course, aware that Spaniards were forbidden to go to Guinea — it was the preserve of the Portuguese — but he had voyaged to the Indies, not Guinea, and he could show as evidence the Indian who differed considerably from any African native.

Most of the reports of the meeting refer to its gracious and honourable nature, but two other views are chronicled. The first contra view is expressed by Ruy de la Peña (or Piña), confidant of the king, who originally criticised the king for not taking Columbus's project seriously enough. Now, he was outraged: the 'Admiral was by his nature a bit haughty and in telling things that concerned him he altered the bounds of truth, moreover he was rude and unruly.'

The second contra view was given by the sixteenth-century Portuguese historian João de Barros. Understandably, he gave a prejudiced view. He considered that Columbus's visit to the king was:

> not so much a wish to oblige the king as to mortify him with his presence, for before he went to Castile he had applied to this same King John entreating to be sent by him upon the enterprise. This the king had refused ... [Columbus] used so great a freedom of language, chiding and censuring the king for not having taken up with his offer, that many of the nobles, stung to resentment by the licence of his tongue, as well as vexed that the king had lost the benefits of the enterprise, offered to prevent his return to Castile by assassinating him ... The king rejected these offers ... and rebuked the nobles who made them, although the business gave him some concern.

Probably, Columbus was unaware of his closeness to death in crossing swords with the king. John was in the prime of life, though he was to die two years later at the age of forty. He was strong, a wilful ruler who had stabbed his own brother-in-law, and treated opposition with fierce aggression. Columbus, perhaps unknowingly, had sailed close to the wind at this confrontation.

Further courtesies were extended to Columbus, though one senses through gritted teeth. He was escorted by De Noronha and some of the king's knights for much of the time. The queen had expressly invited him not to depart without waiting upon her, and this he did, paying his respects, kissing hands and enjoying a courteous visit.

The Admiral returned to Lisbon to find work on the *Niña* well advanced. New sails had replaced the tattered remnants from the storm. Rigging had been repaired, opened seams caulked and damage made good. Columbus weighed anchor on 13 March and put to sea for Seville. The sea was rough, though Columbus may have thought it less so than the diplomatic visit he had just completed. A fair wind from the north-west carried the caravel to Cape St Vincent. The *Niña* entered Spanish waters and stood to the east for Saltes.

* Probably by virtue of the treaty of Alcacobes of 1479 signed by King John's father.

Columbus's priceless holograph to Santángel in 1493 ran to four pages of old Gothic handwriting.
It is still preserved in the Archivo General de Simancas at Valladolid.

SEÑOR por que se que aureis plazer dela grano victoria que nuestro señor me
ha dado en mi viaie vos escriuo esta por la qual sabreys como en veinte dias passe A
las indias con la armada q̃ los illustrissimos Rey e Reyna ñros señores me dieron
dond yo falle muy muchas Islas pobladas con gente sin numero: y dellas todas
he tomado posesion por sus altezas con pregon y vandera real estendida y non me fue
contradicho Ala primera q̃ yo falle puse nombre sant saluador a comemoracion desu alta magef
tat el qual marauillosamente todo esto an dado los idios la llaman guanahani Ala segūda
puse nombre la isla de santa maria deconcepcion ala tercera ferrandina ala quarta la isla bella
ala quita la Isla Juana e asi a cada vna nombre nueuo Quando yo llegue ala Juana segui
ui io la costa della al poniente yla falle tan grande q̃ pense que seria tierra firme la prouincia de
catayo y como no falle asi villas y lugares enla costa dela mar saluo pequeñas poblaciones
con la gente delas q̃les no podia hauer fabla por que luego fuyan todos: andaua yo a de
lante por el dicho camino pensado deno errar grādes Ciudades o villas y al cabo de muchas
leguas visto q̃ no hauia inouacio i que la costa me leuaua al setetrion de adōde mi voluntad
era cõtraria porq̃ el yuierno era ya encarnado yo tenia proposito de hazer del al austro y tan bien
el viēto medio adelāte determine deno aguardar otro tiepo y bolui atras fasta vn señalado puer
to de adōde embie dos hōbres por la tierra para saber si hauia Rey o grādes Ciudades ādoui
erō tres iornadas y hallarō ifinitas poblaciōes pequeñas i gēte si numero mas no cosa de reg
imieto por lo qual se boluierō yo entēdia barto deotros idios q̃ ia tenia tomados como cotin
uamēte esta tierra era Isla e asi segui la costa della al oriēte ciento i siete leguas fasta dōde fa
zia fin del qual cabo vi otra Isla al oriēte disticta de esta diez o ocho leguas ala qual luego
puse nombre la spañola y fui alli y segui la parte del setentrion asi como dela iuana al oriēte.
clxxviii grādes leguas por linea recta del oriēte asi como dela iuana la qual y todas las otras
sō fortissimas en demasiado grado y esta en estremo en ella ay muchos puertos ala costa dela
mar sin cōparaciõ de otros q̃ yo sepa en cristianos y fartos rios y buenos y grandes q̃ es mara
villa las tierras della sō altas y en ella muy muchas sierras y mōtañas altissimas sin cōparaciõ
de la isla de cētre fre: todas fermosissimas de mil fechuras y todas ādables y llenas de arbole
de mil maneras i altas i parecē q̃ llegā al cielo i tēgo pordicho q̃ iamas pierdē la foia segū lo
puede cōpbeder q̃ los vi tā verdes i tā bermosos como sō por mayo en spaña i dellos stauā flor
idos dellos cō fruto i dellos en otro termino segū es su calidad i cātaua el rui señor i otros pa
xaricos demil maneras en el mes de nouiēbre por alli dōde io ādaua ay palmas de seis o o
ocho maneras q̃ es admiracion verlas por la diformidad fermosa dellas mas asi como los o
otros arboles y frutos e ieruas en ella ay pinares a marauilla eay campiñas grādissimas eay mi
el i de muchas maneras de aues y frutas muy diuersas en las tierras ay muchas minas de me
tales eay gēte estimable numero La spañola es marauilla la sierras ylas mōtañas y las vegas
i las campiñas y las tierras tan fermosas y gruesas para plātar y sebrar para criar ganados de to
das suertes para edificios de villas e lugares los puertos dela mar aqui no hauria creēcia su
vista y delas rios muchos y grādes y buenas aguas los mas delos quales traē oro e los arbo
les y frutos e ieruas ay grandes differencias de aquel las dela iuana en esta ay muchas specie
rias y grandes minas de oro y de otros metales La gente desta isla y de todas las otras q̃ he
fallado y hauido: ni aya hauido noticia andan todos desnudos hōbres y mugeres asi como
sus madres los parē avn que algunas mugeres se cobriā vn solo lugar cō vna foia de yer
ua o vna cosa de algodō q̃ para ello fazen ellos no tienen fierro ni azero ni armas ni so
aello no por que no sō gente bien dispuesta y de fermosa estatura saluo que sō muy te
merosos a marauilla no tiene otras armas saluo las r...as delas cañas quando dla ...cōla simiente
eal al ponen al cabo vn palillo agudo eno vsan de aqllas que mi... ...veze... ...
ciuvo embiar anota dos o tres hōbres a alguna villa pa hauer fabl... ...tura

Columbus's Letter to Luis de Santángel announcing his discoveries of the first voyage was published in Spanish, 14 February 1493.

The spartan simplicity of life in La Rábida monastery is exemplified by this corner in the refectory.

The bar was crossed on a good tide at noon on 15 March and *Niña* entered the port of Palos. The Admiral had come back to the very port he had departed eight months previously.

It was to the plaudits and wonderment of the crowds who fêted the *Niña's* sailors and hero-worshipped Columbus that the caravel came to her berth. In the final entry in his *Journal* Columbus praised Our Lord for His creation of all things good and for the miracles of the voyage. The entry was addressed to the Catholic Sovereigns and in it the Admiral could not resist a little prod in his favour. While admitting that Divine Majesty had performed miracles, he claimed his fair share of the kudos and reminded their Highnesses of the opposition of so many principals of their household. It was altogether a very sweet moment for Columbus.

One of the first acts Columbus had performed on arrival at Lisbon was to despatch a copy of his Letter on the First Voyage to the Catholic Sovereigns, known to be in Barcelona. Now, from Palos, he despatched a copy. He also wrote letters to his family in Córdova. These duties done he performed his vows at the churches of Santa Clara de Moguer and Santa Maria de la Cinta at Huelva for deliverance from the storms. He then retired to La Rábida monastery to relax and rest among friends.

14 Return Home: Royal Reception at Barcelona: Pinzón's Death

WE MUST glance over our shoulders for a moment to consider the plight of the *Pinta*. Had Columbus been aware of her predicament he would have judged the moment sweeter than ever. It will be remembered that the two ships had parted company during the violent storm off the Azores on the night of 13–14 February, and Columbus was apprehensive lest Martín Alonso Pinzón should reach home before the *Niña* and claim the honours due to himself. It would have been a cruel injustice had this happened.

While Columbus was in Lisbon, he dwelt anxiously on Pinzón's whereabouts. It was possible – indeed, almost likely – that he had perished with all hands in the storm. Columbus had picked up no intelligence about the *Pinta*, which somewhat mollified him: had the ship put in at any Portuguese or Spanish port ahead of *Niña* Columbus was convinced the news would have reached Lisbon. What the Admiral did not know was that Pinzón was only a matter of hours behind him. Nor was Pinzón aware of exactly how close he was to snatching all the glory and honour of discovering the New World.

After parting company, Pinzón never reached the Azores. He tried to skirt round the storm, which drove him on a more northerly course rather than the easterly one he wanted in order to reach Spain. This served to make his mainland landfall – when he made it – more northerly than had been intended. In fact he landed at Bayona, a small port in Galicia immediately north of the Portuguese border. He sent a messenger to the royal court in Barcelona, seeking an audience.

The reply, when it came after a fortnight, must have been a bitter blow to Pinzón. The Sovereigns made it clear they intended to receive the report from Columbus. It is evident that long before Columbus's audience with the king and queen they must have known of his imminent return with – it is fair to guess – good news of discoveries. The Pinzón letter gave it away, but further evidence must have leaked out of the Lisbon court to reach Barcelona.

We must follow the Pinzón story to its tragic end. On receipt of the damning letter from the king and queen, Pinzón departed from Bayona and sailed south along the Portuguese coast, not stopping at Lisbon – by which time he was a mere thirty miles astern of Columbus.

When the *Pinta* reached Palos – on the evening of the very same day that Columbus had arrived – Pinzón could see the *Niña*'s masts in the harbour and he knew he had been beaten. He was so distraught that he declined to take the *Pinta* into harbour. He climbed into the ship's boat and landed on the shore outside the town's limits. He refused to meet and congratulate the Admiral, nor even to meet his own younger brother, Vicente Yáñez, who commanded the *Niña*. He headed for his home near Moguer and took to his bed. Whether or not he was sick is not known. Perhaps he was exhausted, mentally crushed, and suffering dreadfully from a deep depression; but whether he was organically ill is just not clear. What is tragically plain is that in five days Pinzón — one of the greatest navigators of his time — was dead, aged about fifty-three: dead from exhaustion.

Yet, curiously, it was not the end of the Columbus-Pinzón enmity; that was to continue for three generations, spanning a century. And there is no doubt in the minds of the people of Palos who was the greater discoverer: it is to Pinzón that the monument in Palos credits the discovery of the New World — not Columbus.

> To Christopher Columbus, Our Admiral of the Ocean Sea, Viceroy
> and Governor of the islands discovered by him in the Indies . . .

The message from the king and queen, when it reached Columbus in Seville on Easter Sunday 7 April, made no bones about it: the monarchs addressed him generously and grandly as was his due. He must have felt enormous pride. His mind must have flitted back to the outrageous capitulations he had demanded several months ago and reflected with great satisfaction on the outcome.

The invitation to meet their Majesties in Barcelona reached the Admiral while he rested in Seville. During Holy Week in the city he had been fêted

The magnificent splendour of the cathedral in Seville dominates today's city. Columbus attended mass here during Holy Week in 1493 to celebrate the discoveries of his first voyage.

The starkness of today's Plaza del Rey in Barcelona contrasts with the colourful trappings of regal splendour in 1493 when the Catholic Sovereigns received Columbus on his return from discovering the New World.

and treated with great honours. Crowds of well-wishers thronged the streets and greeted him. One young man, a spectator of these momentous events, remembered the occasion all his life, and was specially fascinated by the Indians: he was the eighteen-year-old Las Casas, later to become the Admiral's friend and the editor of his *Journal*.

Columbus proceeded in triumphal splendour from Seville, adorned in colourful robes befitting his new station in life, flanked by officers, servants, king's men and some Indians. The whole procession was cheered to the echo, the people flocking to see the great discoverer, his Indians and the displays of gold, parrots, amber and spices.

At Córdova, the city he had come to regard as home, the welcome was specially warm. He was received by his two sons, Diego and Ferdinand. His mistress, Beatrice Enríquez de Harana, met him there, where he rested overnight before proceeding to the coast at Valencia. He then travelled the coastal route to Barcelona, where he aimed to arrive on 20 April. There, as a contemporary recorded, the court and the entire city turned out to greet the Admiral.

The king and queen received Columbus at the Royal Palace of Barcelona. The reception was a public one. A stand had been erected in the inner courtyard, which was filled to overflowing with all the pomp and ceremony of the grandest court of Europe, with princes and noblemen, bishops and grandees and their attendants from all over the country clamouring to witness the historic event.

All except the monarchs rose to their feet in honour of the guest, a courtesy normally extended only to grandees. Banners waved, cheers filled the air, applause and shouts of wonderment at the sight of the Indians came from every corner of the courtyard. Columbus entered the great hall of the palace, packed with richly attired nobility.

Ferdinand and Isabella — with the young prince, Don Juan — sat on their thrones and invited Columbus to approach. He mounted the steps, solemnly

The artist Antonio Gonzalez Velasquez painted this fresco in the royal palace in Madrid. It depicts Columbus (holding a globe) in audience with the Catholic Sovereigns.

yet smilingly. It was the greatest moment of his life. He was being hailed as the great discoverer of the New World by the most powerful kingdom in Europe. Nothing else he ever achieved in his life matched this moment of acclaim.

Ferdinand and Isabella rose, extending their hands to be kissed. Columbus knelt to do so, but graciously was asked to rise and was then ushered to a chair alongside the monarchs and the young prince. It was an honour very rarely accorded and the sight of it was not lost on anyone. The correct level of propriety was maintained, however, the chair being backless and not too grand.

Columbus was closely questioned for one hour about the great voyage and about the next expedition, after which the royal party retired to the royal chapel where the *Te Deum* was sung in honour of the great discoveries. It was a fitting end to a memorable ceremony, the like of which had not been witnessed in living memory.

On 28 May a proclamation from the Sovereigns granted rights and privileges to the Admiral in a long, discursive document:*

> . . . We confirm by these presents to you and your said sons,
> descendants and successors, one after the other, now and forevermore,
> the said offices of Admiral of the Ocean Sea, which you have found
> and discovered, and of Viceroy and Governor of the said islands and
> mainland [in fact, Cuba] that you have found and discovered and of
> the other islands and mainland which by you or your industry shall be
> discovered from this time forth in the said region of the Indies.

It has been written by many historians, with their customary benefit of hindsight and not a little tongue in cheek, that the Admiral should now have given up his plans for further exploration and discovery, and retired to a well-deserved rest. He could not possibly earn greater honours or privileges: he had received all that he had demanded and he had won a place in history; surely there were no greater rewards awaiting him.

We cannot let this chapter close without further reference to the Treaty of Tordesillas, made on 7 June 1494.

The two greatest colonising powers at the time were Portugal and Spain. At that time, too, it was the public law of Europe for the Pope to allot temporal sovereignty to any lands possessed by a Christian prince, and the kings of Portugal had been assiduous in acquiring a series of papal edicts regarding the coastal regions of Africa. It was undoubtedly to this situation that King John II alluded in conversation with Columbus in Valle de Paraíso, when claiming the Admiral's discoveries as belonging to him. In short, Portugal was claiming as its own anything discovered west of Africa and south of the Canaries. In a series of papal edicts first Portugal and then Spain became alarmed at the new findings, as the advantage lay first with one nation and then with the other. After years of sensible negotiations, the signing of the Treaty of Tordesillas

---

* Extracted from the facsimile edition of *Christopher Columbus: His Own Book of Privileges*, compiled and edited by B.F. Stevens, 1893, pp.53–62.

COLUMBUS'S COAT OF ARMS

ON 20 May 1493 the Catholic Sovereigns honoured Columbus by conferring the right to bear arms. It was a further step in the ennoblement which Columbus had sought in recognition of his achievements. The patent declared in heraldic terms:

> You may place above your arms a castle and a lion that we grant you for arms, viz the gold castle on a green field in the upper quarter of the shield of your arms on the dexter hand and in the other upper quarter on the sinister hand a purple lion rampant with green tongue and a white field, and in the other quarter below on the dexter hand some gold islands in waves of the sea, and in the other quarter below on the sinister hand your own arms which you are accustomed to bear.

It was a rare honour for the Sovereigns to allow the Admiral to use the symbols of the lion of León and the castle of Castile.

By 1502 Columbus had made some alterations to the arms. The gold castle was now placed on a red field (as in the royal arms) and the lion matched more closely the design on the royal arms. As well as the cluster of islands a mainland was now incorporated to represent more accurately the lands Columbus had discovered. And a new sinister lower quarter was added comprising five gold anchors, horizontally, on a blue field. Presumably this represented the title of Admiral of the Ocean Sea. The Columbus family arms comprised a blue bend (a stripe) on a gold field with a red chief between the third and fourth quarters.

By 1535 the arms had acquired a crest, probably added by the second Admiral, Don Diego, comprising a small globe and red cross with a white motto ribbon reading: *Por Castilla y Por León: Nuevo Mondo Hallo Colon* (For Castile and For León: A New World Found Colon.)

At the same time as the granting of the original arms the Sovereigns accorded Christopher's two brothers, Bartholomew and Diego, the honour and privilege of being addressed as Don.

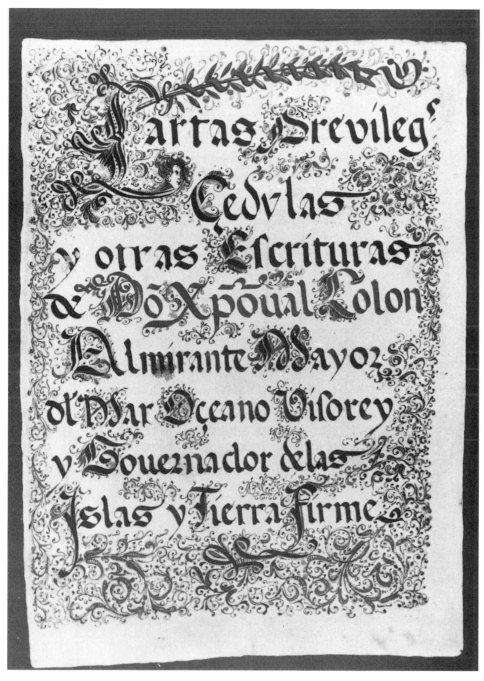

The title page of the rare *Book of Privileges* compiled by Columbus in his latter years. One copy rests in the Library of Congress: the original is preserved in the Biblioteca Columbina in Seville Cathedral.

drew a line of demarcation from north to south along the longitude 46 degrees 30 minutes W. East of this line all discoveries — even if made by Spaniards — should belong to Portugal. And west of it, all discoveries, even those made by Portuguese men and ships, should belong to Spain.

So far, so good: expressed in such simple terms the two signatory powers were able to preserve peace and friendship in matters maritime, until Magellan, a Portuguese in the service of Spain, complicated matters by leading an expedition to circumnavigate the world in 1519. He lost his life in the process, but one of his ships carried on to complete the voyage. It discomfitted both parties and made a travesty of the treaty.

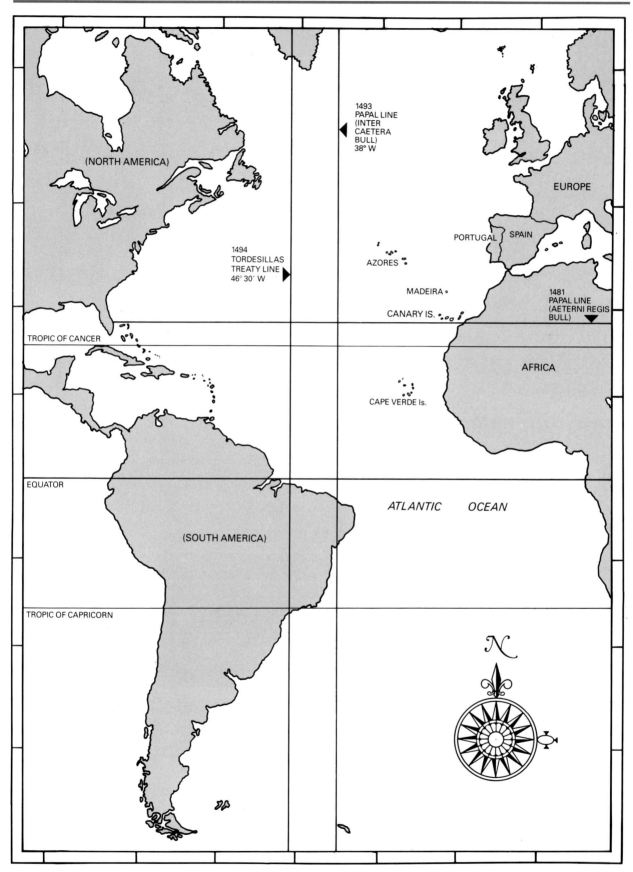

Demarcation lines between Spain and Portugal.

15 The Second Voyage 1493-6: The Navidad Massacre

EVEN BEFORE the first great voyage of discovery was over Columbus was already planning the second. There was never a glimmer of a suggestion that he should retire and rest on his laurels. It came as no surprise to him when the Sovereigns asked him to prepare for the second coming of Columbus to the Indies.

It is a cruel twist of fate that despite all his magnificent discoveries and navigational achievements, the great cosmographical dreams he harboured and statements he made known to the world and held on to for the whole of his life were utterly and totally wrong. And yet he continued to make discoveries for years, all based on these erroneous facts and beliefs. It is a quirk of history, too, that despite all these wrongly-held beliefs, they do not in any way diminish the man and his achievements; for it was those very beliefs which gave him the courage and Christian strength to venture where no one else had ever ventured before and, perhaps an even greater dichotomy, to promote the word of God and the enslavement and near extermination of thousands upon thousands of Indies natives, who within thirty years were to be reduced to a mere handful.

On 20 May 1493 Columbus was appointed Captain General of the new fleet, and a few days later the Archdeacon of Seville, Don Juan Rodriguez de Fonseca, was named as the joint executive responsible with Columbus for organising the preparations of the fleet.

The declared objectives of the second voyage were set out in the Sovereigns' instructions dated 29 May, the first and foremost being to convert the natives to Christianity to which end the Benedictine Father Bernado Buil (sometimes Bruyl) was to accompany the fleet. He was to be assisted by the Jeronymite Father Ramón Pane and by three young Franciscans from Picardy and Burgundy. They had charge of all the equipment necessary to set up the first church in the New World — a gift of the queen.

The second objective was the establishment of a crown trading colony: it was to be a totally nationalised affair, everything conducted with, by and through the government agency with no private trading. One-eighth of the net profits would go to Columbus and the rest to the crown. Cádiz was nominated as the home base through which everything to and from the Indies was to be handled.

Father Fonseca set up a command centre at Seville, appointed a treasurer, Francisco Pinello, and a chief accountant, Juan de Soria, described as 'a tight-fisted administrator'.

Columbus embarked on a pilgrimage to fulfil one of the vows undertaken during the storm off Lisbon. It was a considerable journey, which he made on horseback. He travelled from Barcelona to Saragossa, climbed the sierra to the

Bishop Don Juan de Fonseca, a shrewd administrator who moved smoothly through the corridors of power; he was responsible for organising Columbus's second voyage. The two men never hit it off with each other.

high plain leading to Madrid, and followed the pilgrims' way to the massive monastery of Guadalupe, which lay more than a hundred miles further to the south-west towards the Portuguese border via Talavera de la Reina, then through the foothills of the Estremadura mountains. Here Columbus sought out the ancient image of the Virgin, Nuestra Señora de Guadalupe, said to have been carved by St Luke himself.

The shrine had become venerated and wealthy by its reputation for helping to save soldiers and sailors from death and drowning. The monks of the monastery asked the Admiral to name a newly discovered island after their sacred city, a baptism he was happy to carry out. The long journey continued via Medellín, Trujillo and across the sierra of Estremadura on the long detour to Córdova to say his farewells to Beatrice Enríquez de Harana. His two sons joined him on the last stage of the journey down the valley of the Guadalquivir to Seville. His penance was over. The next great challenge lay before him.

On the Admiral's arrival in July at the base headquarters for the second voyage at Seville, it was to find Fonseca in total command having made considerable progress in the assembly of a fleet and all its paraphernalia. Although the two men failed to see eye to eye on many scores, there was no denying the merit of Fonseca's organising ability, something that was specially necessary for a maritime expedition of this size. However, when Columbus went to Cádiz to inspect the assembling fleet he was furious at the seeming lack of progress there. His hopes of sailing in August – as he had done before, thus catching the best of the fair weather – were dashed. Those ships which had been chartered or acquired seemed to him not of the right quality nor the right type of vessel. He lost no time in telling Fonseca so. The priest gave as good as Columbus, having little patience with the Admiral, genius though he was.

It is unfortunate that the second voyage is not so well documented as the first. There is no *Journal*, but there is Ferdinand's biography of his father and some useful information from Las Casas.

The vessels comprising the fleet of the second voyage looked far more like a fleet than the three ships of the first voyage. There were seventeen ships assembled in Cádiz harbour, but they were a motley collection about which we know little. Columbus's flagship was named – like his first one – *Santa Maria*. Her real name appears to have been *Mariagalante* and she was bigger than the first flagship, some reports say as large as 200 tons.

The Admiral's cabin was more commodious, as befitted his rank. The brother of the governess of the Infante Don Juan was the owner of the ship and therefore her master.

The splendid little *Niña* of the first voyage is believed to have been one of the twelve square-rigged caravels in the fleet; though she now carried the name *Santa Clara* she continued to be referred to as *Niña*. The ships mainly comprised *caravelas rondondes*, vessels which were large enough to prove seaworthy for the voyage but drew little water, enabling them to sail close along shore and to enter shoal waters.

It is believed that 1,200–1,500 men manned the ships (no women were allowed until the 1498 expedition when one in ten emigrants was female). This means an average of seventy and eighty-eight respectively per ship. Even the lower figure seems high bearing in mind the small size of many of the ships. Few names of the crew members are known. Only roll calls for the *Niña*, *San Juan* and *Cardera* exist and analysis of these indicates that there were aboard

Alejo Fernández's allegorical painting of *The Madonna of the Navigators* (*La Virgen del Buen Aire*) shows Columbus, Vespucci and Vicente Yáñez Pinzón on the Virgin's left, and King Ferdinand and Archbishop Fonseca on her right. The painting is preserved in the Alcazar of Seville.

some Genoese and some Basques, but the majority came from the Palos-Moguer-Huelva-Lepe region — like the four Niño brothers of Moguer. Juan Niño and Francisco were the master and pilot respectively of the *Niña*; their brother Cristobal Perez was master of the *Cardera*, and Juan's cousin — another Francisco — had signed on as a lowly gromet. Two other large ships are given names, the *Colina* and *La Gallega*.

Few men's names are mentioned. Juan Aguado commanded a ship but we know not which. Pedro Fernández Coronel was another commander: he later led the advance fleet of the third voyage to the Indies. There were also the following:

Alonso Sanchez de Carvajal, mayor of Baeza, a town which paid his full salary while he enjoyed his sabbatical.

Ginés de Gorbalán and Alonso de Hojeda.

Juan de la Cosa, the second of this name: the chartmaker who signed on with the *Niña* as a mariner.

Ponce de Léon, the future discoverer of Tierra Florida and conquistador of Puerto Rico.

Paul de Terreros, the Admiral's steward who commanded a caravel in the fourth voyage.

Francisco de Peñalosa, commander of the armed forces, was a servant of the queen and uncle of Bartolomé de las Casas, the Admiral's biographer.

Pedro de las Casas, father of the biographer.

Mosén Pedro Margarit, an army officer who commanded a fort in Hispaniola.

Melchior Maldonado, a former envoy of the Holy See.

Diego Alvarez Chanca, a physician of Seville.*

Michele de Cuneo, a childhood friend of the Admiral from Savona near Genoa, who wrote a narrative of the voyage.†

Diego Tristan, gentleman volunteer who lost his life in the fight at Belén during the fourth voyage.

Diego Columbus, the Admiral's youngest brother, 'a virtuous person . . . and of good disposition,' reported Las Casas. He affected an outfit akin to a priest's and it was no secret that the Admiral was grooming him for a bishopric — which he never achieved.

Fonseca and Columbus were overwhelmed with applications for positions in the fleet, two thousand men of all categories and classes applying, all of them sensing a gold rush with jewels and treasures abounding. Young courtiers and men of quality used every means of influence available to secure a post. Sons of aristocrats, artisans, speculators, officials, soldiers, sailors, men from every walk of life pressed for inclusion aboard the crowded ships. They shared accommodation with horses, pigs, goats, fowl and sheep. The ships were packed with European foods and provisions, with enough wines and munitions and weaponry and stores to sustain a colony of white men.

The ships also carried an immense quantity of trashy trinkets, with which to bamboozle the Indians: trinkets for gold. Everyone aboard the ships sailed in

*He wrote a report of the voyage and sent it to the town council of Seville where the letter rests to this day.

†Cuneo's letters to numerous friends in Liguria have been preserved in the Raccaolta Columbiana di Genova (the Columbian Collection in Genoa).

high hopes of personal gain. In the event, few would realise it. Most would be prepared to sacrifice much for the chance of a berth home.

The departure of the fleet was a splendid and great occasion. The white walls of Cádiz formed a clean backdrop for the brightly painted sails. Banners of every colour streamed in the wind, entangling themselves in the rigging. Huge standards flew from the mainmasts, and the waists of the ships were covered with the emblazoned banners of the gentlemen volunteers. It was a grand and colourful spectacle. Noise from the cheering crowds, from saluting cannons and blaring trumpets added to the carnival nature of the scene. Columbus himself was impressed by the spectacle, describing it as 'handsome'.

The fleet was escorted from the harbour by a squadron of Venetian galleys. Sails filled with the light breeze and the fleet set course for the Canaries. The second voyage of discovery, full of promise for everyone, was under way.

On 2 October Grand Canary was reached and three days later all seventeen ships anchored at San Sebastian on the island of Gomera. Without doubt Columbus would have taken the opportunity of seeing his paramour, Beatrice de Peraza. Cuneo referred to her openly in one of his letters: '. . . with whom our Admiral in other times had fallen in love.'

Morison, who described her as a 'handsome and vigorous young widow', regards Columbus as being lucky to have escaped the woman's clutches for 'she was as cruel as she was beautiful'. One anecdote about her will suffice. A San Sebastian man who was rash enough to talk about the lady's lack of chastity was invited to her home to discuss the matter. When she had heard enough

A 19th-century artist's impression of Columbus's departure from Palos for his second voyage of discovery in the autumn of 1493.

she gave a signal whereupon her servants seized the man and hanged him from the rafters. The body was then strung up outside her home as a warning to others to watch their tongues. It was, indeed, a good riddance that Columbus bade her on this occasion. Later, she married Alonso de Lugo, a conquistador, reputedly more ruthless than the widow: she had probably met her match.

The ships embarked fresh supplies, including livestock to introduce to Hispaniola. The animals would have been penned on deck and the congestion and mess and stench must have been almost unbearable.

On 13 October, the fleet finally lost sight of Hierro and course was set for some of the islands in the Indies which Columbus wished to visit en route to Hispaniola. He longed, above all else though, to visit the tiny colony he had left at Navidad.

At this stage we encounter a touch of the masterly navigation that Columbus displayed throughout his several voyages of discovery. First, let it be said that this voyage to the Indies was remarkable for its being so uneventful. This was due almost entirely to the late departure of the fleet. The Admiral had wanted to leave Cádiz in August, or at the worst early in September – certainly not mid-October. In fact it turned out to be a stroke of luck because it resulted in his missing the hurricane season which had by now blown itself out. One fleeting cyclonic incident exploded on the fleet one night and lasted about four hours. On the following morning it was unbelievable that there had been a barrage of storm and wind for 'the sun rose on a sea as smooth as polished marble'.

Otherwise, the twenty-one days of sailing a total of 820 leagues or 2,608 nautical miles on a course of 252 degrees (or west by south half south) at an average speed of 5.2 knots 'must have been very near to the mariner's dream of perfect sailing'.*

The Admiral was taking a more southerly route than on the first voyage and in so doing gained the full force of the trade winds. 'Any fleet of modern yachts,' Morison believed, 'would feel proud to cross that stretch of ocean today in twenty-one days . . . it was a downhill coast all the way from the Old World to the New, not one day of calm or head wind after dropping Tenerife.' Morison expressed it generously: 'Columbus had discovered the shortest and best route from Europe to the West Indies. Put it down to luck, seamanship or the finger of God . . . it was marvellous.'

At the early, faint signs of approaching dawn on Sunday 3 November a lookout aboard the *Mariagalante*, straining his eyes to pierce the lightening gloom, shouted 'Land!' The signs had been there for a couple of days, so Columbus was not surprised, but the excitement of the sighting brought everyone up top to get their first sight of the New World.

The Admiral summoned all hands to a short service where they sang the *Salve*, recited prayers and sang hymns, rendering devout thanks to Our Lord for safe delivery.

The mountainous island that emerged into the bright sunlight, rising loftily from the sea on the port bow, was named after the sabbath – Dominica. The island was deceptively beautiful, its lush green vegetation and beautiful mountain cloaked the fact that the natives were cannibals. For the next century the natives ate anyone they managed to capture. It was fortunate that

*Samuel Eliot Morison, p. 402–5.

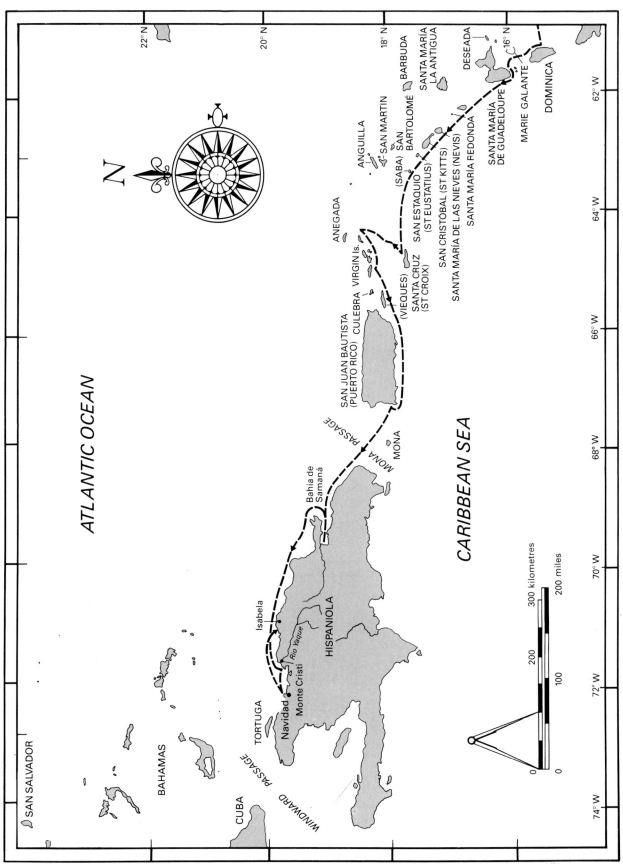

Columbus's Second Voyage. Part 1: Dominica to Hispaniola 1493.

the Spaniards could not locate a suitable landing spot. The story is told that the natives were made violently sick after eating a friar, which thereafter gave a good measure of protection for anyone wearing ecclesiastical clothes. Spaniards compelled to go ashore for any reason dressed as friars as a sensible precaution.

Soon another island came into view, a flat island, close enough on the starboard side for the Spaniards to see the thickly-wooded slopes. Columbus named it Santa Maria la Galante in honour of his flagship. He found a comfortable anchorage and landed there. With suitable solemnity and ceremony he took possession of the island in the name of the Catholic Sovereigns.

More islands came into view the next day and Columbus named one Santa Maria de Guadalupe in honour of the famous shrine of the Virgin of Estremadura, as he had promised.

Landing parties of Spaniards found grisly evidence of the indigenous natives, the cannibalistic Caribs. As if in a butcher shop, large cuts and joints of human bodies hung from huts. Captured natives were fattened like capons ready for the eating. Young women were made pregnant so babies would be produced for feasting: they were regarded as specially appetising. It was all a ghastly discovery and cautioned all Spaniards who ventured ashore to take every precaution against being taken captive.

The island of cannibals.

SOME OPINIONS OF CHRISTOPHER COLUMBUS, ADMIRAL OF THE OCEAN SEA

'Christopher Columbus's voyage to America ranks among history's most important events. It led to lasting contacts between Europe and America. It opened new windows to science and to all knowledge. To few men in modern history does the world as we know it owe so great a debt as to Christopher Columbus.'

Admiral Samuel Eliot Morison USN, 1978.

Columbus had achieved '. . . the greatest thing since the creation of the world'.

Lopez de Gamara, *History of the Indies*, 1544.

'Columbus left in his wake a vast reality that changed the world's understanding of itself, among Europeans and all civilised people.'

Gianni Granzotto, *Christopher Columbus*, 1968.

'The discovery of the New World has been the most disastrous event in the history of mankind.' (Referring to the evil practice of slavery, begun by Columbus. Tens of millions of people were subjected to its misery and pain.)

Cornelius de Pauw, 1768.

'To imagination, intelligence, daring and willpower, he brought constancy and spiritual strength. His deep, unswerving religious sentiment hardened his resolve and brought him serenity, even in the most troubled moments: he was ever aware of being an instrument of Divine Providence . . . and he was one of the giants of human history.'

Paolo Emilio Taviani, *Christopher Columbus*, 1985.

'Christopher Columbus was riding a mule homewards when the queen's messenger caught up with him. He was given everything he asked for — ships, honours, titles and percent of trade. No discoverer was ever promised so much before his performance. No discoverer's performance so greatly exceeded his promise . . .'

Admiral Samuel Eliot Morison USN, 1978.

'The voyage which Columbus tried to find sponsorship for was breathtaking in its daring and imagination.'

Robin Knox-Johnston CBE, RD, 1989.

'It is the object of the following work to relate the deeds and fortunes of the mariner who first had the judgement to define, and the intrepidity to brave the mysteries of this perilous deep; and who, by his hardy genius, his inflexible constancy, and his heroic courage, brought the ends of the earth into communication with each other.'

Washington Irving, *The Life and Voyages of Christopher Columbus*, 1885.

On 17 November, having named dozens more islands, Columbus took the fleet westward from the Leeward Islands into the maze of the Virgin Islands, seemingly infinite in their spell-binding variety and beauty. There are probably one hundred of them. Columbus logged forty-six before coming upon the southern coast of a large island which the Admiral named San Juan Bautista in deference to Genoa's veneration of the relics of St John the Baptist. Early in the next century another explorer, Ponce de León, present also on this voyage, was to found a city about a splendid harbour on the northern coast, naming it San Juan de Puerto Rico, and in time the island became known as Puerto Rico.

The fleet sailed north-westwards from Puerto Rico, as advised by the Arawak Indians on board, and after a run of about sixty-five miles made a landfall on Hispaniola's low-lying eastern promontory. The Admiral led the fleet along the northern waters of the island, hastening with some impatience and anxiety towards Navidad. He stopped momentarily at Las Flechas, where two of the original Indians taken captive to Spain were now put ashore, well clothed and bearing gifts.

At familiar Monte Cristi, a couple of dozen miles away from Navidad, the

The cluster of Virgin Islands today looking west from Tortola: they were discovered by Columbus in 1493.

Spaniards found grisly evidence of trouble ahead. A team of men sent ashore to fill water casks found two bodies lashed together and in an advanced state of decomposition. One appeared to bear the remnants of a thick beard which classified him as Spanish. Altogether, the bodies of what appeared to be four Spaniards were found in macabre circumstances. Alarm and anguish spread through the fleet, which hurriedly weighed anchor for Navidad.

In the early darkness of 27 November the fleet anchored off the little colony, lit flares and fired cannons to summon a response from ashore, but there was no sign of life. A chronicler described the Spanish crews: 'A sadness and profound grief seized their hearts.' It was to be several days before a clear picture of the great tragedy that had taken place began to form.

Soon after the Navidad party of colonists had been left by Columbus they began to quarrel among themselves, and two of the men — Rodrigo de Escobedo and Pedro Gutiérrez — joined forces and killed Jacombe the Genoese. They formed a gang and went in search of gold and women. Instead, they encountered the chief or cacique of the Maguana tribe, a man by the name of Caonabó, who put the whole gang to death, then set out to Navidad.

In the meantime the rest of the colonists had split into more gangs and themselves began roving the island in search of wealth and pleasure. Only ten men remained in the relative security of the fort under the command of Diego de Harana. They had with them numerous women.

The cacique and his men attacked these Spaniards in the darkness of night, killed three of the men and chased the others into the sea where they were all killed or drowned. Caonabó and his men also razed the little colony to the ground, burning and pillaging, leaving the site a wreck and leaving the bodies to rot.

Over a short period the remaining gangs of men were all eliminated by the natives, hunted like animals, receiving short shrift from the Indians whom they had wronged, as Columbus had expressly forbidden them.

Columbus's old friend, the young cacique Guacanagari, claimed that his tribesmen had fought alongside the Spaniards against the marauding Caribs. The Caribs were always a useful scapegoat for any wrongdoing. He claimed he himself had been wounded and invited Columbus to visit him in his village.

Columbus accepted, and made the visit one of great splendour. He mustered one hundred men dressed in all their flamboyant best, headed by musicians drumming a beat and wailing a tune from the pipes, as they marched on the overawed cacique. He was found in his hammock, a thigh roughly bandaged. On pretence of expert medical advice the Spanish physician Chanca unravelled the bandage to expose unwounded flesh. Chanca reported that the cacique was persistent: 'with fox-like shrewdness [he] pretended to feel very sick.'

But not sick enough to decline Columbus's invitation to supper aboard the flagship *Mariagalante* that night. Once on board he had the fright of his life when he saw his first horse.

The cacique probably never knew how close to death he came, for many of the Spaniards considered he should be put to death. Even the Benedictine friar, Father Buil, voted he should be executed as an example to the rest. Columbus displayed a greater depth of compassion than the priest and resisted the pressure. He realised with shock and disappointment that the colonisation of the New World was not going to be the smooth, easy-going business he had believed possible. The honeymoon was over. As one biographer put it: 'The happiness and magic of the meeting between the two worlds had ended at Navidad.'*

It must have been a forlorn and depressing time for the Admiral to have his dream shattered like this, but his achievements already in this second voyage read like a roll of honour. He had discovered twenty new large islands, far more than most explorers had discovered in a lifetime, plus another forty-odd smaller ones. He had commanded the transportation of an enormous fleet, carrying 1,200 men or more across an ocean with the loss of only one Spanish life. Yet it is true, Columbus had reached a watershed and problems were beginning to accumulate, and he now wore a different hat — that of a Governor General — an administrator rather than a navigator, which suited him better.

It had been expected that by the time Columbus returned to the tiny colony he had left behind after the first voyage it would have established itself, arrived at suitable trading arrangements with the Indians, discovered the gold mines, or at least the sources of gold, collected some barrels of the precious metal for shipping home and have carried out some exploratory work on selecting sites for development.

With the destruction of Navidad all of these hopes and expectations had evaporated, and the Admiral was left, instead, with a number of urgent and

*Gianni Granzotto, p. 208.

serious problems. The first priority was given to the search for barrels of gold: perhaps the original colonists had managed to collect such quantities and then, when besieged, had managed to find a hiding place, burying it or hiding it in a cave or burial site. Columbus ordered a determined search but nothing was revealed. Either there had been gold and it had been so well hidden as to prevent discovery, or the Indians had located it and carried it away triumphantly. One further option existed, and its implications worried Columbus enormously: perhaps the colonists had found no gold.

Columbus was clearly disturbed by this absence of gold. The Sovereigns had invested heavily in this large fleet and its train, and that investment demanded a return in gold, precious stones and jewels. Without these the investors and, in particular, the Sovereigns would have much to say to the Admiral. It was evident that the only way to keep them contented was to ship home to Spain large quantities of gold. At last the reality of it all was plain to see. Exploration, discovery, spreading the gospel or the word of Our Lord, bringing Christianity to the Indians: all of these most worthy objectives were as nothing compared with the need to locate gold – in abundance.

The next most urgent item for the Admiral's attention was the need to establish another base, a site suitable for immediate settlement of the many hundreds of men, the establishment of a secure, sustaining and profitable town. He promptly sailed the fleet to locate a new site, heading east, towards the area where the gold mines of Cibao were reputedly to be found.

No sooner had the fleet reached Monte Cristi than the easterly trade winds set in for weeks. Practically the whole of December was wasted in beating to windward, battling laboriously to make good thirty-odd miles in twenty-five days. Two days into the new year of 1494 the fleet anchored in the lee of a peninsula which on the face of it afforded the Admiral all the attributes he sought. He had little hesitation in selecting the site as the foundation of the city of Isabella – named after his queen.

It was an unfortunate choice. The late Admiral Morison visited Hispaniola and commented: 'Great discoverers and explorers seldom make successful colonists, and pioneer colonial expeditions almost never select a suitable site.'*

Isabella was the first of such major colonising sites and perhaps Columbus can be excused because there was no precedent to call upon. At first inspection, all looked well. The peninsula was wooded and it afforded protection to the anchorage from the trade winds. But the anchorage was open to the north and north-west from which direction came the occasional storm in winter. A ravine on one side gave natural protection against predators. A small plain seemed an ideal site for the building of a city, except there was no harbour and the nearest to shore a large ship could anchor was about half a mile. The Rio Bajabonico ('a crossbow shot wide') drained into the anchorage, but it was not navigable, and drinking water was only available about a mile away. Some of the land proved marshy, infertile and unhealthy.

The fleet was wearied by its exertions over the past few months. Columbus himself fell ill and for three months was unable to write up his daily log. The crews' morale was low, livestock were dying, men were sick. Pressures were being imposed on Columbus to select a site. He came to a firm decision, and on this less than desirable site rose the city of Isabella. Men by the hundred

*Samuel Eliot Morison, p. 430.

Columbus is shown
bartering for gold at
Hispaniola in this Jean
de Bry engraving.

and all the livestock were disembarked, cargoes were discharged, hutments and
fencing constructed, defence positions located, the ground tilled and sown with
seeds. Work commenced on building a brick church, public offices and a store.
Private houses were constructed in wood and thatched with grass.

Even as the town was taking shape, Columbus began seeking gold. With
their cargoes discharged, the ships were ready to take on new cargoes for
shipping home to Spain — especially gold.

Columbus's obsession with gold and his belief in its being close to the town-
site of Isabella is understandable even though he was utterly mistaken about it
all. He had been influenced greatly in his reading of Marco Polo, who referred
to Cipango where the sun glistened on the roofs of buildings coated with
burnished gold. It was Cipango and its gold that Columbus dreamed about.

When he discussed Hispaniola with the natives, they spoke of Cibao, a
region of the island, and of the gold to be found there in abundance — 'a
golden mountain'. Columbus believed this Cibao to be the same as Cipango,
and planned an expedition to get it by visiting the dangerous territory, ruled by
the murderous cacique Caonabó. To head this expedition Columbus chose
Alonso de Ojeda, a dashing, daredevil, cavalier character of aristocratic
background. Las Casas described him in graphic terms:

> He was slight of body but very well proportioned and comely,
> handsome in bearing, his face good-looking and his eyes very large,
> one of the swiftest of men . . . all the bodily perfections that a man
> could have seemed to have been united in him . . . He was very
> devoted to Our Lady. He was always the first to draw blood wherever
> there was a war or quarrel.

This was the man that Fonseca had chosen to command a caravel in the fleet. This was the man, too, who seemed to exhibit all the qualities that Columbus sought to lead the venture into the interior of Hispaniola. The second in command was Ginés de Gorbalán.

On 6 January 1494 the Feast of the Epiphany, the first mass celebrated on the soil of the New World, was held by Father Buil and was attended by everyone. Immediately after the mass Ojeda led the squad of men (variously reported as between fifteen and thirty) plus native guides towards Cibao.

It was a difficult journey, with days of strenuous climbing of mountains, and crossing of rivers and streams until the village of Janico was reached. The streams were seen to contain glistening traces of gold brought down from the central mountain range near Janico in the region which the natives called Cibao. The local natives were discovered to be friendly and they presented Ojeda with three great nuggets of gold as proof of the metal's existence in the mountains. Ojeda returned to Isabella and reported enthusiastically about the richness of the gold deposits he had found. Columbus was overjoyed. Cuneo wrote of the occasion: 'The Lord Admiral has written to the king that he hopes soon to be able to send him as much gold as the iron produced in the mines of Biscay.'

Columbus had intended sailing the unwanted portion of his fleet – probably twelve of the original seventeen ships – to Spain with examples of plants, fruit, gold and natives found in Hispaniola. Rain and a dreadful sickness intervened to spoil his plans. Half the population went down with the sickness, a combination of change of diet, climate, hard labour and mosquito bites. Columbus urgently needed supplies of food and provisions to enable the Spaniards to revert to the European diet which the physician Chanca considered essential to their future wellbeing.

On 2 February twelve ships weighed anchor and formed up into a convoy for the homeward voyage. Command had been given to Antonio de Torres, Columbus's second in command on the outward voyage. He took with him a letter from the Admiral to the king explaining the paucity of gold and asking that four or five of the ships should be replenished with urgently needed stores, especially medication, salt meat, wheat, wine, oil, vinegar, sugar and molasses. It seemed an unending shopping list. For the recuperation of the sick Columbus asked for almonds, raisins, honey and rice. He asked for shoes, clothing, mules and other animals, and a list of weaponry which included three hundred cuirasses, one hundred arquebuses and one hundred crossbows.

And finally, the Admiral asked for a squad of miners from Estremadura in the expectation they would open up mines in the Cibao region.

As if compiling a commander-in-chief's report of a campaign, Columbus then mentioned in his despatch for specific commendation the work of the physician Chanca, Margarit, Aguado, Coronel and others. He recommended a pay rise for them and he asked that two hundred gentlemen volunteers be put on the pay roll. It took months to exchange letters, but in due course the Sovereigns replied to Columbus in most generous terms. 'Rely upon it,' they wrote, 'that we consider ourselves well served and obliged by you, so that we shall confer upon you favours, honours and advancement as your great services require and deserve.'

When Columbus had recovered from his sickness he initiated a processional expedition to the so-called gold-bearing region of Cibao, complete with pageantry, banners, standards, cavalrymen, weapon-carrying soldiers and flamboyantly dressed gentlemen volunteers. All of it seemed incongruous in the near-tropical heat of the interior of Hispaniola.

It was a show of strength, a sabre-rattling display of colonisation as well as a practical enterprise in the establishment of a mining camp and a fortress. Ferdinand Columbus described the processional progress:*

> Having crossed the river that lies a musket shot from Isabella, the Admiral forded a smaller river one league further on and marched three leagues more to camp that night on a beautiful plain. This plain extends to the foot of a rugged mountain pass about two crossbow shots high ... Coming out of that pass, they descended to a great plain ... sleeping that night near a large river which they crossed in canoes and rafts.

The historian Las Casas was more lyrical in his description of the large fertile valley into which the cavalcade debauched:

> ... one of the most admirable things in the world ... of such perfection, grace and beauty, so fresh, so green, so open, of such colour and altogether so full of beauty, that as soon as they saw it they felt they had arrived in some part of Paradise ... and the Admiral, who was profoundly moved by all these things, gave great thanks to God and named it Vega Real [the Royal Plain].

The cavalcade proceeded across more breathtaking scenery, forded a river, then carried on south till the Admiral called a halt at Janico.

Near here work began on the building of a combined mining camp and fortress – called San Tomás. The Admiral watched things get under way, then left Mosén Pedro Margarit in charge of fifty or more men to finish construction.

The return trek to Isabella was more gruelling, with bad weather, bad food, bad drink and sickness among the men. Things were little better in Isabella. Flooding had occurred when the river overflowed its banks; it is true the crops were coming on well, but other Spanish foodstuffs were just about exhausted: the men simply had not learned how to stomach the local food of fish, maize, yams and cassava.

A call for help from Margarit impelled Columbus to despatch a powerful force of four hundred or more men under Ojeda's command to defend the new encampment at San Tomás and establish some sort of colonial rule. Such a foray would have the additional advantage of exercising the minds and bodies of the four hundred men.

One injudicious act by Ojeda, however, led to what Las Casas described as 'the beginning of the shedding of blood which has since flowed so copiously in this island ...'.

Ojeda cut off the ears of one of the cacique's men who had been caught stealing some Spanish clothing, and chained the chief, his brother and nephew together and sent them under guard to Isabella.

*Ferdinand Columbus, p. 131.

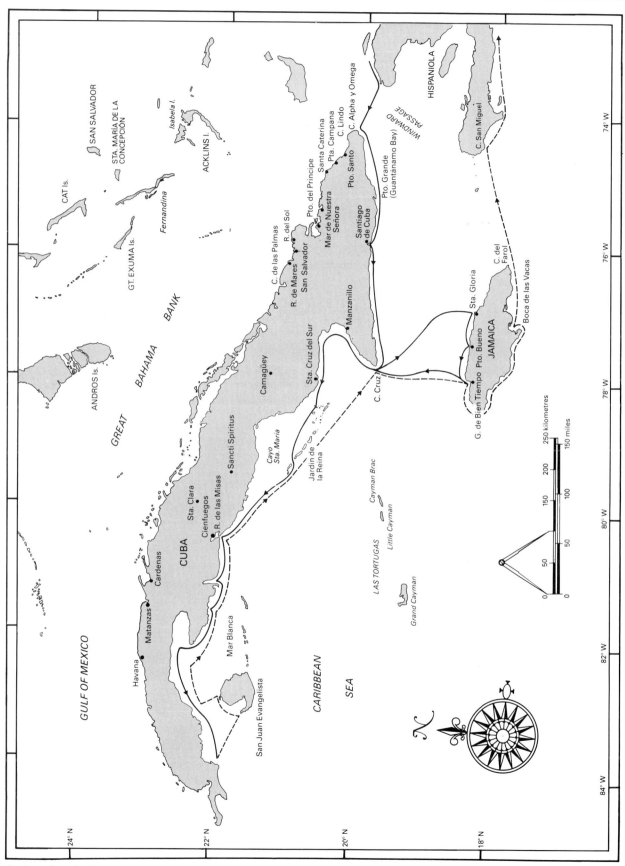

Columbus's Second Voyage. Part 2: Hispaniola to Cuba and Jamaica 1493.

Columbus adjudicated on the matter and decreed execution by beheading on the cacique and his two relatives. It was only on the tearful entreaties of a friendly cacique that Columbus tempered the sentence with mercy. But the damage had been done. Relations between the Indians and the Spaniards, between the Admiral and the caciques, would never again have the trust that had been enjoyed before.

Columbus was now convinced, partly from exchanges with the Indians and partly from his own deliberations, that Hispaniola was not the mainland he had believed it to be; he accepted it was an island and, furthermore, he now accepted that Cibao was not Cipango. Having altered his views like this, it behove him to venture off to sea again to try to discover the mainland of Asia. To this end he designated his brother, Diego Columbus, president in his absence, with four others as governors of the island: Father Buil, Captain Coronel, Alonso Sanchez de Carvajal and Juan de Luxán.

The three caravels *Niña*, *San Juan* and *Cardera* were made ready and left on 24 April, and one senses that Columbus was glad to be back at sea, away from all the bickerings and problems of administering Hispaniola. He was, in fact, setting out on a five-month voyage of discovery and exploration of Cuba and Jamaica of outstanding navigational merit, even judged by his demanding standards.

MASTER OF THE CARIBBEAN

THE PERIOD from the end of April to the end of September 1493 was an example of the brilliant navigation of Columbus in the course of which he explored the southern coast of Cuba and discovered the island of Jamaica. Little information exists about his small squadron of three Portuguese-style lateeners, ideal vessels for this sort of coastal exploration, but what is known amounts to this: the three ships were the *Niña*, *San Juan* and *Cardera*.

Another five men were known to be aboard but are not allocated. Thus the grand total of men involved was 59.

Niña	*San Juan*
Flagship: 60 tons	40 tons
Columbus, Admiral	Alonso Perez Roldán, Master
Francisco Niño, Pilot	Pilot
Alonso Medel, Master	Boatswain
Juan de la Cosa, AB	6 ABs
Pedro de Torreros, Bo'sun	1 Cooper
Diego Tristán, Gentleman	5 Gromets
Volunteer, Gentleman	15 Total
16 ABs and Gromets	
Servant	*Cardera*
Public Notary	40 tons
25 Total	Cristobal Perez, Master
	Fernerin, Boatswain
	7 ABs
	5 Gromets
	14 Total

16 Cuba and the Discovery of Jamaica: Abandonment of Isabella

L EAVING Isabella, the tiny fleet coasted westwards to the Windward
Passage, across which Columbus could vaguely discern Cuba's eastern
extremity about forty-five miles to the west-north-west. On reaching this point
of Cuba he then had to decide whether to explore the northern coast or the
southern one. During the first voyage of discovery he had followed about
150 miles of the northern coast, so it was more enticing and sensible to break
new ground by selecting the southern route.

Columbus soon came upon a harbour which Las Casas described as 'in the
form of a sickle, shut in on both sides by promontories that break the waves;
and it is large and of great depth'. Today, this site is the great US naval base of
Guantanamo Bay, but was named by Columbus Puerto Grande.

The ships entered the harbour and boatloads of men sent ashore helped
themselves to refreshing meals of cooked fish, which natives had abandoned on
the foreshore when they saw the boats approaching. These natives were enticed
back to their fires and hawks' bells and trinkets were exchanged for more fresh
fish.

The next anchorage of any significance was Santiago de Cuba, just forty
miles further west along the southern coast. It first appeared from seaward as a
cleft nearly two hundred yards wide in the steep, rocky cliff face, which then
opened out into an expansive bay. It had little to offer the squadron. No gold,
only fish to eat or to exchange. However, the Indians did mention the
existence of an island to the south which was the source of large supplies of
gold — an island by the name of Yameque or Jameque.

When Columbus reached the end of this leg of the southern coast of Cuba
he named the cape Cabo de Cruz. With almost indecent haste he abandoned
the idea of coasting round the cape to the north-east and instead altered course
to dash southerly to locate Yameque: the lure of gold was powerful.

The Admiral's departure from Cabo de Cruz, resulting in the discovery of
Jamaica, was a small gem of his mastery in navigation and sense of the sea. He
knew only the general direction and the very rough distance of Jamaica. In fact
it was ninety-five miles, and it took forty-eight hours sailing to reach after
experiencing foul weather when the caravels were struck by a north-east trade
wind and ran before it, then hove-to so as not to be swept to leeward of
Jamaica. Most of the time the ships were under bare poles.

When the weather moderated a landfall was made dead centrally on the
north coast of the island.

The Admiral was enchanted with what he saw. Bernáldez described it as 'the
fairest island that eyes have beheld'. Soon the bay where the landfall had been
made was filled with sixty or seventy canoes carrying hundreds of aggressive-

Montego Bay. When Columbus discovered Jamaica in 1493 he named this bay Fair Weather Gulf.

looking, warlike people staring in wonderment at those three enormous ships manned by foreigners whom they could only believe came from heaven. The firing of a few lombard shots (simply to create frightening noises to clear the way) had an immediate effect and the canoes scattered.

From this landfall of Santa Gloria, Columbus headed west and put in to a harbour he named Puerto Bueno, where more warlike natives demonstrated against the Spaniards. Men in feathered headdresses with bodies covered in palm leaves hurled stones and spears at the caravels. The Spaniards responded with crossbows, killing some natives, and they set a big dog — probably a mastiff — on them, which 'bit them and did them great hurt for a dog is worth ten men against Indians'. It is one of the first instances of the barbaric use of a dog of war.

Despite these drawbacks, trading was established and Columbus noted how much more industrious were these Indians. They fashioned and decorated canoes, a particularly large one measuring ninety-eight by eight feet having been hollowed out from one massive tree.

Perhaps it was the evident lack of a gold source on the island that decided Columbus to curtail the visit to Jamaica. After naming today's Montego Bay El Golfo de Bien Tiempo (Good Weather Gulf) he persuaded an Indian to desert his crying wife and children to join the ship. Course was set for Cuba again: to Cabo de Cruz.

Columbus now embarked upon a two month voyage of discovery along the southern coast of Cuba. According to Bernáldez's report, at sunrise on 15 May the Spanish sailors:

> . . . saw the sea full of islands in all four quarters, and all green and full of trees, the fairest that eyes beheld; the Admiral wished to pass to the southward and leave these islands to starboard but remembering that he had read [about the Orient] that all that sea is full of islands, he decided to go forward and to follow and not lose sight of the terra firma of Juana (Cuba) and to see for certain whether it was an island or not. And the further he went the more islands they discovered, and on one day he caused to be noted 164 islands.

Columbus named this long chain of islands El Jardin de la Reina (The Queen's Garden). He must have come close to running out of names for every discovery he made, and settled for a collective name in this instance.

Navigating through these islands must have been nightmarish, especially as each sudden rain squall threatened the squadron with dangers of running aground in shoal waters, as indeed *Niña* did on one occasion, though she was floated clear some hours later.

The voyage along Cuba's southern coast is regarded as one of Columbus's finest feats of exploration and navigation. He handled his three caravels in a masterly fashion despite all the navigational hazards such as the myriad islands, shoals, mud banks, mangrove swamps, cays and shallows where kedging became a regular means of progressing the ships.

The scenery lacked the beauty of other regions, though lightened occasionally by butterflies, turtles and red flamingos. But of gold, there was none. The natives — more friendly than the Jamaicans — wore no golden ornaments and there was no evidence of the precious metal's existence on the island.

Of course, Columbus was still vacillating between its being a peninsula of the mainland or an island. With all these hundreds of islands surrounding the area, surely to goodness this must be the Malay Archipelago: soon he was convinced that Cuba was the Chinese province of Mangi. He was still absolutely wrong in his deductions and beliefs, and yet he was so close (just how close he never knew) to discoveries which had he persevered for a brief while longer would have revised all his evaluations. As it is, he stubbornly accepted that Cuba was the eastern extremity of Asia. At this point he perpetrated one of those curious legalistic charades of the day: he sought written confirmation from his officers, gentlemen volunteers and serving seamen that they believed Cuba to be a continent and not an island. His secretary and lawyer visited all three vessels and solemnly recorded each man's statement and they understood that their deposition would be a life-long declaration, without let of changing on threat of a huge fine and having their tongues cut out.

On 22 June 1494, having completed the depositions, the men knuckled-to and prepared the ships to turn about and make their return voyage. Columbus had finally called it a day. The caravels were in a sorry state, in urgent need of refits, all leaking; seams had opened during groundings, the ships' fabric needed repair or renewal, and more importantly the men were sick to death of the whole business. They were specially apprehensive that each league sailed west made it less likely they would return home safely.

The irony is that Columbus made this decision to return when he was probably fifty miles from the south-westernmost promontory of Cuba. To have reached that point would most likely have convinced the Admiral that Cuba was an island, not mainland, not an archipelago, not Asia . . . Had he dared risk those extra few miles and made that discovery, then other speculations intrude. At that stage it would have taken only a little more than a hundred miles of beating to the WSW for the Spaniards to have reached the Yucatán peninsula of Mexico: and it is mind-boggling to wonder what the Admiral's fate might have been thereafter.

Alternatively — and this would have been more likely — had Columbus rounded the western promontory, the three caravels would undoubtedly have been swept by the Gulf Stream to the Florida Keys and a new chapter in exploration and discovery would have opened.

The voyage back to Hispaniola was a trial. The ships' crews were getting close to the end of their tether. They had signed that incredible declaration and longed to make the return to Isabella. Columbus prolonged the agony by taking a roundabout route, wandering from island to island. He threaded the ships through the labyrinth of islands off the south coast of Cuba, skirted south of the Queen's Garden and reached Cabo de Cruz on 18 July.

From this cape the course to Isabella lay due east, but the winds were contrary and Columbus stood off towards the south to Jamaica. He reached Montego Bay with customary navigational accuracy, then embarked on a curious anti-clockwise south-about coasting of the island. It was a laboured haul which took close on a month to complete, and further weakened the crew.

The open sea passage to the south-western cape of Hispaniola was made easily enough, although Columbus believed the landfall to be on another island, until three days later some natives ashore hailed the ships with shouts of 'Almirante! Almirante!'

By then Columbus was a sick man. When the fleet rounded the south-western cape of Hispaniola, the Admiral collapsed. Las Casas describes the incident with typical colour: 'The Admiral fell into a pestilential sleep that robbed him of all his faculties and strength, so that he seemed as though dead. Everyone thought that he would not live another day.'*

Various symptoms and names have been attributed to the Admiral's state of health. Granzotto described it as 'a form of gout or podagra, aggravated by widespread rheumatic affections, and an overall change in his metabolism'. Morison refers to 'a high fever accompanied by alternate coma and delirium', and suggested a modern nervous breakdown brought on by '. . . extreme exertions, lack of sleep and bad nourishment'.† According to Las Casas, Columbus suffered from arthritis.

Finally, Ferdinand Columbus stated: 'he had a high fever and drowsiness, so that he lost his sight, memory and all his other senses.'‡ Ferdinand also says that it took five months for his health to be restored.

---

*Quoted by Gianni Granzotto, p.219.
†Morison, p.479.
‡Ferdinand Columbus, p.149.

BARTHOLOMEW COLUMBUS (c.1461–c.1515)

BARTHOLOMEW was the third son of Domenico and the younger brother of Christopher Columbus. He lived in Genoa and Savona in Italy, and in Portugal. He was an explorer, coloniser, administrator and cosmographer, having been credited with thirteen geographical and four astronomical charts. He travelled to Guinea, and may have accompanied Dias to the Cape of Good Hope. He was imprisoned by pirates for some time. Christopher sent him to London in 1488 to solicit Henry VII's support for a voyage of discovery. Failing there, he visited France in 1490 and found Charles VIII even less interested.

Bartholomew returned to Spain after Christopher's first voyage and introduced his young nephews Diego and Ferdinand to Queen Isabella as pages for the Prince Don Juan. The queen gave him command of a squadron of ships bound for Hispaniola.

He was appointed Adelantado or provincial governor of the colony by Columbus, who as Viceroy assumed a royal prerogative which simply was not his to assume. The Sovereigns declined to ratify the appointment and it took another two years before they relented and commissioned Bartholomew Adelantado of the Indies. Las Casas leaves us with this description of him:

> A person of very good disposition, tall of stature, although not so tall as the Admiral, good in action, though somewhat severe, of good strength . . . unfortunately in [matters] of severity and cruelty later attributed to the Admiral, the Adelantado was the cause . . .

Crown agent Francisco de Bobadilla imprisoned Bartholomew with Christopher for maladministration, and the brothers returned to Spain in shackles. The Sovereigns released them. Bartholomew sailed with Christopher on the fourth voyage of discovery between 1502 and 1504, and again with his nephew Diego in 1509.

He died at the end of 1514 or the beginning of 1515 and was buried appropriately in the church of San Francisco in Santo Domingo, the city he founded in Hispaniola.

The ships made haste to Isabella, where the first man to board the *Niña* was Bartholomew, Columbus's brother. It was 29 September 1494 and they had not seen each other for five or six years. Bartholomew's journeyings during this lapse of time are a little obscure. We know he was occupied in visiting the courts of the kings of England and France seeking backing for Christopher's enterprise, though no trace of his visits has been found except a report from his nephew, Ferdinand, who says his uncle gave Henry VII of England a world map, and another reference by Oviedo, the historian. He recorded that the Tudor king's counsellors were dismissive of the enterprise. Charles VIII's counsellors seem to have been no more interested than Henry's. However, Bartholomew found a patroness in Anne de Beaujeu, the French king's sister and regent during his minority: he lingered in Fontainebleau for a year or more but it all came to naught and he returned to Spain.

By then, his brother had reached the New World and he made efforts to follow him. The Sovereigns gave him command of three ships to relieve Hispaniola.

He was distressed to find his brother looking worn out and grey. Columbus was laid so low and remained bed-ridden for so many weeks that he appointed his brother El Adelantado (the Leader or Governor) of Hispaniola but this did little to solve the colony's problems. When Columbus had recuperated from the illness it was to find the island still in a mess. This was largely attributable to Mosén Pedro Margarit and his small army, which ranged the Vega Real committing gross acts of atrocity and criminality. The army comprised some 250 hidalgos and crossbowmen, 110 musketeers and 16 troopers.

To feed this army trinkets were bartered for food, and when the trinkets ran out the Spaniards simply confiscated whatever they wanted. The Indians reacted predictably and fighting developed all over the region. Margarit retaliated with increased brutality. It had always been clearly understood that Indians caught stealing would have noses and ears cropped. Now, the innocent suffered too. Gold was extorted from them, wives and daughters were raped and young boys abducted to work as slaves.

This was not so at the fort of San Tomás, where Ojeda managed to maintain discipline among his men and an acceptable form of conduct with the Indians.

Christopher's brother, Diego, wrote to Margarit warning him to obey the Admiral's orders. Margarit reacted by marching on Isabella, seizing the three caravels which Bartholomew had brought from Spain and sailing them home to Spain. A fellow mutineer was Father Buil, who had adopted a hard-line attitude with the Indians and had failed lamentably to convert any to Christianity. When he arrived home he began berating Columbus and his brother Bartholomew, circulating slanderous stories about them, denying the existence of gold, and relating the dreadful conditions in Hispaniola.

These latter were plain for all to see. Anarchy was rife. Armed bands of soldiery roamed the island like brigands. In the course of many skirmishes that developed, natives sought retribution in killing Spaniards. Columbus reacted by sending a punitive expedition to hunt natives with horses and dogs. No fewer than fifteen hundred Indians were captured and taken to Isabella. They were the subject of a barbarous transaction devised and executed by a heartless Columbus. About five hundred of them — the best specimens of men and women — were crammed into four caravels and transported to Seville for sale in the slave market. The remainder — a thousand luckless souls — were given away free to any colonist who wanted them, as many as they liked, to do with them as they wished. Four hundred of these managed to flee to some form of safety.

Three chiefs or caciques, including the warlike Guatiguana, were bound together in readiness for execution by arrows, but they managed to gnaw through their bonds and escaped.

Of those natives transported in the four caravels, two hundred died and were cast overboard like jetsam. Half of those who survived were sick when put ashore. Fonseca put them up for sale and Bernáldez witnessed the sale and remarked on their unashamed nakedness and short expectation of life. It was a squalid and discreditable episode in an otherwise glorious period of discovery.

Meanwhile, back in Hispaniola, a battle was fought in the Vega Real on 27 March 1495 in which a force of Indians led by the escaper Guatiguana was routed by two hundred Spaniards, twenty horses and as many hounds.

Skirmishes and squabbles continued almost without respite until the Indians of Hispaniola were ultimately subdued by force. Columbus ruled despotically and with little seeming Christian compassion. He demonstrated his lust for gold by the adoption of a cruel system of taxation. Everyone over the age of fourteen had to deliver to the Spaniards, each quarter, a hawk's bell full of gold dust. Caciques were required to supply more. People from non gold-bearing areas had to produce instead one arroba (about 25 lb) of spun or woven cotton. On delivery of the tribute, the donor was given a copper or bronze token to hang about the neck as evidence of having contributed.

Columbus introduced an iniquitous tax on the Indians of Hispaniola. Chiefs are depicted here giving their quarterly tributes of gold to the Spaniards.

This tribute proved an impossible burden for the Indians to bear. What gold they had possessed in some quantity had represented generations of collecting. The tribute required daily working in the streams in order to collect the quarterly norm. Those who were unable to meet the tax fled to the hills and were persistently hunted. Starvation took its toll, and thus began the depopulation of Hispaniola. Within two years the original figure of 300,000 or thereabouts on the island when Columbus arrived had been slashed by a third. By 1508 only 60,000 were reckoned to be alive, and forty years later perhaps a mere five hundred indigenous Indians survived.

Columbus began to make preparations to leave for Spain, but a storm struck with the force of a hurricane and his caravel took a battering. *Niña* survived all right, but the *San Juan*, *Cardera* and *Gallega* became total losses. Their remains were cannibalised by shipwrights and carpenters into one vessel like the *Niña* and she was given the name *Santa Cruz*, although the seamen soon adopted the nickname *India* for her, in acknowledgement that she was the first vessel to be constructed in the Indies.

In October 1495 a squadron of four caravels with relief supplies arrived in Hispaniola under the command of Juan Aguado, who had the express instruction to carry out an audit check on the administration of the colony. It was a sorry tale that he unearthed.

Before Columbus completed his preparations for returning to Spain, he took the decision to abandon Isabella, and to construct a new city on a new site on the south coast of the island. Columbus and his brother Bartholomew selected a site and Bartholomew, as adelantado, was charged with the duty of building the new city, to be called Santo Domingo. Construction began in 1496 or 1497. Isabella, deserted, fell into ruin and the flora of the region has reclaimed the land over the years until today there is barely a sign by which the site can be recognised.

Two ships comprised the squadron which returned Columbus to Spain. He sailed on 10 March 1496 aboard the *Niña* in company with the *Santa Cruz* (called *India*). The flagship was commanded by Alonso Medel and the *India* by Bartolomé Colín. All told, the ships were crammed to the gunwales with 255 men, including thirty natives. One of the natives was the belligerent cacique Caonabó — 'the greatest and most famous Indian' — who failed to survive the voyage. It is inconceivable that so many men could ship aboard the caravels and still allow the crew space to run the ships. What no one realised, too, was that it was to be an abnormally long voyage: it was to be almost exactly three months before they reached home.

By 20 May food stocks had been so reduced that each man was rationed to six ounces of bread a day and a pint-and-a-half of water. Some people made two suggestions in the face of dwindling rations: throw the natives overboard to conserve rations, or, *in extremis*, eat the natives. Columbus, to his relative credit, forbade that they be molested in any way.

Then came a demonstration yet again of Columbus's brilliance in navigation. There were eight or ten pilots aboard the two ships, each attempting to calculate his own dead reckoning. Each had his own idea as to where they were. On Tuesday 7 June all the pilots thought they were still several days

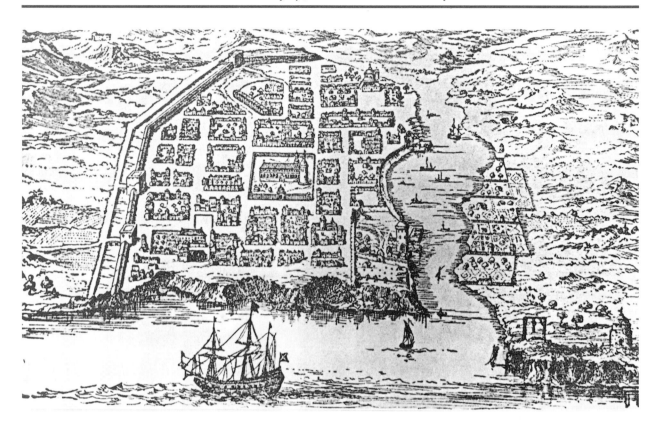

sailing from land, but that night Columbus ordered sails to be taken in for fear of striking land, cautioning everyone that they were near Cape St Vincent. Ferdinand Columbus continues with the anecdote:*

> . . . all the pilots laughed, some declaring they were in the Flemish Channel and others that they were near England. Those who were least mistaken said they were off Galicia and therefore should not take in sails, for it was better to die by running on the rocky coast than to perish miserably from hunger at sea . . .

The next day they made a landfall at Odmira, about thirty-five miles north of Cape St Vincent, Columbus's objective. It was a truly incredible exhibition of ocean navigation, even allowing that he may have got a fix in the Azores — which is unlikely.

The pathetic, care-worn little squadron put a brave face on things and dressed ships with all manner of bunting and flags as they entered the harbour of white-walled Cádiz. The date was 11 June 1496. It had been a long, long second voyage.

Santo Domingo became Columbus's base for operations in the Carribean. It was the first city in the Americas, founded by Bartholomew Columbus and his brother. It claims the first cathedral, hospital, convent and university in America, all of them founded in the early 16th century. The island of Hispaniola today is shared between Haiti and the Dominican Republic.

*Ferdinand Columbus, p. 177.

17 The Third Voyage 1498-1500: Columbus Returns in Chains

T HE TWO years that Columbus spent before embarking on his third fateful voyage in May 1498 marked the beginning of the long downfall of the great Admiral, who by then was entering a period of depression and mental instability leading increasingly to eccentricity.

Yet the third voyage was brilliantly executed. A new continent was discovered and landed upon by Europeans for the first time. This discovery alone opened up measureless areas of new lands and peoples, peoples to convert to Christianity in general and to the Catholic faith in particular. The Admiral achieved all this without the loss of one life, or of a ship, and even without the firing of gun shots. And on top of all this, on a purely commercial basis, he threw in for good measure the discovery of a flourishing pearl fishery. Rarely in history can one man have achieved so much in terms of exploration. And here he was doing it for the third voyage running.

Incredibly though, Columbus ended the third voyage chained like a criminal, prisoner of the state, arrested by a judge sent by King Ferdinand to investigate charges of maladministration and shipped to Spain, fettered to his brother as if they were a couple of petty thieves.

The events leading up to this ignominious return to Spain started with his homecoming at the end of the second voyage. One of the first acts he performed on coming ashore in Cádiz was to adopt the coarse brown habit of a Franciscan friar, perhaps an eccentric way of demonstrating to friends and opponents the humility of the Admiral of the Ocean Sea. Furthermore, he sought the company of ecclesiastics. He took up residence in a humble room at the Seville house of the curate and historian Andrés Bernáldez, who was also chaplain to the archbishop.

It was to Bernáldez that Columbus entrusted his log book and other documents relating to the completed second voyage.

Columbus made the long journey to Burgos, where the court was due on one of its peripatetic visits, and greeted his two sons who were pages to the Prince Don Juan. The Sovereigns received the Admiral with their customary courtesy and kindness and Columbus showed them some of his plunder, the Indians wearing ornaments of gold being a special attraction. Some of them had been baptised as Christians at Guadalupe on the way to the court. Even more attractive was the quantity of gold dust and nuggets which had been extracted as tributes from the Indians of Hispaniola.

While still enjoying much support at court, Columbus also aroused resentment and opposition. It was argued by many that his achievements failed to match his — and their — expectations. Reports from Hispaniola, including Juan Aguado's, told of deep unrest, of fighting, mutiny and maladministration.

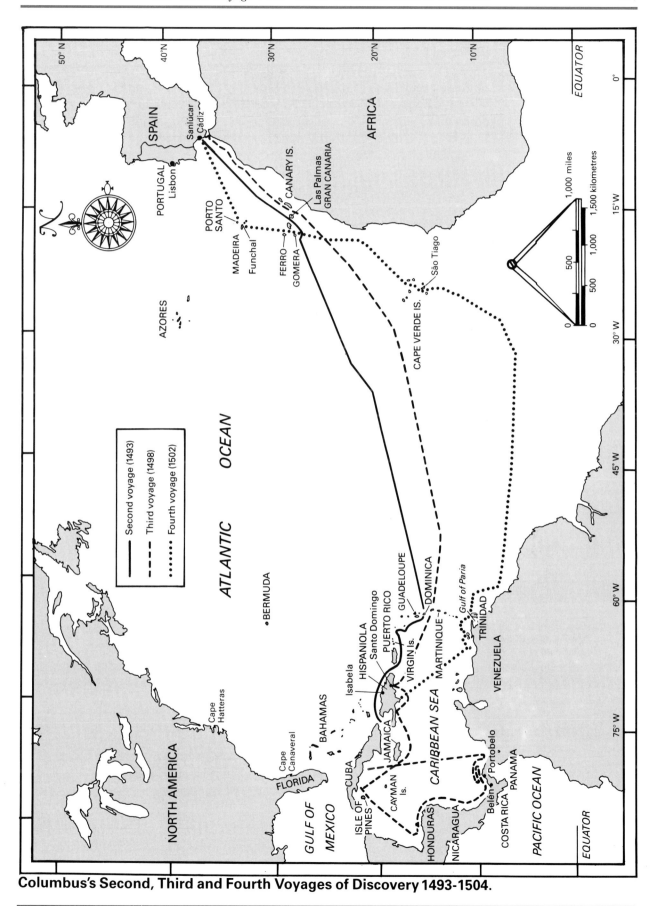

Columbus's Second, Third and Fourth Voyages of Discovery 1493-1504.

Further, many people were increasingly upset by the signs of the Admiral's eccentricity.

Columbus presented his case for a third voyage. He planned to sail further south and south-east of his Indies discoveries to discover a mainland which he knew the king of Portugal believed to exist. The Sovereigns had many pressing duties and problems which engaged their attention and while seeming to give support to the idea of a third voyage they procrastinated.

The first of a series of instructions from the Sovereigns came in April 1497, but altogether it was to be another year before the third voyage got under way, in the last week of May 1498. By then a lot of loose ends had been carefully tied up. The Admiral was confirmed in his original titles and honours, and his brother Bartholomew was formally given royal confirmation of his position as adelantado of Hispaniola. Columbus had been given a seemingly endless stream of instructions about the engagement of priests to convert the Indians; about cows and mares; about gold diggings, logwood and precious metals; about ships and their masters. The ships could be chartered by the Admiral at regular rates; and criminals could be pardoned and enrolled as crewmen and colonists — except those who had been convicted of heresy, lèse-majesté, murder, treason, counterfeiting, arson or sodomy.*

Six vessels comprised the fleet for the third voyage. Three of the ships were to be sent direct to Hispaniola with the majority of the fresh provisions and the colonists: though these ships have never been named, their captains were:

Alonso Sanchez de Carvajal, mayor of Baeza and a captain in the second voyage.
Pedro de Harana, brother of Columbus's mistress.
Giovanni Antonio Colombo, from Genoa, son of Columbus's uncle Antonio.

*Samuel Eliot Morison, p. 510.

THE FIRST WOMEN COLONISTS

THE controversial third voyage of discovery was sanctioned by King Ferdinand and Queen Isabella in a series of edicts, the first of which gave precise instructions about the composition of the people to be given passage. It is dated April 1497.

As regards Hispaniola, Columbus was to convey another three hundred men to the colony at the crown's expense. This number was to be made up as follows:

40 Squires
30 Mariners   30 maravedis per day
20 Artisans
30 Gromets
20 Gold diggers   20 maravedis per day
100 Soldiers/Labourers

50 Farmers
10 Gardeners   6,000 maravedis a year
A special allowance of twelve maravedis a day was due to all categories.

In addition, Columbus was to furnish up to another fifty men prepared to join the enterprise at their own expense.

Finally, thirty women (a ratio of one to ten) should accompany the expedition and work their passage for no pay nor special allowances.

If any women actually sailed — and there is no evidence that they did — they were the first women colonists.

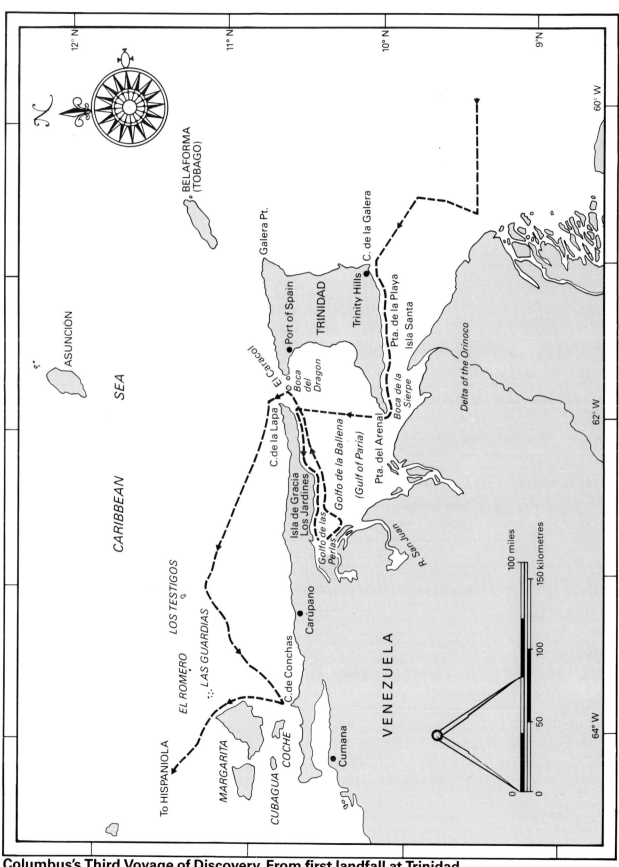

Columbus's Third Voyage of Discovery. From first landfall at Trinidad to the island of Margarita 1498.

Three remaining vessels formed the discovery squadron:

A small caravel, *El Correro* (The Mail).
A seventy-ton caravel, *La Vaquenos*.
The flagship, name unknown, about one hundred tons.

The three captains of these ships were Columbus himself, Pedro de Terreros (Columbus's steward on the first voyage) and Hernán Pérez.

The Admiral boarded his flagship at the bar of Sanlúcar de Barrameda on 30 May 1498 in the Guadalquivir river. Course was set for Madeira, where all six ships anchored in the Funchal roads and replenished stocks of wood and water.

It was here that Columbus had set up home during his early married life. He was well known and the Madeirans gave him a splendid reception.

The ships caught a lively wind to the south for the three hundred miles to the Canaries and anchored in the roadstead of San Sebastian on the island of Gomera, home of his lady friend Doña Beatrice de Peraza y Bobadilla. Columbus's log entry on this occasion, however, makes no mention of her, only to the quality of cheeses taken aboard.

The three supply ships parted company for Hispaniola while Columbus headed SSW for the Cape Verde Islands, a run of about 750 miles which took six days. The islands were new to him, and he found them quite objectionable because of the leper colony, the intense tropical heat and the suffocating dust haze.

On 4 July 1498 the Admiral was relieved to put to sea again. His plan was to sail south-west until on the latitude of Cape St Ann in Guinea − about 10 degrees N − then due west to the meridian of Hispaniola, and then, if no landfall had been made, to head south. And finally, back to Hispaniola. It was planned to be yet another great venture of enterprise and discovery, typical of the man, but it nearly foundered in the first eight days in the doldrums, in what Morison referred to as 'about the hottest and calmest spot on the entire ocean at that season'.*

The heat was so intense that casks of water and wine burst, snapping the hoops of iron, and the stocks of salt meat roasted and rotted. Suddenly a wind arose from the east-south-east and the mood changed from dispirited languor to unexpected activity as sails were filled and the ships gathered way. The air was cleansed, the heat moderated, the spirits heightened.

Success is often accompanied by a little luck: this was one of those occasions for Columbus, although it must not be allowed to detract from his superb display of navigation. Nine days after the doldrums, at midday on Tuesday, the last day of July, 1498, Columbus's servant, Alonso Pérez, climbed to the crow's nest. Las Casas records in his abstract the Admiral's own words:†

... and saw land to the westward distant fifteen leagues, and it appeared to be in the form of three rocks or mountains.

Las Casas continues in the third person:

[the Admiral] named this island La Ysla de la Trinidad because he had determined that the first land he shall discover should be so named ... he gave infinite thanks to God ... and all the people

*Samuel Eliot Morison, p. 523.
†Quoted by Morison, p. 528.

This modern scene of a Trinidad beach would have been familiar to Columbus when he discovered the island in the summer of 1498.

glorified the Divine bounty and with great joy and merriment they repeated, singing the *Salve Regina*, with other devout canticles and prayers which glorify God and Our Lady.

Columbus's intention to give the name Trinidad to the first land sighted seemed to everyone a miracle when three mountains came into view. But the piece of luck which Columbus attracted was Pérez climbing the mast at that very moment and managing to sight the island at a distance of forty-five miles: the squadron might well have sailed into empty waters.

After making his landfall Columbus sailed another fifteen miles along the coast to find a watering place. A landing was made at today's Erin Point or Punta de la Playa, the best watering place on the southern coast of Trinidad. The men stripped off and bathed and splashed in the fresh streams, washing off the salt of four weeks at sea, gulping sparkling clear water instead of the dank warm liquid available on board.

Just before rounding Erin Point, as the squadron coasted westwards searching for an anchorage, Columbus detected land dimly to the south. He named it Ysla Sancta — Holy Island. Heaven knows, he was entitled to think it was an island, having discovered hundreds of them in the past several years. But he was wrong on two counts. It was not an island he was gazing at, but the mainland of a new continent, today's Punta Bombeador, Venezuela. It was Wednesday 1 August 1498, and Columbus was probably the first European ever to set eyes on the South American mainland — but he did not know it!

The second error he made was of little consequence; he made an over-estimation of the distance to this headland he could see dimly in the Orinoco delta. He reckoned the distance to be twenty to twenty-five leagues. It was, in fact, just ten miles.

Columbus did have some reservations about it, some suspicions that it might be more than a mere island. Some days later he was still pondering on it. Las Casas records on 14 August in his abstracted log:

> I believe this land may be a great continent that has remained unknown to this day. Reason bears this out, in light of the immense river and the sea of fresh water formed at its mouth.

The immense river he referred to was the mighty Orinoco, and the rivers Grande and San Juan, and the sea of fresh water was, in fact, the enormous Gulf of Paria; Trinidad forms its eastern and south-eastern coastline. Columbus named the gulf Golfo de la Bellena (of the whale), for no reason which is apparent. He sailed north across the gulf, then westerly along the southern coast of the long Paria peninsula.

On 5 August, along this very peninsula, the first European landing on the American continent was made by Columbus's sailors. History does not record their names. Nor is the site known with any degree of accuracy. It could have been one of four or five. Morison, with no factual evidence but with infectious enthusiasm, makes a compelling argument for Ensenad Yacua.

The three ships coasted along the shoreline, landing men to carry out the ceremony of taking possession in front of an audience of bow and arrow-carrying natives, who Columbus was somewhat disconcerted to find looked very much like the Indians he had encountered throughout the Caribbean, though slightly lighter in colour and of a more gentle nature.

It was from these people that he learned of the pearl fisheries that existed nearby. Columbus failed to cash in on this source of wealth: he was complaining at this time of very sore eyes, sleeplessness and the need to press on to Hispaniola. Pearls, he decided, could wait. In the event, they couldn't. In 1499, Ojeda's expedition made the discovery and revealed a great source of wealth for Spain that was to last a hundred years.

Columbus's three ships explored the Gulf of Paria and the peninsula they thought was an island, turned about and sailed back to the northern exit of the gulf which Columbus named the Dragon's Mouths (Bocas del Dragon) and sailed into the Caribbean. He set a course which arched in a big sweep to the west towards the island of Margarita, eschewed the nearby pearl fisheries and headed north and west to Hispaniola where his main duties lay.

Wittingly or not, Columbus had discovered the mighty continent of America, and Europeans had landed on the mainland for the first time. Yet somehow he failed to capitalise on this achievement: he was still inhibited in his thinking that he was in Asia and it was inconceivable to him that a continent stood between him and the reality of the Orient. He had made so many miscalculations, held so many wrong assumptions, yet here he had made one of the world's most significant discoveries and failed to exploit it.

The pearl fisheries of Margarita Island.

The leg of his voyage from Margarita Island to Hispaniola was another little gem of navigation. These were totally unknown waters necessitating sailing during daylight hours only for fear of running ashore or aground on unseen islands at night, with varying winds, totally unpredictable currents and unexpected changes in compass variations; and yet in setting a course from Margarita to Santo Domingo in Hispaniola, he made a landfall some distance from the one he expected and was extremely annoyed, or as Las Casas expressed it: '. . . it weighed on him to have fallen off so much.' The landfall was a mere one hundred miles to leeward of Santo Domingo. It was an accomplishment of stunning accuracy.

The meeting of the two brothers was affectionate, as befitting a reunion after two and a half years. It was now the last day of August 1498. The Admiral arrived at Santo Domingo to find nothing but problems. The island was in uproar and turmoil.

Bartholomew had become faced with a rebellious situation. Francisco Roldán had been appointed chief justice of the island, but this did not stop him becoming the ring leader of about seventy men who 'went native', living with the Indians and cheating and robbing for gold. Bartholomew led a punitive expedition to the interior of the island and after a long, messy period of guerilla warfare, burning villages and hounding natives, subdued a large part of Hispaniola. Bands of desperate men still roamed the hills and wooded lands. The natives were subdued and exploited.

Roldán was still at large. Spaniards lay ill with fever and sickness and 160 of them were suffering from syphilis.

Roldán's trickery out-manoeuvred Columbus at every turn. He commanded far more men than Columbus could muster and the Admiral made the best of a bad job: he agreed to a form of amnesty, allowing Roldán and his terrorists to embark for Spain together with their concubines, slaves, gold and other possessions. Even this lenient concession failed at the last hurdle and a new

This woodcut of Indians washing for gold in order to pay the Spanish tributes first appeared in the illustrated Salamanca edition of Oviedo's *Historia General de las Indias* in 1547.

arrangement came into force late in 1499: Roldán was cleared of all charges, he was granted tracts of land, and had his office of chief justice restored to him. It was a disgraceful, humiliating episode which not only underlined the folly of dealing generously with a tyrant, but revealed something of the turmoil in Columbus's mind. Rather than commanding the situation, he was constantly reacting to it — and being forced into making concessions.

He wrote to the Sovereigns to keep them informed of affairs in Hispaniola, and mentioned his intention to set up a colony in Paria, an area already being thought of as a Terrestrial Paradise. His letters to the Sovereigns, however, were becoming increasingly rambling and imprecise, lacking the clean-cut authority displayed in earlier letters. Columbus, it seemed, was losing his grip. Others began to take advantage of his mounting problems. For example, Alonso de Ojeda learned of Columbus's discovery of Paria, managed to get hold of a copy of the Admiral's chart, then secured a licence from Don Juan de Fonseca to explore the area. He carried on where Columbus gave up, continuing the voyage along the coast of the mainland, west of Margarita, locating the fabulous pearl fisheries and discovering new islands, including Curaçao and the splendid Gulf of Maracaibo. To this he gave the name Venezuela (Little Venice).

Accompanying Ojeda (who, it could be argued, was usurping Columbus's authority as Admiral of the Ocean Sea) were the map-maker Juan de la Cosa and the Florentine navigator Amerigo Vespucci, the latter of whom wrote an account of this voyage, pre-dated it by two years and conveniently omitted any reference to the expedition commander's name, Ojeda. This report, based on a deception, contributed to his fame and the eventual naming of America.

Another usurper of Columbus's authority was Peralonso Niño, one-time pilot of the *Niña* and *Santa Maria*. He secured himself a licence and helped himself to a personal fortune in pearls from Margarita.

Finally, as further evidence of the Admiral's loss of authority and standing, Vicente Yáñez Pinzón sailed north-west along the whole of the north coast of Brazil, and discovered the mouth of the Amazon in a fine display of navigation and exploration.

The Sovereigns became aware of Columbus's diminishing grasp on matters. They were aware, too, that brother Bartholomew was making no significant contribution, and that brother Diego's contribution was negligible. Columbus had written asking the Sovereigns to send out to the colony a competent judge to help govern the island. It took some months for this to come about and when it did so there was an ironic twist to the appointment. The man selected was Francisco Bobadilla, Knight Commander of the Order of Calatrava, an aristocrat known personally to the king and queen but regarded by Ferdinand Columbus as 'such a bad and ignorant man'.

Bobadilla was granted far-reaching powers, superior to those wielded by the Admiral himself. He arrived at Santo Domingo to discover the Admiral putting down yet another rebellion in the province of Concepción. As Bobadilla landed on the island his gaze was met with seven Spaniards hanging on a gallows: rough justice had been meted out to these rebels.

When Bobadilla learned that another five men were due to be executed a squabble ensued which had dire consequences. Don Diego, temporarily in charge while his brothers Ferdinand and the Admiral were away chasing rebels, refused to accede to Bobadilla's demand to stop the executions. The new chief

WHY AMERICA?

IF IT was Christopher Columbus and not Amerigo Vespucci who discovered the Americas, why are the two continents named after Vespucci and not called, for example, North and South Colombia?

It had much to do with the character of the two men. Columbus did not court popularity. His was not a happy disposition. He lacked a warm personality. Indeed, such was his character that he seemed to reject any close friendship. He was moody, silent, brooding. He was considered mean, devious even, aloof and mystical. He attempted neither to please people nor to befriend them. He drove a hard bargain, and thereby reaped the materialistic rewards of his explorations. He invoked the Capitulations stubbornly and to the point of being tiresome. He even alienated King Ferdinand, despite his son Diego marrying the king's niece.

Columbus did not capitalise on his success by writing a book of his adventures. Nor was there a biography of him in the Castilian language. His fascinating log was not published for centuries, nor did his letters and papers see the light of day. By the time of his death in 1506 — just fourteen years after his great discovery — he had become discredited by the failure of his last two voyages and memories of him had receded: to such an extent that the king was only a few miles away from Valladolid yet knew nothing of the great navigator's funeral.

By contrast the discoverer Amerigo Vespucci was a self-publicist and extrovert. After his discoveries in the steps of Columbus, he published descriptions, in both Latin and Italian, of all he had seen. Either by subterfuge, design or mischance, Vespucci's account of his discoveries bore a date earlier than Columbus's voyages. It was an historical report: 'I have found a continent more densely populated and abounding in animals than our Europe, Asia and Africa. We may well rightly call this continent the New World.'

Amerigo Vespucci (1451–1512)

An influential European writer, Waldseemüller, published *A New Introduction to Cosmography* in 1507 and made this proposal: 'I do not know of any law that would forbid that the land discovered by Amerigo, a man of great wisdom and intelligence, be given his name: and since Europa, Asia and Africa have feminine names, let Amerigo's land be called America.'

The name travelled around Europe and gained general acceptance. A lone voice of protest and indignation came from Bishop Las Casas, but it was not strong enough to arrest the popular misconception that Amerigo Vespucci discovered the Americas. 'It is manifest,' he recorded, 'what injustice he did if he intentionally usurped what belonged to another, namely to the Admiral Don Christopher Columbus, and with what good reason this discovery, and all its consequences, should belong to the Admiral.'

justice clapped him in chains and had him locked in prison. He went further, taking charge of the city, of the Admiral's house, documents and letters. He despatched the priest Juan de Trasierra to Concepción with this royal summons:

> Don Christopher Columbus, our Admiral of the Ocean Sea. We have sent the Knight Commander Francisco de Bobadilla, the bearer of this letter, to say certain things to you on our behalf. We desire you to give him full faith and credit and to act accordingly. From Madrid 26 May 1499.
>
> I the King   I the Queen
> By Their Order, Miguel Perez de Almazán.

On Columbus's return to Santo Domingo, he was peremptorily arrested, manacled and thrown into prison. Later, when Bartholomew, the Adelantado, returned, he too received similar harsh treatment.

Bobadilla held some sort of a court hearing and sentenced all three brothers to return to Spain for trial. It was an incredibly humiliating and frightening twist of fate for Columbus to endure.

Early in October 1500 Columbus, accompanied by Diego, boarded the caravel *La Gorda*. Ferdinand described this incident:*
As soon as they put to sea, the captain who had come to know Bobadilla's malice, offered to remove his the Admiral's chains, but the Admiral refused. He had been placed in chains in the Sovereigns' names, he said, and would wear them until the Sovereigns ordered

*Ferdinand Columbus, p. 219.

Jean de Bry captures the scene of Columbus's arrest for maladministration during his third voyage. He is shown here with his legs being shackled.

them removed, for he was resolved to keep these chains as a memorial of how well he had been rewarded for his many services. And this he did, for I always saw them in his bedroom and he wanted them buried with his bones.

When on 20 November 1500 Columbus arrived at Cádiz, still in the chains which he now continued to wear like a badge of office to the evident embarrassment of the people of Cádiz and to Sevillans, he wrote to the Sovereigns announcing his arrival. On 17 December — six weeks later — the Sovereigns ordered him set free and wrote inviting him to Granada where the court was residing and where he would be treated honourably, to settle his affairs. They also expressed their displeasure at Bobadilla's handling of the affair. Ferdinand continues:

> Their Highnesses received him with friendly and affectionate greetings, assuring him that his imprisonment had not been by their wishes or command, that they were much displeased by it and would see to it that the guilty parties were punished and he was given satisfaction for his wrongs.

What more could a subject ask of his sovereigns? The Admiral graciously accepted the assurances. He felt vindicated.

18 The Fourth Voyage 1500-02: Wrecking of a Fleet: Marooned in Jamaica

A WEEK before Christmas in the year 1500, the ageing Admiral, now in his fiftieth year, accompanied by his brothers Bartholomew and Don Diego, was presented at court at the Alhambra at Granada. The fact that he was fashionably dressed was by courtesy of the compassion of the Sovereigns who sent him two thousand ducats 'so that he could appear in court in a state befitting a person of his rank'. Perhaps they had heard of his eccentricity and feared he might appear in monastic cloak and sandals. It is a curious incident, because he was by no means a poor man at this stage and was not in need of a royal handout.

It was an emotional meeting. The Admiral wept as he kissed the hands of the Sovereigns. Oviedo, at the time a 22-year-old hidalgo, wrote of the occasion:*

> [The Admiral] made his apologies as well as he could; and when they had heard him, with much clemency they consoled him and spoke such words that he was somewhat content. And since his services were so remarkable — although in some measure irregular — [they] could not suffer the Admiral to be maltreated; wherefore they commanded him straightaway to be restored all the income and rights that he held here, which had been sequestered and detained when he was arrested.

For more than a year Columbus suffered the pangs of being wronged as he learned of expeditions being despatched to the Indies — *his* Indies. They were becoming a free-for-all hunting ground, no longer the priceless preserve of the great discoverer. Ojeda was allowed to reap rich rewards; Vespucci explored south to the River Plate; Rodrigo de Bastidas sailed west along the coast of Venezuela to the Gulf of Darien (modern Panama, close to the canal). Other explorers were ranging further and further afield, widening the horizons of man's discovery. The Portuguese Gasper Corte-Real had made landfalls in Newfoundland and Cabral had discovered Brazil; the naturalised English seaman from Venice, John Cabot, was exploring the northern waters for England. The colonisation scramble was on.

The greatest hurt, however, was the despatch from Cádiz to Hispaniola of a fleet of thirty ships with 2,500 men, including the governor-elect, Don Nicolás de Ovando, Knight Commander of Lares, and twelve Franciscan friars. The

*Quoted in Morison, p. 577.

whole force was commanded by Antonio de Torres. It created a grand spectacle at Cádiz, another great enterprise. Its loss after ignoring the Admiral's warnings will be related in due course.

Columbus's spirits must have soared a few weeks later when he received authorisation from the Sovereigns to embark on his fourth (and last) voyage of discovery. From the outset there were differing views on the objectives of this enterprise. Columbus had spent much time in contemplation and planning: he still clung stubbornly to the belief that Cuba was a Chinese province, possibly the Malay Archipelago, and that further west from Cuba lay a great navigable gulf giving passage to the western route to India. Finding it would lead to circumnavigation.

By now others were believing that a continuous land mass extended from Newfoundland to the River Plate. Duarte Pacheco Pereira, the geographer, believed its latitude limits were 70 degrees N to 28 degrees S. Cosmographer Juan de la Cosa showed this same land mass on his famous Mappamonde. But Columbus held fast to his belief in a strait or passage. And this is what he wanted to discover.

He pestered friends and acquaintances from the Pope — Alexander VI who was, no doubt, otherwise concerned with his own interests* — to friars of the monastery, and one senses that the decision by Ferdinand and Isabella to despatch him on another voyage was primarily made in order to get shot of the pestilential Admiral. Their instructions to him made no direct mention — only by implication — of the need to discover this western passage, but otherwise they were quite explicit. The voyage was to be sponsored by the Sovereigns and carried out in their name. A sum of ten thousand ducats was allocated for the necessary preparations. Further, Columbus was instructed to concentrate on gold, silver, pearls, precious stones and spices. He was expressly forbidden to send back Indians as slaves: we detect here the wishes of Isabella, though the dichotomy remains when trying to reconcile this example of her concern with her lack of compassion to victims of the Inquisition. Columbus was also forbidden to visit Hispaniola, except for a brief stop 'if this should be necessary'.

The Guadalquivir river was navigable upstream to the port of Seville. Columbus's four caravels worked their way down the river at the beginning of April 1502, found a suitable beach for careening, then proceeded to Sanlúcar de Barrameda and then Cádiz. There, Ferdinand Columbus, barely into his teens, accompanied his father and boarded the flagship, *La Capitana*. It was to be the boy's first voyage and his father's last. Columbus was now fifty and an aged man by the judgements of his day. It was to be one of the most adventurous voyages ever recorded in the story of ships and the sea and the experiences were to make a man of the boy and were to hasten the end of the great explorer.

To relieve the Admiral of some responsibility, command of the flagship (her true name has never been recorded) was given to Diego Tristán. It was a sensible appointment, contrasting with that of Francisco de Porras to captaincy

*Alexander VI (1431–1503), Pope from 1492. He exhibited three outstanding sins, love for gold, lust for women and nepotism. Bribery, poisonings, murder, immoralities and secularisation of the church are among the many charges laid at his door.

of the *Santiago de Palos*. Bartholomew, the Adelantado, took passage in her, but was compelled to take command of her because Porras, and his brother, the enterprise's treasurer, were 'not only incompetent but disloyal'.

These two ships, plus the *Vizcaína* and *La Gallega*, completed preparations for the voyage at Cádiz. Last masses were heard and confessions dispensed with. After two days in the anchorage under the fortress of Santa Catalena, the vessels put to sea on 11 May.

The ocean crossing from the Canary Islands began after a stop for provisioning on 25 May. It was noteworthy as a crossing only in its speed. Trade winds blew consistently and after twenty-one days a landfall was made a little more to the southward of Dominica than Columbus had planned — at the island of Martinique. Columbus headed north and west, leading the small squadron through the cluster of islands comprising the Leewards, westerly along the south coast of Puerto Rico then, on 29 June, found an anchorage off Hispaniola's new capital, Santo Domingo.

He had, of course, been forbidden quite explicitly to call at Hispaniola except by *force majeure*, but his need for a harbour visit was urgent and genuine. Two things were uppermost in his mind: first he was worried about the *Santiago de Palos*, the second in importance of his four caravels. She was not a good sailer: she was described by Morison as a 'crank', that is a vessel liable to capsize; safe enough to sail home to Spain, perhaps, but not suited to the exploration duties she was being asked to undertake. Columbus wanted to trade her for another vessel.

Secondly, Columbus sensed an approaching storm, and in saying so he gives another example of his innate knowledge of the sea and seamanship. This sense instinctively warned him of the need for caution and protection. Las Casas enumerates the symptoms of the storm: an oily swell to the sea approaching from the south-eastward, an abnormal tide, gusty winds blowing at sea level while high in the sky veiled cirrus clouds sped about. Las Casas also mentioned large numbers of seals and dolphins on the surface. And finally, Columbus's gout and arthritis gave him specially painfully twinges. Further, he had experienced two hurricanes in the Indies.

In Santo Domingo's harbour there were anchored all thirty ships* of the convoy taking Don Nicolás de Ovando to his new post of governor. The fleet was assembled ready for departure back to Spain.

Columbus sent Captain Terreros of the *Gallega* ashore with a message for Ovando, requesting permission to enter harbour. He added a warning that the fleet's departure be postponed until after the approaching storm. Ovando denied the Admiral's request to enter harbour and expressed his disdain of the storm warning by sailing the fleet to sea forthwith.

Columbus's ships weighed anchor and immediately sought a safer lee anchorage, finding one a few miles to the westward where the ships anchored under the land, providing protection from the north and west.

Two days later the storm struck. Columbus's four vessels struggled against the howling fury of the tempest and survived, all four thinking the others had been sunk. Apart from relatively minor damage (including to the crank *Santiago*) and losses (*Gallega*'s boat), there was no loss of life, either.

The homeward-bound fleet, by contrast, suffered fierce ordeals. Of the thirty

*Ferdinand says twenty-eight, Las Casas thirty-two, others say thirty. We quote the mean.

ships, nearly all were lost with heavy casualties among the men. Many ships foundered at sea when the storm struck them from the north-east. Others hove-to but were driven ashore and wrecked, and the seas pounded them to matchwood. Only three of the ships managed to limp back into Santo Domingo harbour, virtually in sinking condition. All told, about five hundred men died in the hurricane. Only one ship of the thirty — the *Aguja* — eventually got home to Spain.

One of the foundered ships — she sank with all hands — was the flagship captained by Columbus's friend Antonio de Torres. Taking passage were many of Columbus's enemies, including his gaoler Bobadilla, so retribution came to the Admiral in a roundabout and extraordinary way. Also lost was the captured warlike cacique Guarionex, and a veritable treasure of gold.

Ferdinand Columbus reported:*

> The fleet carried the Knight Commander Bobadilla, who had made prisoners the Admiral and his brothers, and Francisco Roldán and all the other rebels who had done the Admiral so much hurt. God was pleased to close the eyes and minds of all those men so that they did not heed the Admiral's good advice. I am certain that this was Divine Providence, for had they arrived in Castile, they would never have been punished as their crimes deserved; on the contrary, as protégés of Bishop Fonseca, they would have received many favours and thanks.

In the middle of July 1502 Columbus set course to the west, to the undiscovered western region of the Caribbean, to find the mainland of which Cuba was a peninsula and then to discover the passage to lead him to the wonders of Cathay and Cipango.

The fleet became becalmed for almost a fortnight, carried almost imperceptively by the current towards Jamaica and some sandy islands. A south-easterly wind sprang up and took the squadron past Jamaica, between Grand and Little Cayman Islands to the cays off western Cuba where the ships found an anchorage. On leaving, the ships scudded south-by-west before a north-easterly wind, logging 360 miles in three days.

A lookout seeking signs of sharks for fishing, or a good bottom for swimming, sighted land ahead. It was the island of Bonacca (modern Guanaja), one of the Bay Islands off the coast of Honduras. Once again the mainland of America lay before Columbus.

He sent Bartholomew with two ships' boats to land on the island. By good fortune a large canoe — 'as long as a galley' — about eight feet wide, made of a single tree trunk, came by. It carried twenty-five paddlers and a palm leaf awning fixed amidships to give weather protection to the women, children and baggage. Ferdinand Columbus described the scene of this canoe packed with goods for trading:*

> Our men brought the canoe alongside the flagship, where the Admiral gave thanks to God for revealing to him in a single moment . . . all the products of that country . . . He took aboard the costliest and

*Ferdinand Columbus, p. 227.

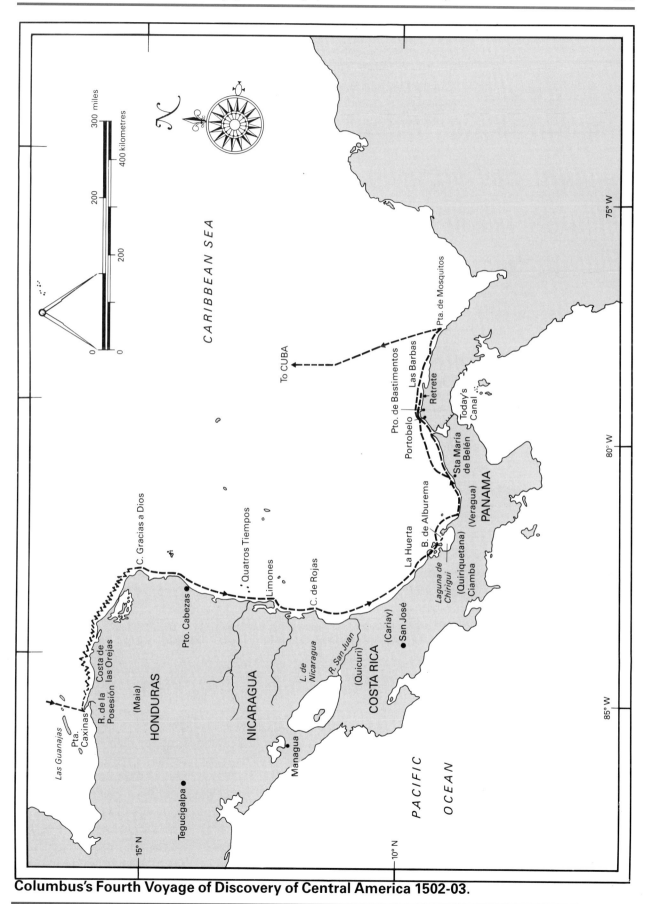

Columbus's Fourth Voyage of Discovery of Central America 1502-03.

handsomest things in that cargo: cotton mantles and sleeveless shirts
embroidered and painted in different designs and colours . . . being
like the shawls worn by the Moorish women of Granada . . . flint
knives, hatchets made of good copper, and hawks' bells made of
copper, and crucibles to melt it.

Evidently Columbus had stumbled upon a civilisation more advanced than
that of the Indians of Cuba, Jamaica and Hispaniola, but it was still centuries
away from the descriptions of the people of Cathay and Cipango.

Columbus decided to press on: he reached the mainland of Honduras about
thirty miles away, then turned east. Had he turned west he would have found
the descendants of the Maya Indians at Yucatán, and further on he would have
reached the treasures of the Gulf of Mexico.

It was Sunday 14 August 1502 when Bartholomew Columbus, the Adelantado,
accompanied by the captains and many others, went ashore onto the mainland
with standards and banners to hear mass. A few days later — on the
Wednesday — he went ashore again and in a simple ceremony formally took
possession of the country in the name of the Catholic Sovereigns. The
Admiral, who had remained aboard on his sickbed, named the land Costa de
las Orejas (The Coast of the Ears) after having been told that some of the
Indians in the vicinity of Punta Caxinas (named after the fruit tree there), who
were nearly black in colour and uglier than others, lived practically wild, ate
raw fish and human flesh, and pierced holes in their ears large enough to insert
hens' eggs.

It was time for Columbus to press on. He sailed to windward, searching for
the elusive strait he believed must exist. The four caravels laboriously beat
south-east along the coast for twenty-eight rainy days. Columbus feared for his
young 13-year-old son, yet the lad took to the task like a born sailor and his
youthful enthusiasm heartened the rest of the crew.

In those twenty-eight days of hard labour the ships managed to cover only
170 miles, an average of a mere six miles a day, before the coastline took a
southerly turn, and at last the sailors felt a wind on their backs. It took them
along the coast of today's Honduras, Nicaragua, Costa Rica and Panama.
At one point Columbus thought he had found the strait which would lead
him through the land mass, but on investigation it proved to be a beautiful,
large lagoon. It ended abruptly at the mountains' edge. There was no
strait. The fleet took advantage of the place's beauty and rested for several
days.

It was the end of the first week of October when the fleet entered this
tropical paradise of Chiriqui lagoon, and Columbus and his men spent ten days
idling through its warm transluscent waters, trading trinkets with the Indians'
necklaces of gold, the men regaining strength and health. Two curious things
happened here and, like so many incidents in the great discoverer's life, they
are so hedged about by mystery that five centuries later we still ponder the
puzzle.

The first concerns the time he spent in the Chiriqui lagoon: it was here that
he learned with conviction that he was on an isthmus: that another ocean lay
across the land, a mere nine days' travel by foot. It is as if the mere relating of

the fact confirmed Columbus in his belief that a strait must therefore exist and having that knowledge meant there was no need to continue searching for it. Whatever the reason, the Admiral seems to have put it out of his mind and never again referred to the strait which had been the prime objective of this fourth voyage.

From now on — 16 October 1502 — only one thing seemed to matter: gold, the lure that never left him.

As the fleet left the Chiriqui lagoon it headed east into the Golfo de los Mosquitos in the region of Veragua, supposedly where gold mines lay. The gulf was 125 miles broad with a coastline devoid of harbours. Here, a violent storm struck the ships and they ran before it 'without power to resist'. The present site of the Caribbean end of the Panama canal was passed on 2 November 1502 and the Admiral discovered a large, fine harbour 'encompassed by well-tilled country'.

By the end of the month Columbus gave up his coasting to the east: he had reached a point he called Retrete. It was the tiniest harbour the fleet could have squeezed into. The shore was inhabited by Indians in great numbers, of a good physique which Ferdinand Columbus described as 'tall and spare, not potbellied, and handsome of face'.*

The ships lay alongside the rocky harbour for nine days and traded quite peacefully until a number of Spaniards crept ashore — 'a greedy and dissolute set of men' — and traded with the Indians at gunpoint and 'committed a thousand outrages'. The Indians were intimidated and provoked into fighting the sailors. They also responded by gathering in large numbers to attack the ships. A lombard shot intended to disperse them only had the effect of retaliatory action — banging staves against trees and much shouting of defiance.

To demonstrate further his firm intention, the Admiral fired at a group of natives, and the gunshot let them know that the thunder concealed a shot far more dangerous than just noise.

From Retrete Columbus retraced his steps, to search again for the gold mines of Veragua. The ships were struck by violent storms. Columbus described the experience in graphic terms:†

> The tempest arose and wearied me so much that I knew not where to turn; my old wound opened up and for nine days I was as lost without hope of life; eyes never beheld the seas so high, angry and covered with foam. The wind not only prevented our progress but offered no opportunity to run behind any headland for shelter hence we were forced to keep out in this ocean, seething like a pot on a hot fire. Never did the sky look more terrible; for one whole day and night it blazed like a furnace and the lightning broke forth with such violence that each time I wondered if it had carried off my spars and sails . . . All this time the water never ceased to fall from the sky . . . it was like another deluge. The people were so worn out that they longed for death to end their dreadful sufferings.

*Ferdinand Columbus, p. 239
†Quoted in Morison, p. 617.

The caravel *Vizcaina* lost touch with her consorts for three whole days, during which time she lost her boat and at one stage had to cut her anchor cable.

In two days of calm, sharks by the hundred surrounded the ships. They were hauled aboard by hook and chain in a grisly, bloody scene. Fresh steaks of shark meat proved better fare than maggoty hard tack.

The four ships put in at Santa Maria de Belén in the Veragua region on 10 January 1503. All ships were the worse for wear, and the crews seemed lifeless. It proved an ideal base for bartering and exploring the hinterland. The ships and men settled down to let the rainy season pass. Disaster almost overtook them when floodwater cascaded down the Rio de Belén, taking with it everything in its path. It struck the *Capitana*, damaging her in a number of ways, and partly dismasted the *Gallega*. Then both ships fouled each other and it seemed they would founder with all hands, but the danger passed and all survived.

When calmer days returned all vessels were repaired, re-rigged, re-caulked and spruced up. Far worse ordeals lay before them in the three months they were to remain in Belén.

Bartholomew Columbus led a search party of three boats and eighty-six men up the river Veragua, through wild and inhospitable country, in a climate of sweating savagery for white men, mountainous and floodswept, thickly wooded with dense undergrowth. The area secreted gold, it is true, and at first discovery the Spaniards were able to extract it with no other tools than their knives, but the conditions – and the warlike Indians – overcame all the stubborn persevering attempts by Bartholomew and his tough seamen to locate and exploit the source of the precious metal.

Columbus was overjoyed with the gold discoveries and he determined to build a small colony on the site which he had already named Santa Maria de Belén – Our Lady of Bethlehem. About a dozen wood-and-thatch houses, a stout store and a fortress were built, and the Admiral's plan, like the Navidad experiment of ten years before, was to leave fifty men ashore under the command of Bartholomew together with one of the caravels – the *Gallega* – to mine the gold, while he hurried to Spain for reinforcements. But the plans went dreadfully awry.

When the rains stopped the floodwater level subsided to such an extent that the clearance of the bar at the entrance to the river dropped to a couple of feet. The Admiral's ships were virtually trapped, close to the shore with no possibility of clearing the bar. There was no option but to settle down and await favourable conditions for escape. Bartering with the Indians continued apace, trinkets for great numbers of gold discs worn about the natives' necks.

However, before the favourable conditions came along the Indians adopted an increasingly belligerent attitude.

When the floodwater rose and allowed the caravels to be towed from their anchorages, farewells were exchanged between the Spaniards about to go home and the settlers. Bartholomew and his lieutenant Diego Mendez were still ashore with about twenty of the seventy men remaining behind when several hundred Indians appeared in the hills overlooking the settlement. They were armed with spears, staves and stones plus bows and arrows tipped with sharp fish bones.

In a series of disconnected skirmishes the Spaniards were pressed hard. In one incident Indians crept to within fifty feet of the settlement huts, then attacked, damaging the huts and wounding several Spaniards. Bartholomew seized a lance and, mustering seven or eight men and a wolfhound, counter-attacked and put the natives to flight. The Spanish casualties amounted to one dead and seven wounded, including the Adelantado who received a spear wound in the chest.

In a separate incident the flagship's captain, Diego Tristán, in charge of a boat with seven crewmen and two or three soldiers, had rowed ashore to top up with fresh water. They were ambushed and all were killed except one man who made an incredible escape. Tristán died by a spear thrust in the eye.

Later, the evidence of their deaths was only too clear as their mutilated bodies floated downstream 'accompanied by croaking carrion crows'.

The Spaniards ashore became increasingly restless. They had been confined for several days in the fortress they had built and had fended off persistent attacks by groups of natives.

They begged to be allowed to rejoin their ships — except for the poor old *Gallega*, no longer seaworthy and abandoned within the bar. The Spaniards adopted a mutinous attitude, refusing to be condemned to death by being left behind. It was clear that evacuation and abandonment of the venture was the only sensible course of action.

Aboard the *Capitana* the Admiral was suffering bouts of malarial fever: he raved deliriously for days before the fever passed and evacuation began. Diego Mendez came to the fore. He supervised the construction of a substantial raft, capable of crossing the bar, and in this fashion the whole garrison, its stores and equipment were transported to the three caravels outside the bar. Mendez received the warm embraces of a relieved Admiral, and was given command of the flagship.

The intention was to sail to Santo Domingo: suitable winds were picked up and course was shaped. But the ships gave cause for great concern. All had been at sea in tropical waters for a year and all were being attacked by shipworm, the dreaded teredos which riddled ships' timbers, weakening structures and causing leaks impossible to caulk or seal. Hardly had the return journey got under way — on 23 April — than the *Vizcaina* succumbed to the worm. Efforts to save her failed. She drew more and more water until she became unhandy and dangerous. She was abandoned at Puerto Bello.

Columbus continued the eastward haul until Monday 1 May 1503, then headed north. He was pressed by the pilots aboard the two ships, and against his better judgement set course as near to north as the wind would allow. It was a fateful decision.

Nine days later the two ships, getting spongier by the day as their riddled timbers became waterlogged, fetched up at the two very small islands of Little Cayman and Cayman Brac, more than 130 miles north-east of Jamaica and hundreds more from his intended destination.

Two days later, on Friday afternoon, the ships made a Cuban landfall in the myriad of islands comprising El Jardín de la Reina. That night a storm brewed and the *Bermuda* [*Santiago*] dragged her anchor and collided with the *Capitana*. Both ships fouled each other's sterns and created serious damage. Men already weakened by months of exertion and poor victuals were strained to the limit labouring to save their ships in the wind and rain. The storm lingered for days. The damaged ships, now quite unseaworthy, nevertheless set sail to the east,

Fourth Voyage	3 April 1502–7 November 1504		**Admiral – Christopher Columbus**	
SHIP	Flagship. Name not known. Called *La Capitana*	*Santiago de Palos* Nicknamed *Bermuda*	*La Gallega or El Gallego* (The Galician)	*Vizcaína or Vizcaíno* (The Biscayan)
TONNAGE	70	Not known	About 60	Not known
CAPTAIN	Diego Tristan	Francisco de Porras* (Titular captain)	Pedro de Terreros. He took part in all Columbus's voyages	Bartholomew Fieschi from Genoa
MASTER/ OWNER	Ambrosio Sánchez	Francisco Bermudez (Owner)	Juan Quintero (Probably Master and Owner)	Juan Perez. He sold the ship to Columbus on the voyage
CREW/ PASSENGERS	Juan Sánchez (Pilot-brother of the Master) Ferdinand (son of the Admiral) 14 Able Seamen 20 Gromets 1 Cooper 1 Carpenter 2 Gunners 2 Trumpeters	Bartholomew (brother of the Admiral) Diego de Porras (brother of the captain – auditor, clerk and crown representative)* 11 Able Seamen 12 Gromets 1 Boatswain 6 Gentlemen Volunteers 1 Cooper 1 Caulker 1 Carpenter 1 Italian Gunner	9 Able Seamen 14 Gromets 1 Gentleman Volunteer 1 Boatswain	8 Able Seamen 9 Gromets 1 Boatswain 2 Gentlemen from Genoa 1 Chaplain (Fray Alexander) 1 Page

Summary of Losses

All four vessels were lost.

According to the pay rolls there were between 135 and 140 men on the voyage.

One quarter never returned, say	35
Deserted at Hispaniola	4
Drowned, died of disease, killed by Indians or in the mutiny	30
Total losses, about	69

*These brothers were incompetent and disloyal. Alonso de Morales, treasurer at Castile, forced these two men upon Columbus. His mistress was the brothers' sister.

the *Bermuda* secured to the *Capitana* by a line, and when anchored, lashed together alongside.

Jamaica was the objective – as a stepping stone towards Hispaniola. By 25 June the waterlogged *Capitana's* deck was almost awash and the three pumps were losing the contest. The two ships limped into a tiny harbour on the north coast, which Columbus had named – about ten years before – Puerto Santa Gloria (today's St Ann's Bay).

Ferdinand described the sad end of the two ships:*

> We ran them ashore as far as we could, grounding them close together, board and board, shoring them up on both sides so they could not budge ... the tide rose almost to the decks. Upon these,

*Ferdinand Columbus, p.255.

and the fore- and sterncastles we built cabins where the people could lodge.

Christopher Columbus, famed Admiral of the Ocean Sea and master mariner, suffered the ignominy of being marooned. He had with him 115 men, and their chances of survival were desperately low. The two fortified ships, like two wounded animals shouldering each other for support 'a crossbow shot from land', had foundered on a foreign shore thousands of miles from home in a tropical and merciless environment on an island only recently discovered and unlikely to be visited for years: their neighbours were natives of unknown friendliness yet upon whom the Spaniards would need to rely for their everyday sustenance. It seemed a position beyond hope and prayer even. Only God knew how the great discoverer could overcome it . . .

19 Survival, Mutiny and Death

THE PRIME task for the Admiral and his companions was to establish friendly contact with the neighbouring tribes of Indians, for their very survival depended on an acceptable system of barter for food. The Spaniards' provisions were virtually all gone, so the collection of food became an important item on their agenda. Providentially, an abundant supply of fresh water was available from two nearby streams.

The establishment of a bartering charter devolved on Diego Mendez, who emerged as one of the great characters of the fourth voyage: valiant, resourceful, intelligent and a powerful leader. He helped in fortifying the ships. Lombards and muskets were sited to give cover from areas of possible attack: an arc of 150 degrees of sight preserved to watch for any passing sea traffic. The ships were shored with newly-cut timber and sand ballast was added to give better stability.

Mendez visited the neighbouring caciques. He found the natives to be friendly and gentle folk eager to barter their wares and provisions from their canoes. In order to set up an equable exchange rate the bartering was regulated. Officers were put in charge of the trading, and the receipts of all transactions were shared to the benefit of the ships' community as a whole.

Further, Mendez won the confidence of the natives by assuring them that all Spaniards would remain aboard and only be allowed ashore with permission — similar to liberty runs ashore in modern navies. Thus there would be no parties of Spanish seamen, noted for their rough, tough, ill nature, running wild, thieving, marauding and carrying off women. Mendez agreed the following rates of exchange, according to Ferdinand Columbus:

For one or two large rodents called *hutias*, we gave them a lacepoint.
For a large cake of cassava bread we gave them two or three strings of
    green/yellow beads.
For a large quantity of anything, we gave them a hawk's bell.
To caciques or nobility we gave an occasional gift of a mirror, red cap or pair
    of scissors.

In his travels visiting the Indian caciques Mendez collected a good supply of provisions and employed two Indians to carry his hammock and packages of food. His greatest *coup* came in his dealings with a cacique named Ameyro, with whom he struck up a great friendship. For a brass helmet, a cloak and a shirt, Mendez purchased a splendid dugout canoe into which he stacked his purchases and in which he returned to Santa Gloria in triumph with six hired canoeists paddling rhythmically, to the delight of the Admiral and the Spaniards.

For the next most urgent item on the agenda — to determine ways and means of returning to Castile, or at least to Hispaniola — Columbus sought the help of his brother and Mendez. It became evident that the only means of rescue would be to despatch an Indian canoe with a messenger to Hispaniola, and there to charter a rescue caravel loaded with provisions and ammunition, and capable of embarking well over one hundred men. The Admiral asked Mendez to be that messenger. Not surprisingly he was not happy with the suggestion. To their knowledge, such a venture entailed a canoe trip across what is known today as the Jamaica Channel, more than one hundred miles from the eastern tip of Jamaica to the western point of Hispaniola — against both wind and current. Nor did it end there: there would then be a journey of 350 miles paddling to reach Santo Domingo. It was an awesome prospect.

The Admiral called all officers together to seek volunteers to act as the messenger. None offered. Mendez was persuaded.

The first attempt was aborted and Mendez was captured by Indians. He escaped and immediately prepared for a second attempt.

This time two canoes took part, plus a considerable number of dugouts to act as escort to the eastern point of Jamaica. It was planned that Mendez and Bartolomeo Fieschi, a gentleman from Genoa and captain of the *Vizcaina*, should each take a crew of six Christians and ten Indian paddlers to Hispaniola. On arrival there, Fieschi should return to Jamaica with the news of Mendez's safe arrival.

We must leave the marooned Spaniards to their predicament while we follow the fortunes of Mendez in his desperate and courageous flight to Hispaniola, in itself a saga which Morison generously called 'one of the most daring adventures in the history of the sea'.

The canoes, fragile and unstable coastal craft, were made more robust and seaworthy in preparation for their journey. Keels were fitted, the bottoms scraped and pitched and boards fixed across the bows and stern. Boards were also fitted in the waists to give a better freeboard. Masts were fitted to carry simple sails. The finished craft were filled with provisions and gourds of water to sustain the crews. Each captain carried a compass.

It was a hot July day with a flat calm sea when the canoes set out, the sails useless and the paddlers setting up a sensible rhythm. It was exhausting work and in the blazing heat the paddlers working in shifts drank their fill of fresh water, emptying their gourds. Dehydration and thirst became a problem; the captains' small reserves were rationed out to the crews. One native died and was slid overboard. The Indians refreshed themselves at times by swimming. The captains steered as best they could in the contrary currents, and by the end of the first day land had disappeared astern of them.

The second day followed the pattern of the first, leaving the Spaniards and the Indians exhausted with sheer physical effort, lack of good food, sips of water and the sweltering heat.

A third day followed. The canoes were making good about ten leagues a day, probably the maximum to be expected under the conditions. It was hoped that a rocky islet named Navassa, about three-quarters of the distance across the channel, would be sighted and water supplies replenished before embarking on the final leg to Hispaniola.

The islet, virtually a bare rock, came into sight, a landing was made and water brought aboard from rock pools because there were no fresh water streams or springs. The Indians drank so copiously that some died and others writhed in agony with stomach pains.

On the fourth day the two canoes made a landfall at Cape San Miguel in Hispaniola where they rested for two days, recuperating after their exertions. Bartolomeo Fieschi was prepared to make the return journey to Santa Gloria to carry the good news of the successful crossing as instructed by the Admiral, but the Indians and Spaniards proved mutinous and flatly refused to make the trip. Fieschi accepted the reality of the situation, though he deplored leaving the marooned Spaniards in ignorance of the position, and pressed on following astern of Mendez towards Santo Domingo.

This is the last we hear of Fieschi until he returned to Castile with the Admiral. He witnessed Columbus's will and later commanded a fleet of fifteen galleys in a war with France.

It was a very long, exhausting haul of something between 300 and 350 miles in prospect. When Mendez put in to the harbour at Azua, three-quarters of the way to Santo Domingo, he learned that the governor, Don Nicolás de Ovando, was away campaigning to subdue the Indians of a southern kingdom of the island. Mendez quit the canoe and set off by foot to the governor's field headquarters.

Ovando had no wish nor any intention to go to the assistance of Columbus and his marooned men. Columbus meant trouble for Ovando. The Admiral's presence in Hispaniola could only adversely affect Ovando's position. In the expectation that the Admiral would be claiming more glorious discoveries the Sovereigns might reinstate his viceroyalty, putting Ovando's nose nicely out of joint. The date was August 1503. Mendez could wait. The Admiral could wait. Ovando had a job to complete. He delayed Mendez by procrastinations of every sort while he waged his gruesome and bloody campaign for a period of seven months until March 1504, during which time something like eighty caciques were hanged or burned alive.

Once back at Santo Domingo, Ovando made Mendez wait another two months for a caravel from Spain. In due course three ships arrived from Castile, one of which, described as a *caravelón* or little caravel, was chartered by Mendez and was fitted out suitably as a rescue ship. Mendez gave command of the ship to Diego de Salcedo, a man loyal to the Admiral. Mendez himself returned to Spain as instructed in order to deliver the Admiral's letters to the Sovereigns.

We must now return to Columbus whom we had left about a year before languishing aboard his fortress at Santa Gloria in Jamaica. During all this time he had been without a word of the success or otherwise of the Mendez-Fieschi venture. Ignorance of the situation gave rise to discontent, to conspiracy and to outright mutiny. The ageing Columbus, racked with arthritic pain and the agony of gout, strove courageously to cope with the situations as they arose, but it was an endless struggle, dispiriting and draining; enough to kill an ordinary man. Only the Admiral's strength of will enabled him to cope.

Conditions conspired to bring discontentment. Confining the men aboard the ships, restricting liberty ashore, subjecting them to non-European food, denying them female company and enduring the tropical seasons fomented

TRICK OF THE MOON'S ECLIPSE

WHEN, IN February 1504, the Indians refused to supply any more food to the fifty-odd Spaniards marooned in the small bay of Santa Gloria in Jamaica, Columbus conceived of a ploy to trick the Indian caciques. He had aboard the *Capitana* a copy of Johannes Müller's *Calendarium* published in Nuremberg about 1474. It contained predictions of lunar eclipses for many years ahead. It revealed that a full eclipse was due on 29 February 1504 – leap year.

On this day Columbus entertained all the local caciques aboard the *Capitana*. He addressed them all. He explained that the Spaniards were Christians, that they believed in one God who lived in the Heavens, rewarded the good and punished the bad. His God, he warned them, was about to punish them with pestilence and famine if they did not supply food to the Spaniards.

As a mark of His intent He would display a sign in the sky – a blacking-out of the moon. 'Some feared and others mocked', Thacher reports, then right on cue a dark shadow began to pass over the face of the moon. Abject fear gripped the Indians. They begged Columbus to intercede on their behalf. He retired to his cabin for one hour and fifty minutes, then returned to the caciques. God, he informed them, was prepared to withdraw the threat of punishment so long as they behaved themselves and resumed supplies of food and other necessities to the Christians, and to pardon them, in token of which he would withdraw the shadow over the moon. They all agreed.

As the eclipse cleared the Indians marvelled. 'From that time forward, they always took care to provide what [the Spaniards] had need of.'

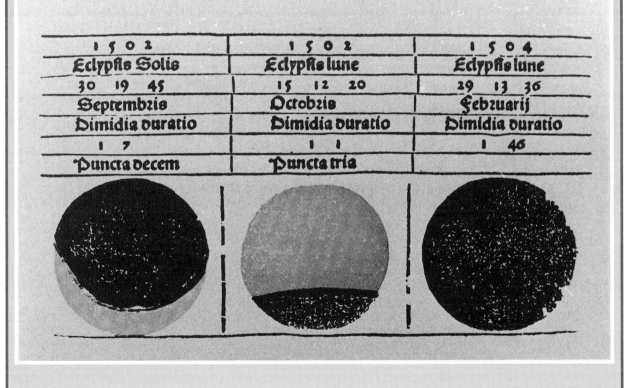

mutiny. Leaders, trouble-makers, emerged. The Porras brothers – Captain Francisco of the *Santiago* and Diego – incited the others to revolt. They recruited support from forty-eight sailors, roughly half the total number of castaways.

On 2 January 1504 the conspirators took action. Francisco Porras boarded the *Capitana* and burst in upon the ailing Admiral. The mutineers took over the two ships and only the actions of loyal servants managed to prevent both the Admiral and his brother Bartholomew from being murdered.

Ten dugout canoes lay alongside. The mutineers scrambled into them in response to the ring leaders' calls of 'I'm for Castile!' then paddled off eastwards. As they progressed along Jamaica's north coast they robbed Indians of food, took prisoners to paddle the canoes, then left the easternmost point of the island astern of them to attempt the channel crossing. Rough weather scotched the attempt. Canoes were lightened and all goods other than guns thrown overboard until, in a final attempt to stay afloat, the Indians were jettisoned like bad cargo; they drowned or had their hands hacked off as they clung to the gunwales. The sea defeated the mutineers and they put back to Jamaica.

Two more attempts were made in the ensuing months, but both failed and the disconsolate mutineers, ill with fatigue and malnutrition, set out to return to Santa Gloria on foot, scavenging for food, to surrender to Columbus and submit to punishment.

Aboard the two-ship fortress starvation faced the loyal supporters. The Indians now had so many trinkets they were not interested in any more. The Admiral's lunar eclipse ploy solved the immediate food problems, but it still left unresolved the problem of how to escape the island and return home. Spirits among the Spaniards were roused to near delirium in March 1504 – over eight months since the gallant canoeists had paddled off to seek help. A small caravel was sighted entering the bay: she anchored close to the marooned ships. As soon as her captain, Diego de Escobar, called upon the Admiral it was realised that the visit was a cruel deception by governor Ovando of Hispaniola.

He had despatched the caravel to spy upon Columbus and his survivors. The choice of Escobar as a messenger was itself an insult to the Admiral, for the captain was an officer who had rebelled against Columbus years ago in Hispaniola. However, it was not all bad news. Escobar brought gifts of two casks of wine and a huge slab of salt pork. He also brought a letter from Mendez announcing his safe arrival at Santo Domingo, expressing the intention of despatching a relief ship as soon as possible. That same evening, the little caravel sailed. Columbus could have claimed a berth aboard her, but he expressed a preference to remain with his loyal men. Salvation sailed away . .

By now the Porras mutineers were camped nearby and Columbus made efforts to reconcile the situation. He despatched two officers to parley with them, and they took as a measure of their good intent a hefty chunk of the slab of pork. Discussions were broken off when it was seen that the mutineers' terms were too demanding.

Another parley was arranged when the mutineers marched on the loyalists. The Adelantado led the band of loyalists, strongly armed with swords and cudgels. The mutineers were intent on fighting and a fierce skirmish ensued, watched with great interest by the Indians.

A number of the mutineers were struck down, Captain Porras was captured and others taken prisoner. The rest fled for their lives into hiding. The following day they emerged sheepishly and surrendered after pleading for a pardon. In an act of great generosity, Columbus granted the pardon.

The anniversary of the ships' marooning at Santa Gloria was celebrated with the arrival of the small caravel chartered by Mendez in Santo Domingo towards the end of June 1504. She was in poor condition, almost unseaworthy. About one hundred men crammed aboard her and endured a dreadful voyage lasting six and a half weeks. On arrival at Hispaniola's capital Columbus was greeted by Ovando in an outward display of cordiality. His real sentiments were made evident when he released from custody the two Porras brothers whom Columbus had kept imprisoned.

A ship was chartered for Columbus, his brother Bartholomew and son Diego and twenty-two others for the return to Castile. She sailed from Santo Domingo on 12 September. Like all Columbus's voyages, this one, too, had its elements of drama. Very soon the mainmast 'split right down to the deck'. It was the two Columbus brothers who brought their seamen's skills to bear and rigged a working jury mast. They also helped repair the foremast which sprung in a storm.

It was fifty-six days out of Santo Domingo before Columbus arrived off Sanlúcar de Barrameda on 7 November 1504. It marked the end of Columbus's seagoing career. He went to Seville to await a royal summons that never came. Indeed, Queen Isabella was too ill to see him and before the end of the month she was dead. The date was 26 November.

The rooms that Columbus rented in Seville were finely furnished as befitted a man of considerable wealth. He was to live out his relatively short life in material riches with all the trappings of a wealthy man, but broken in heart and in spirit. He became embittered and obsessed by imaginings of being denied his rights, titles, honours and monetary rewards. Yet in truth he received substantial revenue from his years of discoveries of gold. His tenths,* eighths† and thirds‡ originally negotiated in the Capitulations had paid off handsomely.

He persisted in his complaints to such an extent, though, that he lost the favours of his friends and acquaintances. He became a bothersome old man, enfeebled by his painful infirmities. No wonder the king had no inclination to afford him an audience. But, as ever, his persistence paid off and he received an audience before Ferdinand at Segovia in Old Castile in May 1505, having travelled three hundred miles across country on the back of a horse or mule. But it gained him nothing. The king simply could not be bothered to deal with the carping claims of a broken man. Columbus followed the court for a few months but the end was coming nearer.

On 20 May — Ascension Day — 1506 the end came in Valladolid with merciful release from pain for the great man. The cause of death could have been a combination of several elements: certainly grief played a part, as did the

*10% of the net production of the world he discovered.

†One eighth of the profits that Columbus's own ventures gave him.

‡One of his presumed prerogatives as an Admiral.

The house in Valladolid where Columbus died on 20 May 1506. It has long since been demolished.

infirmities brought on by gout, arthritis and the exhaustion of years of worry, anxiety and endless squabbling. Others attribute his death to diabetes, others to syphilis. Others think he simply lost the will to live — and quietly gave up the ghost.

Around his bedside were his closest relations: his son and heir Don Diego; his son and future biographer Ferdinand; his beloved younger brother Diego (Bartholomew was away at court). The captains of his last voyage, Diego Mendez, and Bartholomeo Fieschi, were there together with a few other close friends. Beatrice Enríquez de Harana, mother of Ferdinand, was not there yet she was still alive at the time.

Nor did any member of the royal family attend the death scene, though the king was staying at Villafuerte at the castle of the Kings of Aragon just a few miles away. He was unaware that the great discoverer who had brought nothing but glory to the name of Spain had died, and he knew nothing of the funeral arrangements until after Columbus was buried.

A priest administered the Eucharist and the dying Admiral whispered his last words: *in manus tuas, Domine, commendo spiritum meum*: Into Thy hands, O Lord, I commend my spirit.

The story does not end there. Two more elements intrude, one of which need only detain us for a moment: it relates to the years, decades and generations of petitioning and litigation which were to blight the lives of the second Admiral, Diego, and his wife Maria de Toledo, niece of the king and a descendant of the great family headed by the grandee the Duke of Alba. Their son, Luis, inherited the legacy of litigation, and by profligacy squandered the patrimony and even the memory of his grandfather.

The other element does concern the Columbus story, and – like the series of mysteries which comprise the birth and life of the Admiral – the story ends with yet another question mark.*

His body was laid to rest in the church of San Francisco de la Santa Maria de la Antigua in Valladolid, whose twelfth-century tower still holds a commanding position in the city. But some say he lay in the crypt of the Franciscan abbey: throughout his life he had always felt comfortable in the company of friars, and one senses he would have been content to rest in peace in the crypt at Valladolid.

Some time between the years 1509 and 1514 his remains were transferred to Seville – not to the cathedral, but to the Carthusian monastery or convent of Nuestra Señora Santa Maria de las Cuevas, immediately across the Guadalquivir river from Ferdinand Columbus's house.

About twenty years later, probably in 1536 or 1537, the daughter-in-law, Maria de Toledo (already widowed for ten years or so since Diego died prematurely, aged a little under fifty in 1526) and their son, Don Luis, now the third Admiral, asked the king, now Charles V, for permission to disinter the remains and transfer them to the cathedral at Santo Domingo in Hispaniola. The request was granted promptly.

However, problems arose when the clergy of Santo Domingo objected to the proposal of burying the Admiral's remains in the mortuary chapel of the high altar – after all he was both a foreigner and a layman. As a consequence, it was at some point between 1541 and 1547 that Columbus's and his son Diego's coffins were buried in the vaults beneath the cathedral in the New World.

Son Ferdinand was buried in Seville cathedral, Bartholomew in the monastery of San Francisco in Santo Domingo and Luis, the grandson and third Admiral, with the first and second Admirals.

Politics and war now intervened. France occupied the western half of Hispaniola from 1697, and in 1795 Spain ceded all the rest of the island of Hispaniola to France. It was thought proper that the remains should find rest in Spanish not French soil, so they were removed and carried to Havana in Cuba where they were once more put to rest on 19 January 1796 in the wall of the high altar of Havana cathedral.

Just over a century later Cuba proclaimed her independence and in 1899 the coffin was disinterred, carried aboard a Spanish cruiser and delivered to the cathedral in Seville where it remains to this day lying at the foot of the marble monument sculpted in the Admiral's honour.

However, the story continues . . .

In September 1877, another vault was discovered next to that once occupied by Columbus's coffin in Santo Domingo, in which was found a battered lime-encrusted coffer, inscribed: 'The Illustrious and Excellent man Christopher

*The story is related in full in Granzotto, pp.282–3.

The grandiose tomb of
Columbus in Seville Cathedral
was sculpted by Arturo Melida
when the remains were taken
to the cathedral in 1899
from Havana.

Columbus.' The contents of the coffer were spilled and it is some of these ashes and dust which have found their way to Genoa, Paris, New York and Rome. In the bottom of the box a small silver plate was found with the inscription 'The Last Part of the Remains of the First Admiral, Christopher Columbus the Discoverer'.

Thus, we have two claimants for the remains of the Admiral — Santo Domingo and Seville. A thorough examination in 1960 by the American Professor Charles Goff of the dust, bones and ash in the leaden coffer in Santo Domingo convinced the professor there was a mix of two bodies — presumably Christopher's and his son Diego's, a mix up which probably occurred in 1795.

Geographer Dr Robert Fuson* relates that a convincing piece of evidence was found in the coffer: it was a small lead pellet. Could it, he asks, have been the result of a gunshot wound Columbus received during his fourth voyage? Even after centuries of death, the Admiral still leaves us puzzled and in doubt.†

The late biographer Gianni Granzotto leaves us with an even more quizzical thought. He believes Columbus's remains were never allowed to be taken from the Franciscan monastery in Valladolid, whose friars were stubbornly possessive of the discoverer's remains. Today, on the site of the old monastery there stands the Del Norte café with its billiard room. If — and it is a big if — the remains are still there, then the relics of Christopher Columbus may well lie beneath the billiard room floorboards.

The end of the Christopher Columbus story deserves something on a plane higher than the level of these two anecdotes; yet perhaps it is more in keeping with this Master of the Atlantic, discoverer of the unknown, navigator-extraordinary, that his end, like his signature, should leave us mystified and puzzled.

* Robert Fuson, pp. 239–40.

†This is conjecture. There is no evidence of a gunshot injury other than a letter from Columbus to the Sovereigns during his fourth voyage in which he wrote 'My wound has opened again'.

This massive monument to Columbus's memory at the Punta del Sebo dominates the river entrances to Huelva, Palos and Moguer.

Select English Bibliography

T HERE seems little point in providing a bibliography of the rich array of works about Christopher Columbus in Italian, Portuguese, Spanish and other languages. The following select bibliography covers the major works in English, including translations of the more important works from the Spanish into English. The list which follows is not necessarily a recommendation. I have copied a procedure adopted by a respected Italian author, though he displayed greater courage by refusing to nominate more than three books as his choice. I pay tribute to the late Gianni Granzotto and his *Christopher Columbus: The Dream and The Obsession*, William Collins, 1986 and Grafton Books, 1988, wherein he gives the timely reminder that the countless scholarly books on Columbus available to today's students are all derived from material to be found in Columbus's near contemporaries – Las Casas, Bernáldez, Oviedo and Ferdinand, Christopher's son.

His first choice is a Spanish work compiled by Salvador de Madariaga – available in English translation – a scholarly, standard work marred only by the author's tiresome attempt to establish that Columbus was descended from Spanish Jews.

Granzotto's second choice of special merit is Samuel Eliot Morison's splendid two volume version of *Christopher Columbus: Admiral of the Ocean Sea*. As a doyen historian of sensitivity, and an admiral in the US Navy, Morison was a man of the sea, perhaps able to understand the feelings of the discoverer better than most. He also followed Columbus's wake across the ocean to gain an intimate knowledge of his subject.

The third work to receive Granzotto's accolade is fellow Italian Taviani's *Christopher Columbus: The Grand Design*, a book overflowing with half a century's treasure trove of learning and scholarship about his subject. His analysis is masterly and conclusions compelling.

I suspect that few scholars would disagree with these choices. I would hazard adding Granzotto's own work, and for the pleasure of reading a modern translation of the Admiral's log, the 1987 translation by Dr Robert H. Fuson – *The Log of Christopher Columbus*. Mentioning these few works does not detract from the merit of the other titles listed. I commend Ernle Bradford, Washington Irving, Dr Benjamin Keen's translation of Ferdinand's biography of his father, and Spotorno's *Memorials of Columbus*. Finally, do not miss John Boyd Thacher's three volumes.

BECHER, A.B., *The Landfall of Columbus on his First Voyage to America*, J.D. Potter, 1856.

BERNALDEZ, Andrés (trans and ed) with an introduction and notes by Cecil Jane, *The Voyages of Christopher Columbus, being the Journals of his 1st and 3rd and the letters concerning his 1st and last Voyages, to which is added an Account of his 3rd Voyage*, Argonaut Press, 1930.

BRADFORD, Ernle, *Christopher Columbus*, Michael Joseph, 1973.

BREBNER, J.B., *The Explorers of North America*, 1933.

CASTLEREAGH, Duncan, *The Great Age of Exploration*, Reader's Digest/Aldus Books, 1971.

CHAPMAN, Paul H., *The Man Who Led Columbus to America*, P. Judson, Atlanta, 1973.

COLLIS, John Stewart, *Christopher Columbus*, Macdonald & Janes, 1976.

A Columbus Casebook, Supplement to Joseph Judge, 'Where Columbus Found the New World,' *National Geographic Magazine* (vol 170, No. 5, November 1986), pp. 562–99.

COLUMBUS, Christopher, JANE, Cecil (trans) and VIGNERAS, L.A., *The Journal of Christopher Columbus*, Hakluyt Society, 1960.

COLUMBUS, Christopher and FUSON, Robert H. (trans), *The Log of Christopher Columbus*, Ashford Press Publishing, Southampton, 1987.

COLUMBUS, Christopher and SPOTORNO, Giovanni Batista, *Memorials of Columbus: or a collection of authentic documents of that celebrated navigator . . . preceded by a Memoir of his life and discoveries*, Treuttel & Wurtz, 1823.

COLUMBUS, Christopher, *The Journal of his First Voyage to America*, Jarrolds, n.d. (c.1930s).

COLUMBUS, Christopher and COHEN, J.M. (trans), *The Four Voyages of Columbus*, Penguin, 1969.

COLUMBUS, Christopher and KEEN, Benjamin (trans), *The Life of Admiral Christopher Columbus*, Folio Society, 1960.

CRONE, Gerald R., *The Discovery of America*, Hamish Hamilton, 1969.

DUFF, Charles, *The Truth About Columbus and The Discovery of America*, Grayson and Grayson, 1936 and Jarrolds, 1957.

DUNN, Oliver, 'Columbus's First Landing Place; The Evidence of the Journal', *Terrae Incognitae* (vol 15, 1983), pp. 35–50.

DUNN, Oliver and KELLEY, James E., *The Diario of Christopher Columbus's First Voyage to America: 1492–1493*. Norman, University of Oklahoma Press, 1987.

FERNANDEZ-ARMESTO, Felipe, *Columbus and the Conquest of the Impossible*, Weidenfeld and Nicolson, 1974.

FISKE, John, *The Discovery of America*, 2 vols, Houghton, Mifflin & Co., 1902.

FUSON, *see under* COLUMBUS and FUSON.

GIARDINI, Cesare and LANZA, Frances (trans), *Christopher Columbus*, Collins, 1986.

GRANZOTTO, Gianni and SARTARELLI, Stephen (trans), *Christopher Columbus: The Dream and The Obsession*, Collins, 1986.

HAMILTON, E.J., *Money, Prices & Wages in Valentia, Aragon & Navarra, 1351–1500*, Cambridge, Mass., 1936.

HARRISSE, H., *The Discovery of North America*, Parish, 1882.

HELPS, Sir Arthur, *Christopher Columbus*, J.M. Dent, 1910.

HUMBLE, Richard, *The Explorers*, Time-Life, Amsterdam, 1979.

INNES, Alexander, *The Life and Adventures of Christopher Columbus*, David Bryce, Glasgow, 1892.

IRVING, Washington, *The Life and Voyages of Christopher Columbus Together with the Voyages of his Companions*, John Murray, 1849. Original edition 1827, 3 vols. Revised edition, Cassell, 1885.

JOHNSON, W., *Genoa The Superb: The City of Columbus*, 1892.

JUDGE, Joseph, 'Where Columbus Found The New World', *National Geographic Magazine* (vol 170, No. 5, November 1986), pp. 562–99.

LANGSTROM, Bjorn, *Columbus: The Story of Don Cristobal Colón and his Four Voyages Westward to the Indies*, Allen & Unwin, 1967.

MADARIAGA, Salvador de, *Christopher Columbus, Being the Life of The Very Magnificent Lord Don Cristobal Colón*, Hodder and Stoughton, 1939. Reprinted Hollis and Carter, 1949.

MAJOR, R.H. (trans and ed). *Select Letters of Christopher Columbus, With Other Original Documents Relating to His First Four Voyages to the New World*, Hakluyt Society, 1870.

MAJOR, R.H., *The Bibliography of the First Letter of Christopher Columbus, Describing His Discovery of the New World*, Meridian, Amsterdam, 1971, a reprint of a London edition of 1872.

MARKHAM, Sir Clements R., *Life of Columbus*, 1892.

MARKHAM, Sir Clements R., *The Journal of Christopher Columbus During His First Voyage, 1492–93*, Hakluyt Society, 1893.

MARTINEZ-HIDALGO, Jose Maria and CHAPELLE, Howard I. (trans). *Columbus's Ships*, Barre Publishers, Barre, Mass., 1966.

MERRIEN, Jean and MICHAEL, Maurice (trans), *Christopher Columbus: The Mariner and the Man*, Odhams, 1958.

MORISON, *see also under* COLUMBUS and MORISON.

MORISON, Samuel Eliot, *Christopher Columbus, Admiral of the Ocean Sea*, 2 vols, Little, Brown & Co, Boston, 1942: also published as a single volume edition with the title *Admiral of the Ocean Sea: A Life of Christopher Columbus*, Little, Brown & Co.

MORISON, Samuel Eliot, *Christopher Columbus, Mariner*, Little, Brown & Co, Boston, Mass., 1955

MORISON, Samuel Eliot, *Journals and Other Documents on the Life and Voyages of Christopher Columbus*, The Heritage Press, New York, 1963.

MUSMANO, M.A., *Columbus Was First*, New York, 1968.

NUNN, G.E., *The Geographical Conceptions of Columbus*, New York, 1924.

PARRY, J.H., *The Discovery of South America*, New York, 1979.

SPOTORNO *see under* COLUMBUS and SPOTORNO.

TAVIANI, Paolo Emilio, *Christopher Columbus: The Grand Design*, Orbis Publishing, 1985.

THACHER, John Boyd, *Christopher Columbus, His Life, His Works, His Remains, As Revealed by Original Printed and Manuscript Records, Together With an Essay on Peter Martyr of Anghera and Bartolomé de Las Casas, the First Historians of America*, 3 vols, A.M.S. Press, Kraus Reprint Corporation, New York, 1967.

VIGNAUD, Henry, *A Critical Study of the Various Dates Assigned to Christopher Columbus; The Real Date 1451, With a Bibliography of the Question*, Henry Stephens, Son & Stiles, 1903. Also published in 3 vols, 1967.

WASSERMAN, Jacob and SUTTON, Eric (trans). *Christopher Columbus*, Christopher Columbus Publishing, New York, 1979.

Index